UNIVERSITY OF
EXETER

WOMEN'S RIGHTS AS MULTICULTURAL CLAIMS

WOMEN'S RIGHTS AS MULTICULTURAL CLAIMS

Reconfiguring Gender and Diversity in Political Philosophy

Monica Mookherjee

Edinburgh University Press

© Monica Mookherjee, 2009, 2011

First published in 2009 by
Edinburgh University Press Ltd
22 George Square, Edinburgh
www.euppublishing.com

This paperback edition 2011

Typeset in Goudy Old Style by
Iolaire Typesetting, Newtonmore, and
printed and bound in the UK by
CPI Antony Rowe, Chippenham, Wiltshire

A CIP record for this book is available
from the British Library

ISBN 978 0 7486 4296 0 (paperback)

The right of Monica Mookherjee to be identified
as author of this work has been asserted
in accordance with the Copyright, Designs
and Patents Act 1988.

Contents

Acknowledgements

I have incurred many debts in the course of writing this book. My colleagues at the University of Keele have provided a greatly valued working environment. The Research Institute for Law, Politics and Justice at Keele kindly granted me sabbatical leave during the Autumn Semester, 2007. This book was completed during the tenure of a research award from the UK Arts and Humanities Research Council, whose assistance is gratefully acknowledged.

Andrea Baumeister, Paul Bou-Habib, Gideon Calder, Lynn Dobson, John Horton and Jonathan Seglow provided generous and exceptionally valuable feedback on draft chapters. Cécile Laborde, Stephen Macedo and Tariq Modood patiently responded to my queries; and Deen Chatterjee enthusiastically supported the initial book proposal. I am indebted to Peter Jones for supporting my AHRC grant application and for his steadfast encouragement throughout my career so far. I have benefited enormously from the support and intellectual stimulation of a community of scholars working on issues of gender and culture in the UK. This book is intended as a contribution to ongoing discussion with, amongst others, Dr Baumeister, Anne Phillips, Sawitri Saharso, Oonagh Reitman and Samia Bano. I would also like to express my special thanks to Glen Newey and Sorin Baiasu at Keele, who have provided invaluable help. I also thank Clare Chambers, Rowan Cruft, Duncan Ivison, Graham Long, Cillian McBride, Ian O'Flynn, Fariha Thompson, Simon Thompson and Judith Squires.

I would also like to thank my editor Nicola Ramsey at Edinburgh University Press for her advice and unstinting kindness. I am also deelpy grateful to Eddie Clark for his expert guidance and assistance preparing the manuscript for publication; to Patricia Marshall for her extensive bibliographical assistance; and to Teresa Sinclair for her assiduous and patient work compiling the index.

Finally, my deepest thanks go to Celia Robson, Joshua Mason and Prem Chaudhury for their companionship; and my endless gratitude, of course, goes to my family. This book is dedicated to my parents.

Chapter 1 draws upon my 2003 article, 'Exclusion, Internalisation, Harm' in *Ethicnities* (2003), 3:3; and Chapter 5 draws from Mookherjee (2005). A modified version of the latter sections of Chapter 3 appears in Mookherjee (2008b).

Monica Mookherjee

Preface

Women activists in India lead marches to denounce the glorification of acts of widow immolation and campaign for greater state intervention into the problem of dowry death. On the other side of the globe, immigrant women contest the sensationalising images of forced marriage, honour crimes and female genital mutilation portrayed in the international media (see Baker et al.: 1999). Women worldwide campaign for change and yet the local and context-specific character of their claims appears increasingly more salient than the universal commitments to freedom and equality that historically underwrite feminism. At the same time, support for the ideal of multiculturalism, understood as the equitable recognition of all cultural, religious and ethnic groups, appears more precarious than ever in the post-9/11 world. This instability has manifested itself clearly in heightened anxiety over women's rights in non-liberal cultures. In light of these pressing issues, one of the most controversial questions in contemporary political philosophy concerns the possibility of integrating the discourses of feminism and multiculturalism.

The issue was presented starkly a decade ago by Susan Okin's provocatively titled essay, 'Is Multiculturalism Bad for Women?' (1999a). Notwithstanding her subsequent qualifications, Okin answered this question in the affirmative, arguing that the majority of the world's cultures are patriarchal and that liberal policies that protect minorities typically entrench gender hierarchies. Unsurprisingly, this perspective has been contested by postcolonial feminists and defenders of multiculturalism (see, for example, al-Hibri 1999; Hutchinson 2000; Steans 2007), who warn against oversimplifying women's interests or simply equating them with Western liberal priorities. They recommend an explicit acknowledgement of the neo-imperialism to which non-Western women often react in their emancipatory struggles. Their observations are apt not least because envisaging a stark opposition between commitments to feminism and multiculturalism belies the fact that the two movements share important objectives, such as their mutual challenge to the emphasis usually placed by liberals on uniform rights and laws at the expense of recognising valuable human differences.

My contribution to this debate addresses two concerns that arise from Okin's claim. The first and most obvious issue is whether women can be understood to share universal interests that transcend the particularities of their cultural location. Specifically, the concern is that, if such interests cannot be identified, feminism's credentials as a viable political project would be compromised and, to put the point starkly, multicultulturalism would 'triumph' over feminism. If women differ in terms of values and goals, and if they interpret their biological or anatomical identity in culturally variable ways, can their struggles be aligned within a coherent political project? The second, less direct but no less pressing, problem is whether the interests of diverse people should be conceptualised in terms of rights at all. The problem is acute, as discourses of universal rights have often been charged with Eurocentrism and androcentrism (see Robison 1996; Rao 1999). A masculine and typically Western emphasis on what some view as the antagonistic claims of bourgeois, self-owning individuals might be thought to obscure the disadvantages that have historically beset women in the domestic sphere. One might thus risk prioritising formal freedoms at the expense of attending to the marginalisation of non-liberal people's cherished forms of life. Taken together, these concerns prompt liberal philosophers to ask whether discourses of rights can be used to theorise women's interests in an age of cultural diversity.

I respond to this question by reconfiguring feminism to respond to cultural diversity through a flexible interest theory of rights. In doing so, I reject the idea that gender equality and cultural diversity are opposed; and, instead, conceive women's rights as multicultural claims. The central idea that motivates this synthesis is that the meaning of feminist justice, of multiculturalism and, indeed, of rights can only be articulated by paying attention to the interplay between the universality and cultural particularity of human interests. One must recognise that women – and, indeed, human beings generally – share certain needs and capacities, but that these are interpreted and instantiated in infinitely variable ways. The framework of rights proposed in this book thus acknowledges the cultural variability of women's interests globally and the fact that their struggles are often linked with a postcolonial resistance to the apparent imposition of 'Western' norms. Moreover, it also establishes how a discourse of rights can protect women's substantive capacities to resist structural disadvantages that pervade most human communities. In brief, my approach proposes a multicultural form of feminism and a feminist form of multiculturalism. While activists involved in the practical task of defending rights in the world today may find the call to attend to the cultural particularity of human interests uncontroversial, it is important to explain philosophically how the commitment to examining the specificities of time, place and culture interacts with and contributes to supporting a certain form of universalism. I contend that the insights revealed through attending to the particular problems confronted by diverse women serve to unsettle, challenge and finally 'reconfigure' the meaning that liberal feminists attribute to terms such as gender justice, equality or freedom in an ongoing theoretical process that expands a collective understanding of justice. If meaning is created through the practical use of language, as Wittgenstein (1968) supposed, a feminist theory relevant to an age of cultural diversity must acknowledge the interplay between the universal and the particular, and sometimes grant priority to the latter in policy terms.

My defence of this claim draws on Iris Young's influential account of 'gender as seriality' (1994). While Young did not only have in mind cultural and religious differences between women, she nonetheless aimed to respond to the arguments of third-wave feminists (for example, Spelman, 1988), who emphasised multiple differences between women in terms of geographical location, ethnicity, sexuality and disability. These feminists sought to allay worries about 'substititutionalism', or the universalistic representation of the interests of one category of woman only – typically Western women. Young's anxiety that third-wave claims would cause feminism to fragment irretrievably, on account of the implied conclusion that women rarely share any concrete interests, led her to conceptualise women as a 'self-alienated series', or as a collective bound together not by common experiences but in terms of the loose relation that their actions have to material structures such as normative heterosexuality, the rule-bound body and the sexual division of labour. The opening chapter of this book accordingly explains how Young's perspective offers a theoretical line of departure that acknowledges the particularity of women's interests whilst keeping in view their shared investment in overcoming gender hierarchies. By explaining the implications of her account for a theory of rights specifically, the book as a whole proposes an innovative framework of entitlements to political deliberation and individual agency that is appropriate to sustaining commitments to feminism and cultural diversity.

Young's conception of gender is particularly helpful in exposing the difficulties with liberal rights in the context of the now prolific debate about feminism and multiculturalism. The rare practice of *sati*, or widow immolation, in India provides a foundation in Chapter 1 from which I highlight the problems with the dominant paradigm of 'rights as trumps' (Dworkin 1979). A rigid conception of rights as moral absolutes, or as interests of the highest, uncompromising priority, encourages states to place individual rights to sex equality in opposition to group rights to cultural self-determination and to demand that one of these rights be considered normatively prior, without establishing how that ranking can be legitimised. This antagonistic approach casts the debate about sati in terms of a non-negotiable dilemma, and fails to respond to the complex interests of women who are affected by this practice. For this reason, I ask instead whether the interests at stake in this debate should be articulated by drawing on liberal theories of *recognition* or *capabilities*. On the face of it, these approaches respond to the different kinds of harm to human interests that should be theorised in a feminist and multicultural account of rights. However, despite their insights, which assist in setting the agenda for my proposals in ensuing chapters, neither of these accounts succeeds in demonstrating how women's rights can be configured as multicultural claims.

Taking up the recommendation of certain theorists of recognition to proceed in terms of an intercultural dialogue, I articulate an alternative approach in Chapter 2 by remaining focused on India and concentrating on the much-debated Shah Bano controversy. This case involved an elderly Muslim woman who won, but then renounced, a Supreme Court judgment in favour of her right to claim alimony from her ex-husband. The judgement was widely understood as a challenge by Hindu elites to Muslim divorce conventions in a country where religious strife has a complex history. The judgement serves as an instructive starting point from which to challenge Okin's perspective as well as an influential response to it – namely, Ayelet Shachar's theory of transformative accommodation (Shachar 2001). While Shachar's account does not surmount all the difficulties arising from Okin's universalistic approach, she rightly highlights the need for a form of multiculturalism that alters gender hierarchies in majority and minority groups. Her approach therefore paves the way for my own defence of a 'right to mediation', which I propose as the first component of a feminist and multicultural theory of rights. This group right prioritises democratic consultation between state and community according to a culturally sensitive account of public reasoning. The term 'mediation' refers to the fact that the meaning of the human values that underpin rights – that is, values such as equality and freedom – is always conveyed through citizens' diverse conceptions of the good. Thus, positive conceptions of gender identity can be non-liberal without being unreasonable, irrational or unjust. The dialogues prioritised by the right to mediation promise imaginative forms of protection for women such as Shah Bano without leaving them prey to what Shachar calls the 'multicultural paradox' (Ibid.). This is so even though this right must be supplemented by a defence of a universal entitlement that secures the substantive capacities of individual women to resist coercion and to voice their needs in political dialogue.

My account therefore recognises that, while minority groups should have a high-priority entitlement to engage with the state on substantive questions of value, deliberation alone should not be regarded as a panacea when configuring the discourses of feminism and multiculturalism. The ever-present risk that women's voices would be suppressed due to informal gender hierarchies emphasises the need to focus equally on an individual right that protects the capacities of historically vulnerable internal minorities to participate in the deliberative process. This right also justifies direct assistance by states in extreme situations to protect human interests (see Green 1995). Chapter 3 accordingly contends that women should enjoy the right to 'plural autonomy'. This is to say, while autonomy takes a plurality of cultural forms, it comprises a mental ability reflectively to endorse one's life decisions in the sense of not being alienated from them. I defend this capacity as a high-priority entitlement by focusing on the debate about arranged and forced marriage in Britain, arguing that attention to the cultural specificity of autonomy skills is vital if states are to identify when core human capacities have been denied. This approach is preferable to the abstract definitions of autonomy usually found in liberal theory in terms of sovereignty, self-authorship or rational revisability. Equally, it provides an antidote to Kukathas' (1995) 'right to exit' thesis, which offers sparse protection to internal minorities who find themselves under serious psychosocial pressure to comply with cultural or religious norms.

While the political imperative to protect culturally plural forms of autonomy justifies, in some instances, state intervention and protective legislation for individuals at risk of intra-community harm, the difficulties associated with ascertaining whether a person endorsed a particular life decision prompt an examination of extra-legal means to secure the framework of rights defended in this book. These measures are not only necessary in order to challenge the gendered structural inequalities that pervade practically all communities, including the majority society of liberal democracies, but also in light of the need to encourage women's involvement in the dialogues of the right to mediation and to ensure the inclusive negotiation of multicultural claims over time. While education constitutes an important means of empowering women, substantial problems arise from requiring that all sectors of a multicultural society partake of a uniform programme of instruction. If protecting individual rights in a liberal state involves exposing all young citizens to the fact of diversity, including the existence of non-traditional accounts of gender relations, this form of education could be thought to alienate those who espouse non-liberal world views and undermine the cultural sources of young women's auton-omy. At the limit, it could be argued that emphasising civic educational ideals to protect the rights defended in this book would simply reinstate the perfectionist liberal defence of autonomy associated with writers such as Joseph Raz (1986). Yet, as Chapter 3 explains, this perfectionist account does not acknowledge the cultural variability of autonomy skills or, there-fore, the interplay between the universal and the particular in a feminist and multicultural account of rights.

My central claim in this context is that all persons have interests in reflecting on their religious and cultural mandates, as well as in cultivating the civic virtues of reasonableness and tolerance that would enable them to participate as citizens of the wider multicultural society. Chapter 4 therefore defends a form of liberal education that would recognise gender equality and cultural justice as equally valuable goals by examining Stephen Macedo's (1995; 2000) political liberal objections to the accommodation of the demands of evangelical Protestants in the USA. Macedo's assertion of a strong religion–state separation in the educational sphere is, I contend, untenable for many future citizens of faith and is, therefore, inappropriate to a feminist and multicultural theory of rights. By focusing on a case in which a group of evangelical Christian parents sought to exempt their children from civic classes which would have familiarised them with ethical diversity and non-traditional gender relations, I defend a presumption for accommodation in this sphere which is constrained by requirements of non-discrimination necessary to secure the sources of citizens' autonomy. Civic education must, I argue, aim to fuse the cultural sources of a future citizen's autonomy with her public capacity for tolerance. A policy of integrating civic and cultural commitments is needed for this purpose. This claim further demonstrates the dynamic interplay between the universality and particularity of gender interests on this account.

While my claim is not that education constitutes the sole means through which multicultural liberal states could meaningfully address the structural inequalities associated with gender hierarchies, states that are concerned to protect the rights defended in this book should nonetheless strongly prioritise the task of ensuring that an ethos of non-discrimination prevails in the educational sphere. Yet the implications of this claim will not always be straightforward. Chapter 5 addresses the educational accommodation of the muslim veil – the debate about which has been intense in France, a country that prioritises commitments to secular neutrality and republican citizenship. Public figures in France have been divided on this issue with some interpreting the veil as an example of religiously sanctioned sexual domination that threatens the stability of the political order and, thus, the basis of all persons' rights. Engaging with the French republican critique of this practice draws together the different themes addressed in the book – namely, rights to mediation and autonomy and the presumption for educational accommodation. Focusing on this case also enables me to articulate the furthest reaching implications of Young's account of gender as seriality for an interest theory of rights. It demonstrates why the political recognition of diverse practices can be instrumental to evolving a universalistic feminist understanding of issues that warrant collective scrutiny, even if they do not amount to a serious violation of moral rights.

I appeal to theories of citizenship to support these concluding claims. Arising from the writings of Tariq Modood (2005), a commitment to civic reciprocity between diverse citizens entails that an educational ban on the veil would be counter-productive, as it would fail to secure the basis on which young Muslim women might integrate the public and private sources of their autonomy. The ban would thus inhibit them from affirming their commitment to a just state under conditions of freedom. Arguments from civic reciprocity also show that the ban would decrease Muslim women's opportunities to participate in the dialogues of the right to mediation in the long term. If, however, they were to take part, debate could be fostered between diverse women regarding the social constraints that shape their choices, including their choice to wear the veil. The fact that the veil is not itself physically harmful suggests that states would not be justified in prohibiting this symbol in schools. However, this does not mean that feminists should not react critically to the complex conditions under which some women choose this practice. Eschewing a liberal defence of the veil in terms of a simple right to express one's personal tastes, arguments from civic reciprocity indicate strongly that freedom and force are contextual issues; and that the distinctive pressures on some Muslim women to take up their traditional practices should be discussed responsibly through dialogue, whilst acknowledging the problems, such as 'Islamophobia', that often inhibit them from speaking openly about pressures internal to their communities and forming broader alliances aimed at equality and justice.

Whilst recognising the real-world difficulties of instituting a sensitive dialogue about such issues, the final stage of my analysis nonetheless reveals the full implications of conceptualising women's rights as multicultural claims. Conceiving women as a series does not rule out the possibility of cultivating cross-cultural awareness of the subtle constraints that arise in relation to gender hierarchies. The commitment to understanding the particularity of the pressures that structure women's decisions in different cultural locations is underwritten by an ongoing concern about the risk of substitutionalism. To configure women's rights as multicultural claims is to insist that the particular provides a critical lens on, and a means of reformulating, the universal in light of actual human experiences. It suggests a dynamic agenda for feminism as well as for multiculturalism and takes both movements to be concerned with the equitable protection of the sources of bodily, cultural and religious identity through which human lives gain meaning. In brief, cultural particularity is the starting point through which diverse women may achieve justice and, sometimes, find common feminist ground. This is so however elusive the achievement of unity and commonality may be in an imperfect world, in which inequalities of power are pervasive and human values cannot be perfectly reconciled.

CHAPTER 1

Beyond the Liberal Dilemma – Rights as Trumps, as Recognition and as Capability

I Introduction

The normally quiet village of Deorala in the Indian state of Rajasthan witnessed, in September 1987, a controversy that revealed deep social conflicts, when an eighteen-year-old named Roop Kanwar was burned alive on her husband's funeral pyre. News of her death provoked widespread debate about women's status in India and, in particular, about sati or widow immolation (Sen 2002: 2). The practice had been outlawed by the British administration in 1829 and was widely thought to be obsolete in the modern day. While most Indians oppose it, a number of Hindus affiliated to the right-wing Bharatiya Janata Party supported its legalisation in 1996 (Hardgrove 1999: 723).[1] Two years before the Deorala sati, moreover, in her novel *Rich Like Us* (1985), Nayantara Sahgal had portrayed the relationship of this practice to the colonial project and to the independence movement. Her account of the modernity of this tradition is echoed in one feminist's insistence that the Deorala incident 'should not be viewed as a remnant of a feudal past but as an expression of . . . the contemporary denigration of women' (Loomba 1993: 247).

Other feminists are worried, however, about the political risks involved in focusing on rare practices in non-liberal cultures. Uma Narayan (2000: 88), for instance, draws attention to Mary Daly's (1978) reproduction of an 'essentialist packaged picture of "Indian culture"', which effaces the challenges posed to sati in history. To emphasise cultural or religious justifications for this practice, Narayan argues, plays into the hands of fundamentalists who invoke it as a central component of 'Indian culture', even though it has all but disappeared (2000: 89; Oldenburg 1994). Yet, while it is apt to heed Narayan's admonition against permitting feminist analyses to be co-opted for dubious political ends and against allowing them to deepen Westerners' 'arrogant perceptions' of non-Western women (Frye 1983), her warning should not be interpreted as a repudiation of the fact that sati presents a feminist problem in which culture matters. Narayan does not deny that even an isolated incident of sati presents a humanitarian issue. She does not claim that it would be misguided to focus on the cultural norms that are likely to shape women's responses to it. Her point is that such norms should not be invested with an implausible degree of authenticity or explanatory force. Notwithstanding Narayan's important point, then, Roop Kanwar's death presents a problem[2] that would not be so complex if sati were simply assumed to represent egregious coercion. However:

> [t]he abolition of this rite by the British has generally been understood as a case of 'white men saving brown women from brown men'. White women, from the nineteenth-century British Missionary Registers to Mary Daly, have not produced an alternative understanding. Against this is the nativist argument, a parody of nostalgia for lost origins: 'The woman actually wanted to die'. (Spivak 1988: 93)

On this account, it is difficult to dismiss the possibility that sati might at least sometimes constitute an 'existential free choice', one which is premised on the widow's right to exercise courage (Spivak 1988: 96). However contentious asserting this right may be in view of the stigma associated with widowhood in India (Agarwal 1988), the concern is that rejecting this interpretation outright cannot but appear imperialistic. A feminist and multicultural theory of rights must confront the problem apparently presented by Spivak's account which, albeit unintentionally, seems to offer the stark options of either challenging sati in a paternalistic vein or simply accepting the assertion of the widow's free will. Significantly, such an either/or dilemma arises also in the tendency of contemporary liberals to interpret rights as non-negotiable interests or, in familiar terms, as 'trumps' (Dworkin 1979; 1984). The liberal dilemma (Eisenberg 2003: 43) typically constructs a conflict between rights to cultural autonomy and to sex equality (Okin 1999c; Kukathas 2001). This understanding of rights, however, fails to respond to the need to react appropriately to the significance of women's cultural and religious affiliations in debates about justice, whilst retaining a commitment to certain universal feminist ideals. The popular understanding of liberal rights does not appear to help to clarify the issues at stake in sati. It seems to hinder the project of theorising women's rights as multicultural claims.

The tendency to assert a conflict between cultural justice and women's rights is not confined to liberal theory (see Bannerji 2000; Bunting 1993; Pham 2006); but is particularly prominent within this tradition. In order to elaborate on this problem fully, I postpone until Chapter 2 a detailed analysis of liberal feminist Susan Okin, who, as noted in the Introduction, takes the conflict between feminism and multiculturalism to be inevitable. I begin instead by acknowledging the general problems that have been thought to beset liberal discourses of rights in debates about gender and culture. Apart from the widespread disagreement that exists between liberals over the normative basis of rights (for instance, whether in rationality, sentience or mere life; and whether rights are pre-political or artefacts of political institutions), one prominent worry about this discourse is its purported individualism, which, according to one writer, is inevitably hard to 'parse into a communitarian framework' (Ignatieff 2003: 67). Following the observations above, one might also be concerned about the absolutism of liberal rights, which has been thought to 'promote unrealistic expectations . . . and inhibit deliberation [between groups] that might lead to consensus' (Glendon 1991; 14). This complaint echoes Marx's concern about the rights-bearing individual as an isolated nomad, withdrawn behind his bourgeois interests (Marx 1844). Finally, liberal rights could be charged with excessive abstraction and therefore with being politically naive in the face of the deep injustices experienced by women around the world. In brief, for many women who experience violence and poverty today, the assertion of these entitlements could seem merely rhetorical (Yasuaki 1999: 9).

By focusing on the issue of sati in this opening chapter, I challenge these criticisms by arguing that a response to the issues raised by the debate over gender and culture can and should be formulated in terms of a schedule of high-priority rights. However, this task must involve deconstructing the liberal dilemma. The trumping metaphor popularised by Ronald Dworkin (1979) presents rights as fundamental moral entitlements that serve as powerful reasons for compulsory state assistance or the forbearance of other citizens. These entitlements have been taken by later writers not only to override non-right objectives, such as ensuring state security, as Dworkin intended. While some influential thinkers have argued that all rights must be 'compossible' or mutually realisable (Steiner, 1994), the trumping metaphor has been pushed further than Dworkin proposed to create the impression that, where rights seem to conflict, there is no rational way of resolving the situation (Eisenberg 2003: 44). The 'losing claim' is dismissed entirely and, from the perspective of the losing party, arbitrarily. Moreover, this problem may be thought symptomatic of liberalism itself, since this tradition attributes maximum importance to formal rights but does so in full recognition of irresolvable differences between the moral sources and conceptions of the good that ground the ethical commitments of diverse persons (MacIntyre 1981).

However, the assumption of a fundamental incompatibility between rights not only fails to respond to the crucial issues confronting women of non-liberal groups, but also fails to do justice to the elasticity and radical potential of an interest theory of rights (McKinnon 2006: 90). Interest theories generally conceive rights as registering the investment of all persons in being treated with equal dignity and entail that a person 'has right to x when her interest in x is sufficiently important to hold other people to a duty to provide her with x' (Waldron 1993: 72; Raz 1984: 194–214). This account could conceivably accommodate a combination of interests since, as Catriona McKinnon points out, 'the fact that we can discuss . . . what constitutes an important interest explains familiar disputes about the rights that we have and what to do when they clash' (McKinnon 2006: 91). Moreover, an interest theory could recognise the *special* rights of minority cultures as well as those of internal minorities. While it might initially seem that the requirement that rights relate to universalisable interests (Dworkin 1984: 44) rules out special entitlements, members of cultural groups are likely to have non-universal interests that derive from general claims to, say, freedom of association. In sum, the impression of incompatibility generated by the idea of rights as trumps should be countered both for conceptual *and* political reasons. The injustices suffered by women arising today seem absolutely to require a response grounded in this high-profile moral language (Deveaux 2006: 57). Significantly, rights discourses have been taken up by women of remote cultural groups (Merry and Stern 2005). To assume that they are simply vehicles of Western imperialism or that they are inevitably too individualistic to respond to debates about gender and culture would only lead to the trumping of women's claims on grounds of culture-based justifications for gender discrimination (Mayer 2000; Deveaux 2006: 59).

Therefore, there are strong reasons to retain faith in an interest theory of rights and, in doing so, to outline two forms of harm to human interests to which a feminist and multicultural account of these entitlements should respond. These forms of harm will structure my discussion in this chapter. First, some multiculturalists voice the concern that assertions of universal rights run counter to community values (Kymlicka 2002). This problem gives rise to what I call the 'harmful exclusion' of their cherished values from political debate. Multiculturalists often contest the priority that liberals accord to first-generation rights such as freedom of expression and, consequently, the subsidiary role that they leave for community norms (Gehring and Galston 2002; Gunew 1997). This worry cannot necessarily be addressed by calling collective rights human rights (Torbisco Casals

2006; Symodides 1998). For there is controversy over how a group could possess the moral agency necessary to be the subject of a right (Van Dyke 1982). Moreover, if group rights are justified on account of their role in promoting their members' autonomy (Kymlicka 1989), it is not clear why groups that espouse collective goods would be supported (Smolin 1995; Cassatella 2006).[3] While multiculturalists generally eschew extreme forms of cultural relativism, they are correct to be concerned about the hubris of universalistic theories that fail to take diversity seriously, since it is likely that such theories would also fail to respond to the interests that many women have in retaining their cultural and religious identities.

The second form of harm with which we shall be concerned can be explained by referring again to the tendency of rights discourses to fail to account for the systematic inequalities associated with gender subordination (Schwartzman 1999; 2006; Lacey 1998). The problem is that the formality of liberal entitlements can obscure the fact that people often lack the power and psychological preconditions truly to benefit from them (Kingdom 1996). Whilst efforts have been made, in theory and practice, to meet this concern by defending socio-economic rights,[4] many feminists remain rightly concerned that increased material resources do not necessarily lead to enhanced capacities for agency, as the latter are dependent on psychological goods such as self-esteem. The worry is, therefore, that the assertion of rights would only be useful in the debate about sati if they respond to the structural nature of gender injustice, or if they address the way in which vulnerable members of groups internalise social norms harmfully and, thus, fail to contest injustice.

I shall elaborate on these conceptions of harm as my argument progresses. For now, however, let me emphasise the importance of accommodating these concerns in a discourse of rights, if we are to take seriously the insights offered by Iris Young's (1994) notion of 'gender as seriality'. This conception of gender recognises the deep particularity of women's interests, as well as the reality of gender hierarchies that transcend the boundaries of ethnic, cultural and economic groups. To be specific, Young invokes the notion of seriality to explain why women should not be assumed to constitute a cohesive group with common purposes (1994: 724). For one thing, this is because all social groups are internally differentiated and relationally constituted (Young 1995). For another, the account aims to respond to the problem of 'essentialism' or swift assumptions that women share a universal bodily or social reality. Third-wave feminists (Gatens 1996: 76; Spelman 1988), as I noted in the Introduction, contest such claims, contending that, if female bodies are pervasively acculturated, there is no natural body that precedes the phenomenological way in which it is lived. Moreover, the claim that women share a social reality appears false when one considers their diverse life conditions globally. Yet, *anti-essentialism* threatens to lead to political paralysis – if women do not share any interests, how can feminists conceptualise the disadvantages that women suffer as systemic? Young responds to this problem by conceiving women as a 'self-alienated series', arguing that 'their womanliness will not be the only thing that brings them together, since there are other concrete details of their lives that give them affinity, such as their class or race position' (1994: 737).

While this point appears compelling, what, however, is a 'series'? Drawing on Sartre's account of this term (1976: 256–8), Young explains that, while social groups are defined through a set of mutually acknowledged objectives, members of a series are united only in terms of the fact that certain social structures passively organise their lives. The way that they experience what Sartre (1976: 257) called 'practico-inert' structures varies enormously. Young illustrates this point by referring to listeners to a radio programme. While the timing of the programme structures the listeners' lives in an important sense, the programme might be the only thing that they have in common. Due to their diverse life experiences, they might interpret the programme in infinitely variable ways. Extending this point, Young holds that women's lives are passively organised by structures such as the sexual division of labour and normative heterosexuality. Like those who listen to the radio programme, women may become conscious of their relationship to one another in certain circumstances (1994: 740), but their thoughts, reactions and perceptions of the world are importantly shaped by their local contexts. While Young does not explain the implications of the idea of 'gender as seriality' for a feminist and multicultural theory of rights (and, in fact, would probably have been opposed to doing so, given her strong criticism of much liberal theory), it is useful, as we shall see, to adopt this account of gender as a starting point from which to conceive women's rights as multicultural claims. To be specific, Young's approach provides conceptual support for the claim that women's interests cannot be straightforwardly universalised, and that the dynamic interplay between the particular and the universal should be recognised in order to respond equitably to their needs. Assuming, then, that women's experiences in their lived social contexts are likely to shed light on a universalistic feminist understanding of justice, this chapter proceeds to focus on harmful exclusion and harmful internalisation, as outlined above, as key issues in responding to practices such as sati in rights-based terms. In doing so, I seek to go beyond the liberal dilemma. I pursue a rights-based response to the issues raised by this practice in a manner that is informed by Young's conception of gender.

My discussion is structured as follows. Section II explains the need to respond to sati in terms of universal rights by focusing on Michael Walzer's (1994) theory of thin minimalism. I contend that, despite its advantages over standard liberal accounts of rights, it ultimately reinstates the dilemma typically constructed within this tradition. The following sections examine recent approaches in liberal philosophy – namely theories of recognition and capabilities – as sources of an adequate rights-based account. I set out their advantages in terms of responding to the forms of harm outlined above. Section V concludes that neither theory provides the basis for an interest theory that responds to the debate over sati, even though they contain important insights in theorising the 'serialised' interests of women. In sum, this chapter's discussion highlights the issues central to configuring women's rights as multicultural claims, and sets the agenda for the framework of rights to be defended in ensuing chapters.

II BEYOND THE 'LIBERAL DILEMMA'? WALZER'S THIN MINIMALISM

While Walzer is not widely known as an advocate of rights, his theory of thin minimalism (1994) promises to respond to the two harms delineated above through its central premise that a condemnation of injustice exists 'reiteratively' in all world views. Walzer dissents from the assumption generally made by political liberals that norms of justice can be articulated by people who bracket their cultural commitments in political debate (Habermas 1990; Rawls 1971). While each world view, he believes, contains its own thick forms of justice, such as Hinduism's celebration of the principle of dharma, or its imperative that each person carry out the moral duty prescribed by their social role (Babb 1975), each tradition shares with others a minimal notion of how people should never be treated and, thus, an account of which rights should never be infringed. The premises of Walzer's thin minimalism promise a way out of the liberal dilemma by assuming that, while all cultures contain their own historically contingent conceptions of justice (1987), they all reject the idea of extreme coercion (1994: 23). For instance, even if some claim a religious justification for sati, it is more than possible to find alternative voices that either reject the practice entirely or emphasise the injustice of forcing the widow to die (Srivastava 2004). To conceive basic rights in terms of thin minimalism[5] therefore appears to accommodate concerns about the exclusion of non-liberal values from rights-based theories *and* the need to protect the basic psychological capacities of vulnerable insiders in non-mainstream traditions.

The ability of this theory to respond to these issues is questionable, however, when we consider that apologists for sati could simply claim that the issue of choice is not paramount (Major 2006). For instance, some Hindu caste revivalists asserted after the Deorala sati that, through the act of immolation, a widow achieves self-realisation which is morally required (Dickie 1988: 8). However one reacts to this claim, and notwithstanding the evident point that defenders of this practice constitute a very small minority, this issue unsettles the assumption that empirical agreement on the morality of human rights can always be found. Indeed, when Walzer considers sati specifically, he concedes this point, arguing that, while non-liberal practices may be accommodated in certain regimes, liberal values are simply more important than cultural and religious justifications in modern democracies. This is because the state 'grants equal citizenship to all its members, including Hindu widows and Mormon wives', and sati should therefore not be tolerated (1997: 61–2). Yet this view excludes the non-liberal views of defenders of this practice, and seemingly precludes a cross-cultural debate about gender subordination. In brief, the approach seems simply to presume a clash between women's rights and non-liberal claims and, thus, in spite of its aspirations, reinstates the liberal dilemma.

Moreover, this problem recurs in Walzer's earlier account of a society in which women are understood as 'objects-of-exchange'. Even if members of this society endorse this convention, Walzer insists that women 'have . . . the right of agents to refuse a[n] object status' (1993: 173). However, he does not consider the observations of defenders of the 'Asian values' perspective on human rights, who contend that many non-Western traditions prioritise duties, leaving rights with a marginal role (Robison 1996, J. Donnelly, 1989). Even if the right of agency could be taken to be universal in these contexts, it is not clear why it would not include the right to submit to an 'object' status. Walzer's reasoning about this case once again indicates his underlying assumption of a conflict between sex equality and cultural autonomy, without responding to the difficulties with this assumption for women in non-mainstream cultures (Anthias 2002). Furthermore, the fact that Walzer himself is uneasy about this assumption is reflected in his concession that a woman who agrees to her role as an object should both be respected *and* be considered contradictory (1993: 174; compare Putnam 1993: 184). In conceding this point, he acknowledges the 'self-enforcing' nature of many gendered practices (Mackie, 2000),[6] or the way in which women often adhere to practices that seem to undermine their interests (Hellsten 1999). While Walzer indirectly acknowledges the complexity of the debate about culture and gender, his positive proposals do not seem to respond to them.

This cursory critique of Walzer's theory usefully emphasises that a rights-based response to sati should begin with an explicit acknowledgement of the fact that different cultural groups and political communities interpret rights in their unique ways, and that rights always require clarification of the needs of actual persons (Baumeister 2003b: 744). It draws attention to the fact that an interest theory that responds to feminist and multicultural issues should recognise that the particular mediates the universal in important ways, and that not all rights claims in conditions of deep cultural diversity are consistent with liberal values (Tamir 1995). The theory must engage with the specific content of different world views without assuming a zero-sum conflict between them. One important reason for this, given our focus on sati, is that it is likely to be impossible to distinguish the 'gender part' of women who are risk from this practice from the 'religion', 'class' or 'race part' (Spelman 1988: 13). *Pace* Walzer, we must recognise that women cannot be abstracted from their cultural particularity.

III Rights, Recognition and Harmful Exclusion

Let us then attempt to conceptualise the rights at issue in this debate according to a comparatively recent approach in liberal political theory, which takes seriously what I have called the harmful exclusion of minority values. The politics of recognition promises to meet the challenge of inducing liberal defenders of rights to engage with the specific content of non-liberal world views. Since the literature on recognition is prolific, and as some of its proponents are suspicious of rights-based approaches (for example, Fraser 1997), I limit my focus to two major conceptions of recognition that are germane to our theme. Generally, theorists of recognition emphasise that subaltern groups have suffered injustice in the history of many contemporary states, and that this problem continues to undermine their members' dignity (Honneth 1995: x). The 'grammar' of recognition is thus moral and political, in the sense that the feelings of humiliation and injustice driving them imply ethical judgements about the legitimacy of existing arrangements (ibid.: xii). Yet, while the writers that we shall consider advocate an important method for evaluating issues such as sati from a rights-based perspective, their predominant focus on collectivities with a common experience of injustice does not respond to Young's insight that the 'serialized experience of being gendered is precisely the obverse of mutual recognition and positive identification of one oneself in a group' (1994: 731).

While the recognition of difference implies a transformative project that is not limited to protecting rights, Charles Taylor defends recognition in these terms. He argues that, as individual dignity is developed through patterns of inter-subjective recognition between and within groups (1992a: 64), equal dignity should be secured by according marginalised groups special rights (Taylor 1993). As people derive their self-understandings from communities of shared values or 'webs of interlocution' (Taylor 1979), liberals must concede that not all human beings subscribe to their priorities, and should acknowledge that a neutral meta-standard to determine the legitimacy of many claims is likely to be unavailable. Liberals must therefore 'weigh the importance of certain forms of universal treatment against the importance of cultural survival, and opt sometimes in favour of the latter' (Taylor 1992a: 61).

Although Taylor refers in this context to the thin demand of the Québecois to safeguard their language and culture, his claim also supports a form of intercultural deliberation that promises to render universalistic theories of rights responsive to thick diversity. Engagement between widely divergent groups is possible because people in modernity are generally aware of pluralism, or the multiplicity of plausible ethical views that arise out of human diversity (Taylor 1999: 123). Thus, the human interests at stake in a practice such as sati could be clarified if, for instance, liberals considered the merits of pursuing spiritual fulfilment at the expense of physical well-being; and if apologists for this practice, for their part, recognised the exploitation that could arise from supporting such an extreme act. While appreciating the merits of alternative world views could be easier for a secularist than for a religious devotee, Taylor assumes that even strongly orthodox groups are aware of pluralism in modernity (1999: 124). Moreover, although the goal of reaching inter-civilisational understanding may appear utopian, the aspiration to construct limited forms of consensus by engaging with groups that traditionally impugn one's conception of justice is productive (ibid.: 125). The idea is not for liberals to listen sympathetically before imposing their values on others but for everyone's understanding of value to be transformed (Taylor 1992a: 72). On this basis, liberals might support, say, certain restrictive educational programmes or forms of genital mutilation for reasons that they could not have appreciated *before* the dialogue. On account of his belief in a 'fusion of horizons' (ibid.: 72), Taylor urges liberals to recognise that their cherished values are historically contingent and that, while fundamental freedoms remain sacrosanct in a liberal order, their pursuit should not involve de-legitimising other goods. 'It would take,' he argues, 'supreme arrogance to discount the possibility' that most cultures 'are almost certain to have something that deserves our admiration and respect' (1992b: 256). In supporting a presumption for the equal value of cultures, Taylor's account indicates the need for a deliberative process to reach a conclusion with respect to practices such as sati. The idea cannot be that anything that diverse individuals find valuable is admissible: such a perspective would be patronising, ethnocentric and, ultimately, 'homogenizing' (1992a: 64). Rather, the idea is to engage imaginatively with others' views in order to expand the moral horizons of all.

Taylor's approach can be supplemented usefully by James Tully's, whose civic or participatory account of recognition also highlights intercultural deliberation as a means of transcending the exclusions resulting from overly swift assertions of universal liberal rights. Tully recalls that pre-modern polities were an assemblage of jurisdictions which recognised diversity in ways that have been brushed aside by the strong demands for uniformity imposed by the modern state. Referring to these earlier modes of civic belonging, he argues that the alienation of indigenous groups can be addressed by encouraging states to engage with different self-understandings found in a diverse civil society. There is no closure to be found in this process, because struggles for recognition represent a continuing battle against injustice and an incessant practice of freedom (Tully, 2000; Thompson, 2006: 183). This 'agonic' practice promises to alter a group's own self-understanding as well as that of the polity. Anticipating the criticism that his account is best placed to recognise the demands of groups that resemble the modern nation in structural terms, such as national minorities that typically have what Kymlicka (1995a: 13) calls a 'societal culture' consisting in a shared history and institutions (Milde 1998), he insists that his account applies to a diversity of subaltern struggles, and would equally encompass feminist campaigns (Tully 1995: 24). While we shall take issue with this point shortly, Tully does appear to offer a productive approach to ascertaining rights that recognises women's potentially divergent goals and priorities cross-culturally and, thus, their serialised location in culture. He does so by adhering to three insights: (a) that language is 'aspectival', in the Wittgensteinian sense that the meaning of values varies according to forms of life; (b) understanding is achieved in dialogue; and (c) that disputes should be regulated by flexible conventions rather than comprehensive principles (ibid.: 111).

More specifically, Tully supports the conventions of consent, continuity and mutual recognition (1995: 116) which were observed in the culturally respectful treaties formed between settler-colonists and indigenous peoples in early modern times (ibid.: 165–82). This mode of engagement evokes not an image of participants in a hypothetical situation forging consensus on abstract principles from behind a veil of ignorance. Rather, it is one of cultural values playing a key role in mediating conflicts (Ivison 2002: 82; Owen 1999). Consensus on each and every human right is neither necessary nor possible since 'there is always much about the others that we may not understand' (Tully 1995: 89). While Tully (2000) now also evinces universalistic commitments to personal autonomy and human rights, the constitution that he proposes accommodates the idea that the value of freedom, for instance, can be interpreted in different ways – even as the pursuit of spiritual liberation. He therefore implies that diverse interpretations of value could legitimately inform the struggles of all vulnerable persons, including women of non-mainstream groups.

How convincing are these claims? The requirement to 'audi alteram partem', or to listen to the other side (Tully 1995: 135), is important strategically, given the significant number that celebrated the Deorala sati (Jarman 2002). It is prudent to engage with defenders of controversial practices, not least because excluding their perspectives summarily risks provoking a backlash against vulnerable individuals (Kasturirangan 2004). Tully is also correct to discourage liberals from conceptualising non-liberal diversity as the cause of intolerable repression; and he effectively counters the 'boutique multiculturalist' view that evinces sympathy for cultural difference only to a point that is congruent with liberalism (Fish 1997: 378). The approach appreciates the depth of value disagreement in modern societies. Both Tully and Taylor assume, plausibly, that while cultures are internally contested, they are also contexts in which meanings are produced and a framework through which life becomes intelligible. They therefore rightly indicate the need for a deliberative approach to assessing conflicts through an understanding of culture as both constraining and enabling (Gedalof 1999). To this extent, they support a 'serialised' understanding of gender. They emphasise the fact that to conceive the debate about gender and culture as inevitably harbouring intolerable conflicts between sex equality and cultural autonomy is unsatisfactory. One reason for this is that it could mean that many women, confronted with having to make a choice, would renounce feminist campaigns out of reactive defensiveness, opting to put faith behind their communities, irrespective of the inequalities that they experience within their groups (Eisenberg 2003: 46).

At the same time, however, theories of recognition do not respond fully to the issues raised by a practice such as sati. A key problem is that Taylor's dialogue risks producing not a fusion of horizons so much as fundamental disagreement. While he is correct to believe that no neutral meta-standard is available to adjudicate many disputes in complex polities, some guiding conventions would have to regulate the dialogue in order to mediate specific claims in a rights-respecting state. Here, Nicholson (1996) argues that Taylor offers few solutions because he is ultimately torn between the hope that cultures will be transformed by their engagement with liberalism and a respect for diversity that seeks to protect groups' 'authenticity'. The compromise that he suggests in terms of a distinction between fundamental rights and a wide range of discretionary immunities and privileges (Taylor 1992a: 61) is not convincing, as even basic rights can be interpreted in conflicting ways. Moreover, if all persons are assumed to agree on the interpretation of fundamental rights, the point of 'fusing horizons' appears unclear. Therefore, it is not evident how Taylor can avoid, in his own language, 'cramming others into our categories' (ibid.: 74).

Tully's approach poses difficulties too. The endless public assertion of different value perspectives risks inflating rights claims to the point of devaluation (Wellman 1999). Moreover, if different interpretations of universal values are presented as equally legitimate in principle, a diverse polity would, again, require more specific guiding conventions than the norms of consent, continuity and recognition to mediate local interpretations of value and establish mutually persuasive judgements and outcomes, especially on issues of gender justice. For one thing, the indigenous demands for sovereignty on which Tully focuses are likely to raise thorny issues concerning collective goods such as economic efficiency, and the liberty rights of other citizens. Moreover, Monique Deveaux pertinently warns in this context that 'groups that experience systematic forms of . . . subordination . . . are by no means immune from practising their own internal forms of discrimination' (Deveaux 2006: 151). While the conventions that could regulate intercultural dialogue need not be typically liberal ones, as I shall argue in Chapter 2, they should recognise that women do not always share common goals that could easily be voiced within political debate. Tully might reply to this concern by emphasising that a group *discovers* its interests through civic engagement (Tully 1999), or by emphasising that deliberation is indeed often marred by structural inequalities in the real world (Tully 2000: 422). However, is it hard to see how deliberation could be equitable if it simply concedes the fact of structural disadvantage or, more deeply, whether it should be assumed that groups always do have a discoverable collective voice. For instance, indigenous women in Canada have been deeply divided over how gender equality is best conceived (Platiel 1992; Turpel-Lafond 1997; Krosenbrink-Gelissen 1991). In light of these issues, Tully's claim that his conventions apply to cultural groups *and* gender relations appears contentious.

These problems suggest that ascertaining rights in the case of sati cannot simply be a matter of recognising that women across cultures have different histories and political goals. The process must also be geared, as one critic of recognition puts it, towards 'transforming the context in which differences are lived' (Henrietta Moore 2000: 1131). The challenge for a *feminist* theory of recognition, one which could genuinely inform a feminist and multicultural theory of rights, is to analyse how cultural meanings express aesthetic, spiritual and moral matters (Bloch 1993: 95) *and* inequalities of power (Baum 2004: 1086). Moreover, the issue for many women is not simply to make visible that which has been invisible in the political order since, in history, women have been recognised only too readily in terms of their gender (Wolf 1992). In other words, the dialogues proposed by Taylor and Tully do not distinguish adequately between 'cultural domination' (the subjection of a group to another's values) and 'disrespect' (the subjection of a group member to belittlement by stereotyped images) (Fraser 2003). While other accounts of recognition, such as those of Fraser (2003) or Honneth (1995), would be better placed to respond to the structural disadvantages often experienced by internal minorities, it is fair to say that the form of political deliberation evinced by defenders of recognition to address the problem of cultural injustice fails to respond to the deepest inequalities at issue in a debate about sati. Whilst they generally indicate an important method for deconstructing the liberal dilemma, they do not ultimately show how their proposals balance women's rights and multicultural claims.

IV Rights, Harmful Internalisation and Capabilities

A rights-based approach to sati must respond not only to the harmful exclusion of non-liberal values, but should also address the concern that oppression may not be revealed through deliberation alone. Moreover, it must respond to the fact that holding a right does not entail a capacity to exercise it (Obando 2004). These problems call for an account of the structural constraints that give rise to what I have called the 'harmful internalisation' of social norms. This issue is crucial for feminists, because gender disadvantage does not always manifest itself in the formal denial of rights or in overt acts of violence.[7] Rather it is often revealed in women's tendency to internalise a lowly self-conception and therefore to accept a truncated quality of life. While women in different cultures have varying priorities and experience discrimination in different ways, they sometimes internalise cultural beliefs in a manner that feminists rightly wish to call objectively or universally harmful. This point bears directly on our analysis of sati; it emphasises that a theory of rights must include a normative commitment to safeguarding the human capacity to resist injustice, even whilst recognising the significance of cultural affiliations. Of course, one might ask how the *harmful* internalisation of cultural beliefs can be distinguished from their routine internalisation in many cases, given that people are always 'pervasively socialised', to use Robert Post's language (1999: 67). While I turn to this key question in later chapters, I concentrate for now on how this problem can be acknowledged in a culture-sensitive theory of rights. The point is to render a theory of rights responsive to the fact that, while cultures differ widely in their definitions of harm, an interest theory should not always accept a superficial account of a person's preferences, but must ensure that they have the capacity to attain a substantive level of well-being.

A possible means of recognising this issue appears to lie in drawing from the capabilities approach (Sen 1982, 1985a, 1985b, 1995a; Nussbaum 2004). Defenders of this perspective define a capability as a person's effective freedom to convert their rights or resources into well-being or, in simpler terms, their ability to use their goods and entitlements to achieve what they value.[8] On the face of it, capabilities are not tied to any world view but provide a framework for developing cross-cultural judgements about the central capacities of persons. As Duncan Ivison explains, they 'get more directly than rights-talk to the conditions required for the effective exercise of the kinds of interests that rights are often thought to promote' (2002: 130). Thus, if basic capabilities were incorporated into a theory of rights, their depth and cross-cultural applicability promise to respond to issues of structural disadvantage within and across groups. The question, however, is whether the insights of this approach do indeed challenge the liberal tendency to view sex equality and cultural autonomy in terms of an essential dilemma.

IV (i) Sen on Gender, Capabilities and 'Co-operative Conflicts'

Amartya Sen proposed the idea of capabilities to address the limitations of approaches based on well-being or resources such as classic utilitarianism or Rawlsian theory. He argued that a person's capability is their 'ability to do valuable acts or reach valuable states of being' (Sen 1985b: 208). While a person must have money and civil liberties, she must also have the capacity to transform them into 'functionings', or actual states of doing and being, which range from elementary matters such as being adequately nourished and avoiding escapable morbidity to more complex issues such as achieving self-respect (Sen 1995b: 267). Some capabilities, such as the ability to breathe unpolluted air or to receive the positive judgement of others, depend heavily on environmental conditions. However, they generally involve a combination of external and internal factors. For instance, my capacity to breathe unpolluted air in Mexico City depends in key part on my ability and willingness to move. The list of capabilities must be 'deliberatively incomplete' because people must decide which capabilities are valuable and, hence, how they wish to function. The approach therefore holds that to act freely is to have the capacity to 'question those norms of recognition and distribution that govern access to the means [to freedom]' (Ivison 2002: 132–3); and a capability refers to an 'evaluative space' (Sen 1995a: iv–v), or a space of contestation with respect to the forms of a functioning life.[9] As noted above, this approach appears sensitive to cultural difference *and* responsive to gendered structural inequalities.

The theory, moreover, sheds important light on the issues raised by sati. The idea of a capability reveals the failure of standard egalitarian theories to appreciate that people of different genders, cultures and physiological conditions are likely to require different resources or rights in order to achieve an equal amount of well-being (Sen 1995b: 266). A person's capability has to be seen 'not just in terms of permissible possibilities, but with note of the psychological constraints that may make a person (e.g., a housewife in a traditional family) desist from taking steps that she could, in principle, freely take' (ibid.: 267, n. 15; Laden 1991). Thus, assessing whether a person suffers an injustice might involve asking whether they are subject to pervasive norms of social discouragement (Ivison 2002: 134). A person's preferences can be 'adapted' to the point where they do not want what may seem a normal level of well-being. Adaptive preferences raise problems of justice, as any theory of human entitlements must acknowledge that 'long-established deprivation may lead to a realistically low level of desires. People with [such a] truncated psychology . . . may have nearly all their desires satisfied in a way that masks their fundamental deprivation' (Crocker 1995: 123; Sen 1995a: 265–6).

An added advantage of this approach, given our focus on widow immolation, is Sen's insistence that cultural and religious norms per se cannot wholly explain the structural inequalities associated with gender. Gender relations, according to Sen, are often sustained through 'cooperative conflicts', in which the adherence to gender-unequal norms brings benefits to all within a community. The 'relatively inferior role of women and shocking treatment of young girls,' he writes, 'are implicitly "justified" by alleged efficiency considerations' (Sen 1995b: 270). Yet different material and psychological factors are likely to cause a person's preferences to maladapt. That cultural and religious norms are unlikely to be the sole cause of capability failure is illustrated by the contrast that Sen draws between a fasting monk and a starving child (1995a). While the child and the monk experience equal nutritional deficiency, the monk has an opportunity to be adequately nourished, a functioning that he voluntarily foregoes, whereas the child has not chosen her condition. By extension, ensuring that women such as Roop Kanwar avoid a violation of their basic interests is not just a matter of securing external conditions, such as economic independence or their adherence to values such as individual autonomy. Rather, it lies in the interaction between internal and external factors. In spite of the attractions of this claim, however, it has a crucial problem. To accept the legitimacy of, say, the monk's decision to forego physical well-being, arguably he must already have secured certain capabilities, such as a capacity for choice. Yet, keen to preserve the flexibility and culture sensitivity of his account, Sen refuses to define basic capabilities universalistically and rejects the claim that everything that he counts as a capability is related to choice. He insists that sometimes we have the capacity to do things without being able to do the reverse – for instance, one might be able to end one's life without always being able to keep on living (Sen 1995b). Yet, the potential objection to this view is that, although the capability to do 'X' does not imply the ability to do the opposite, Sen's example does seem to indicate that choice of some sort, if only, in this example, to postpone ending one's life and letting oneself die naturally, is essential to this perspective (Crocker 1995; 164). If this is so, arguably Sen cannot abstain from the question of which capabilities are basic and, by extension, which should be regarded as universal interests in a theory of rights.

IV (ii) Nussbaum – Universal Capabilities, Cultural Human Beings

On the other hand, if it is plausible to insist that the theorist cannot determine abstractly which capability failures indicate injustice in all cultural contexts, we should simply concede that this approach would not help to theorise the issue of harmful internalisation. Fortunately, Martha Nussbaum promises to revive the potential of this theory by defending a determinate list of capabilities, on the understanding that those who act beneath a threshold level of each do not have the conditions for adequate functioning (Nussbaum 2000: 97).[10] In my terms, those who lack these capacities would be prone to the problems associated with harmful internalisation. However, the list of capabilities that Nussbaum puts forward as 'a good idea [for] politicians in India' (ibid.: 104–5) is controversial, and it would be contentious to incorporate them within a feminist and multicultural theory of rights. Her proposed list includes abilities relating to 'life; health; bodily integrity; freedom from various kinds of violence; recreation and play; the ability to use one's intellectual faculties and emotional sense; practical reason; affiliation; and the social bases of self-respect and non-humiliation' (ibid.: 78–9). With this list in mind, Nussbaum contends that 'our rights can only be secured when the relevant capabilities to function are present' (Nussbaum 2003: 18). Her plausible claim that one cannot realise rights without focusing on substantive capacities (Nussbaum 2000: 121) is undermined, however, by the thickness of the capacities that she takes as indispensable to human life, as we shall now see.

Whilst Nussbaum once acknowledged 'the possibility of learning from our encounters with other human societies to recognise things about ourselves that we had not seen before' (Nussbaum 1995: 87), her current list of capacities rules out the potential for intercultural conversation advocated by defenders of theories of recognition. By claiming that a 'woman's affiliation with a certain group . . . should not be taken as normative for her, unless, with all the capabilities at her disposal, she makes that norm her own' (Nussbaum 1999a), her account regards with suspicion a woman's decision to adhere to non-liberal norms, such as those underlying sati, for reasons that might seem arbitrary from the point of view of those who endorse them. For, while it is likely that the denial of some of the capabilities on Nussbaum's list could imply an injustice, the claim that a life devoid of, say, recreation is subhuman is not persuasive (Wolf 1995: 109). It is also implausible to think that a person deprived of intellectual fulfilment does not function meaningfully as a human being. Moreover, while Nussbaum claims that the list amounts only to a 'partial and not comprehensive theory of the good' (Nussbaum 2000: 96), this is not necessarily the case, as her account does not acknowledge the different cultural ways in which notions such as non-humiliation can be interpreted. These issues are highly relevant in assessing the legitimacy of practices such as widow immolation, as well as a broad range of issues affecting women around the world. Moreover, although not every capability on Nussbaum's list is too 'intellectualised' for cross-cultural application (compare Okin 2003), she does not recognise the conflicts between them. For instance, it is unclear how one should evaluate the situation of an Orthodox Jew who enjoys religious affiliation in a community that demands rote learning from the Talmud as the sole form of education, and which may be interpreted as denying his intellectual capabilities. These difficulties make it hard to see how Nussbaum achieves her twin aims of: (a) avoiding the deterministic claims about human nature which she believes to beset much liberal philosophy; and (b) defending capabilities that are 'frankly universalistic and essentialist' (Nussbaum 1995: 63). Whilst some believe that Nussbaum recognises the 'complexities . . . of other women, and [seeks] to see them through their own eyes' (Charlesworth 2000: 75), on closer inspection it appears that the perfectionist character of Nussbaum's list does not enable her to respond to cases in which gender justice and cultural autonomy appear to conflict. Furthermore:

there is no harm in admitting . . . that our ability to recognise a common humanity is apt to outstrip any lists of criteria that theorists are likely to come up with. We theorists can offer a list of basic human functions . . . without going out on the . . . presumptuous limb of suggesting that any life or form of life without some one or other of these functions is to be ruled nonhuman. (Wolf 1995: 109)

While Nussbaum does not claim that a person who fails to function in the manner that she recommends is not human at all, this point indicates that her approach is liable to be highly paternalistic towards women in non-liberal groups in practice. This is due to an inevitable slippage between the notion of a capability (an opportunity to be or do) and a function (an actual state of being or doing). As Deneulin points out, when states make decisions about the need for intervention, the distinction between capabilities and functionings narrows, because 'freedom cannot be easily observed unless it has been exercised' (Deneulin 2002: 502). The slippage between capabilities and functionings is evident also in Nussbaum's analysis of adaptive preference formation in different cultural contexts, in which she considers the situation of an American student who diets and uses cosmetics (Nussbaum 1999a: 123). While she concedes that women in affluent nations can be subject to adaptive preferences too, the position of the student is nonetheless different in terms of access to nutrition, education, employment and marital choice (ibid.: 151–2) from that of women who are likely to commit sati – a practice that Nussbaum condemns as a human rights violation (ibid.: 89). Yet, it is hard to see how this claim can be supported in terms of her list of capabilities. For, at least in the Deorala case, the young woman came from an educated and comparatively well-off family (Rajan 1993: 45–7). Thus, she might be assumed to have possessed some measure, if not all, of Nussbaum's capabilities. Her death raises questions concerning how the particular cultural pressures that women experience can be acknowledged, whilst also recognising the need to address structural inequalities associated with gender subordination. Nussbaum's capabilities approach does not supply an adequate basis on which to evaluate these issues.

To be sure, Nussbaum attempts to respond to this problem by prioritising what she calls the 'intrinsic value of religious capabilities', defined as the 'ability to search for one's own good in one's own way' (Nussbaum 1999b: 108). While she concedes that it is hard to know how far states should accommodate non-liberal religious and cultural diversity, she outlines three indicators to guide judgements on this issue (Nussbaum 1999a: 149). These include a person's: (1) lack of or false information; (2) lack of reflection; and (3) lack of options. These conditions seem more flexible than her full list of capabilities. Yet, it is still unclear why the Deorala sati would be deemed a human rights abuse on this account, as the young woman probably did have information, options and, most likely, the capacity to reflect on her practices. For it is reasonable to assume that, given the extreme consequences of self-immolation, a person in this situation would view even a socially ostracised life as a live alternative. Thus, while it is notoriously difficult to assess a person's state of mind, and the extent to which she can contemplate the options formally open to her, there is reason to suspect that Nussbaum indicts practices such as sati on the grounds that they deny women thick liberal capabilities for individuality and independent choice. This concern is borne out by her claim that the capability of 'practical reason' is most important or basic in her list (Nussbaum 2002: 62). Ultimately, then, it would seem that her combination of Aristotelian idealism, political liberalism and Kantian ethics yields a commitment to eradicating a wide range of 'cultural choices' that women might make. As Deveaux aptly explains, women in Nussbaum's view ought to:

> choose to secure basic capabilities and the circumstances that support [them] before they pursue other capabilities and goods . . . associated with traditional cultural roles . . . such as a life of religious devotion which may include the deliberative sacrifice of several [capabilities] and even suffering. (Deveaux 2006: 78; see also Phillips 2001)

Finally, therefore, Nussbaum's approach seems only to reconstruct the opposition between cultural justice and gender equality and, thus, to reinstate the liberal dilemma. In sum, on the one hand, the capabilities approach rightly encourages defenders of rights to look beyond formal freedoms and to respond to the problem of adaptive preferences and structural inequalities with a substantive conception of human freedom. However, on the other hand, the sheer difficulty involved in identifying the basic capabilities suggests that the account cannot be taken up in order to deconstruct the opposition between rights suggested by the liberal dilemma.

V CONCLUSION

By using the feminist controversy over sati as a point of reference, this opening chapter has highlighted the challenges involved in outlining an interest theory of rights that reacts critically to the liberal perception of a basic incompatibility between entitlements to sex equality and cultural justice. While we have postponed until Chapter 2 a detailed critique of an influential liberal writer who asserts this incompatibility strongly, my aim at this stage has been to emphasise the difficulties involved in conceiving rights according to the 'trumping metaphor' which has become salient in liberal theory. This approach assumes that conflicts can only be resolved by positing one right as the non-negotiable winner, whilst dismissing the losing claim entirely. Although it is sometimes likely that rights will not all be 'compossible', swift assertions of fundamental incompatibility in this debate ignore the costs that forcing a choice between feminism and multiculturalism would impose on women who are located serially in different normative orders. I have emphasised this problem in this chapter by focusing on the issue of sati. As Young explains, women conceive goals according to their different cultural, religious and economic standpoints, whilst being related to one another in terms of the relation that their actions have to pervasive structures of gender subordination. Adhering, then, to the notion of 'gender as seriality' served to support my claim that theorising women's interests must involve appreciating how the particular provides a critical perspective on the universal. My purpose in highlighting the rare practice of sati in this context was not to present a packaged picture of Indian culture, or to provide a 'solution' to the social problems that this practice reflects. Rather, it was to provide a vivid focus for the problems of harmful exclusion and harmful internalisation and, thus, to respond to the complex interests of women with affiliation to communities that differ from liberal norms.

In review, Walzer's theory seemed only to reinstate the liberal dilemma. Therefore, we considered two recent approaches in political philosophy as theoretical sources for a rights-based account. The insights of these approaches help to set the agenda for the task I undertake in the following chapters. Whilst theories of recognition respond to the problem of harmful exclusion by highlighting the importance of an inclusive dialogue that acknowledges the depth of cultural diversity, they fall short on account of their tendency to presume a readily discoverable common experience of injustice within groups. By contrast, the capabilities approach emphasises the problem of adaptive preferences arising through structural disadvantages to which theories of rights are often unattuned; and it stresses the need to theorise the issue of harmful internalisation in terms of substantive capacities for agency in different cultures, rather than in terms of formal rights alone. However, the thick liberal requirements for human flourishing presupposed by Nussbaum's account do not leave room to engage fully with non-liberal diversity. In brief, while the proposals of theorists of recognition and capabilities each has a problem, their accounts nonetheless advance insights into how a theory of rights might be taken beyond the liberal dilemma, in order to respond to urgent issues of justice for women around the world today.

NOTES

1. Sati involves a widow's act of immolating herself on her husband's funeral pyre. Extremely rare in India today, it is, however, often associated loosely by various commentators with a Hindu ideal of femininity understood in terms of self-sacrifice. For historical accounts, see Datta (1988), Mani (1989) and Mukhopadhyay (1969). On the death of Roop Kanwar, see Kishwar and Vanita (1987), Rajan (1993), Sangari and Vaid (1991) and Hawley (1994).

2. Narayan concedes that 'anti-essentialism' should not impede feminist efforts to defend rights, even though feminists must relentlessly question generalisations about cultures in terms of their 'empirical accuracy and political risk' (Narayan 2000: 97).

3. I elaborate further on Kymlicka's account of group-differentiated rights in further chapters.

4. Most of the major international covenants on human rights, which states such as India have ratified, include provisions against sex discrimination. Amongst these are the Universal Declaration of Human Rights (1948), the International Covenant on Civil and Political Rights (1966) and the Convention on the Elimination of All Forms of Discrimination against Women (CEDAW, 1979).

5. The voluntary nature of the sati's decision is emphasised by many studies of this practice in colonial times (Sangari and Vaid 1991).

6. Vijayraje Scindia, the Maharani of Gwalior in Madhya Pradesh, who has emerged as a powerful Hindu nationalist, claimed publicly that 'a voluntary act of self-immolation does not constitute an offence' (cited in Crosette 1991: 1).

7. This point is important because my focus on this book is not on egregious nonconsensual violations of rights which most communities are likely to indict. Rather, my focus is on the more complex question of how individuals internalise norms and voluntarily submit to contentious cultural and religious practices.

8. As Ivison (2002: 194, n. 49) explains:

   > a capability is a kind of power to do or be something. It can be more or less developed and more or less feasible, in relation to both internal factors with regard to the agent and external factors to do with the context in which the agent acts.

   While the capabilities approach was presented initially as a response to what Sen called the 'commodity fetishism' of economic theory, it also responds to the excessive abstraction of many theories of rights (Sen 1982).

9. Sen distinguishes between 'agency objectives' and 'wellbeing objectives' in order to address the issue of whether his approach fundamentally values human choice or certain objective states of being (see Sen 1985a; Olsaretti 2005).

10. For a full account of the differences between Sen and Nussbaum's approaches, see Crocker (1995).

CHAPTER 2

The Right to Mediation – Recognising the Cultural Particularity of Interests and Vulnerabilities

I INTRODUCTION

A crucial stage in deconstructing the dilemma examined in the previous chapter is to regard a minority group's values as relevant to an assessment of its members' interests in a robust, deliberative approach. Doing so does not mean that we should ignore the admittedly sizeable risks involved in 'talking "culture"' (Razack 1984), or the dangers of presupposing that cultures have timeless, immutable 'essences'; but it does involve accepting that, on account of the plurality of values and inequalities of power that pervade human lives, women's interests are likely to vary according to their cultural location[1]. Accordingly, this chapter defends what I call 'the right to mediation' or the right of minority groups to participate in consultative fora in order to articulate the values that inform their practices in the course of justifying their claims. This approach does not deny that human beings share certain interests cross-culturally, such as in health, nutrition, literacy and a degree of control over their environment; and it does not entail an uncritical acceptance of all minority demands. Yet it acknowledges that we cannot begin to understand women's differences and their similarities nor, therefore, the relation between the universal and the particular in a multicultural feminist theory until, in Chilla Bulbeck's words, 'we question ethnocentric descriptions of . . . cultural practices and the universal applicability of individualistic rights-based discourses' (Bulbeck 1998: 218).

Following the previous chapter's overview of theories of recognition, one might be wary, however, of relying on intercultural deliberation as a means to respond to feminist and multicultural concerns. One reason for this is that the focus on cultural values seems too often to slide into 'culturalism' (Dirlik 1990), or the view that discrete cultural groups with unified voices may advance non-negotiable claims about which rational debate is impossible. Moreover, a pressing concern is that the conversation would covertly support the efforts of community elites to justify the abuse of historically weaker individuals. While these concerns are sometimes compelling, much depends on the form that deliberation takes. When formulated as a means of promoting an interactive and critical dialogue, intercultural deliberation not only builds productively on the insights of theorists of recognition but also responds to difficulties with liberal attempts to balance women's rights and cultural diversity (Shachar 2001; Kymlicka 1995a). The right to mediation identifies issues of justice that would be obscured if states evaluate minority demands simply by ascertaining their conformity to liberal priorities. Specifically, the approach has the advantage of recognising that: (a) non-liberal practices may often promote women's interests, as liberal priorities do not account for all dimensions of the good; and (b) women experience culturally-specific vulnerabilities that are not always detected through a defence of abstract and universal liberal rights. Thus, the right to mediation 'multiculturalizes' liberalism (Parekh 2000a) and responds to the complex relationship between the particularity of women's experiences and universal feminist ideals. By proposing a feminist form of multiculturalism, it adheres to Young's idea of gender as seriality; and her claim that, while no woman's identity will 'escape the markings of gender', these markings are shaped by her specific location in morally and politically; relevant ways (Young 1994: 735).

While I intend my arguments to apply to minority claims broadly, this chapter focuses especially on the issue of religious divorce conventions. The recognition of these codes has become a point of contention in many contemporary liberal states. The controversy is exemplified by the fraught dispute over the incorporation of Islamic sharia law into the British legal system (Modood 2008). In this chapter, however, I continue to concentrate on India, which, unlike Britain, currently recognises the legitimacy of religious laws relating to marriage, inheritance and divorce.[2] In particular, I refer to Shah Bano's case, which involved an elderly Muslim woman, who was divorced by her husband by way of an informal talaq in 1978. After being thrown out of the family home, she petitioned state courts to obtain alimony from her husband even though, under the dominant interpretation of Muslim law, she was entitled to maintenance only for three months after the divorce, for the period known as the *iddat*. After a long legal battle, the Supreme Court ruled in favour of Shah Bano, ordering the husband to pay 179 rupees, about £10, per month in accordance with the Code of

Criminal Procedure, which forbids anyone of adequate means to allow relatives to remain destitute. The Hindu judge held that, as the purpose of the law was to protect the needy, its 'moral edict . . . should not be clubbed by religion' (Shah Bano: 948).[3]

Key figures in the Muslim community were immediately outraged by what they took to be an assault on their traditions, while feminists voiced concerns about the 'hijacking' of human rights by Hindu elites (Cossman and Kapur 1999: 23–5; Kishwar 1986: 13). If the price of establishing respect for human rights was the suppression of cultural and religious diversity, then some believed that this could not work in women's favour (Mullally 2004: 673). This concern was borne out by subsequent campaigns by Muslim groups to exempt Muslim women from state protection after divorce. Furthermore, swayed by charges that she had betrayed her community, Shah Bano later renounced the court's decision (Shah Bano 1985). According to some, she was forced to choose between her culture and her rights (Das 1992: 84–117; Pathak and Rajan 2001: 204). This case appears to exemplify the liberal dilemma acutely, as many women are disadvantaged in the context of divorce, especially during the religious arbitration of laws relating to child custody and property (Gray and Kevane, 1999; Smock, Manning and Gupta 1999). In response to these problems, I argue that the mode of deliberation encouraged by the right to mediation should play a key role in determining just solutions that promise to enable multicultural states to transcend the liberal dilemma in crucial ways.

One reason for this is that the right to mediation recognises openly that cultural and religious conventions are likely give rise to complex benefits and burdens for women.[4] In preserving a high-priority entitlement for different sectors of minority groups to engage with the state in deliberation, this approach enjoins the state and communities to bring about gender justice collaboratively, without assuming that liberalism fares better than other cultures with respect to gender equality. The right to mediation recognises that cultural and religious misrecognition often compound intra-group sex discrimination. Communities often implement their rules in restrictive ways as a result of a perceived need to shore up collective self-determination, and they typically vest special significance in women's symbolic roles as reproducers of the community at times of social crisis. Thus, while identity in Orthodox Jewish communities, for instance, is traditionally marked via 'control over the womb' and 'by assuring a husband's ownership over his wife's reproductive capacities' (Reitman 2005b: 237; Hauptman 1998), these norms are likely to be enforced in especially rigid ways as a result of pressures on the community to assimilate.

For these reasons, the governments of Israel and Kenya also recognise religious laws (Rajan 1993: Chapter 3) and, amidst much controversy, proposals to do so have arisen in the USA and Canada too (Bainham 1995; Mumtaz Ali 2004). Therefore, given the increasing difficulties associated with denying minority religious and cultural codes some form of recognition in multicultural states, but considering also that these conventions often have gender-discriminatory implications, the right to mediation promises innovative solutions by assuming: (a) that it would be unjust to impose a uniform conception of gender identity on all women; and (b) that contextual solutions to the hardships that they experience should be found through deliberation. This approach responds to the needs of individuals such as Shah Bano, whose interests were not addressed by pronouncing a clash between her religion and her rights.

In sum, the right to mediation recognises that minority practices are likely to represent goods to which women are committed, as well as containing elements that are in need of reform. Since women are located differently with respect to cultural values as well as class, disability and experiences of racism (Ramazanoglu 1989), the effort to apply generally applicable liberal rights in all situations would fail to acknowledge that 'good feminism sometimes requires acts of multiculturalism' (Saharso 2003b: 9). While I ultimately concede that the equity of any deliberative procedure is often dependent on extra-political contingencies, such as a community's willingness to deliberate, that dialogue alone does not always suffice to respond to cultural conflicts, and that further commitments must be specified that encourage participants in dialogue to respond to gender concerns, nonetheless the right to mediation represents a crucial component in a feminist and multicultural theory of justice.

The chapter is structured as follows. Sections II and III reinforce the case for a culturally particular account of women's interests by going back to the liberal dilemma in order to highlight difficulties with Susan Okin's (1999b) liberal universalism. I also consider Ayelet Shachar's response (2000; 2001) to her account. While I argue that Shachar's approach does not surmount all the shortcomings of Okin's approach in relation to cases such as Shah Bano's, it is profitable to build on her proposal to avoid a stark choice between feminism and multiculturalism and to outline a 'transformative' multiculturalism that strives to alter gender hierarchies in the course of supporting minority cultures' forms of life. In the following two sections, I render my own account in terms of the right to mediation, outlining three conventions that guide the dialogues involved in practising this right. I explain how this account responds to the issues raised by Shah Bano. Section VI concludes by arguing that the normative limitations of deliberation entail that the right to mediation must presuppose at least one freestanding universal right, the definition of which poses challenges to which I turn in Chapter 3.

II THE STRONG UNIVERSALISM OF HUMAN RIGHTS: LIBERAL FEMINIST VIEWS

Susan Okin famously accepts the assumption of a basic incompatibility between feminism and multiculturalism, and argues trenchantly in favour of the priority of women's universal human rights. While she acknowledges that minorities may sometimes require special assistance (1998b: 664; 1999b: 131), policies such as group rights must usually be rejected when women's interests are at risk. Despite her contention that there is no simple response to the issue of whether multiculturalism is bad for women, she believes that minority women's prospects for enjoying freedom (2005: 75, 79) and equality (1999b: 21, 23; 1998b: 683–4) would generally be enhanced if they assimilate to the wider liberal society. Thus, she is unmoved by global feminists' observations that universalistic feminist movements risk playing down valuable differences that derive from diverse women's cultural and religious identities (Rajan 2003: Chapter 5), or that it would be unjust to assimilate all women's identities under a typically western liberal model of what it means to be a human being (Hutchings 2005: 158).

To be specific, Okin responds to these claims by insisting that no argument can be made on the basis of self-respect or freedom that female group-members have an interest in preserving patriarchal norms (1999b: 22). Other feminists echo her views: for instance, in *Generous Betrayal* (2002), Unni Wikan analyses the predicament of immigrant women in Norway who tried to escape arranged marriages, and argues that the state, 'deluded by anti-racism and Orientalism', seriously compromised women's interests (2002:210). Yet of those who defend feminism against multi-culturalism, Okin's arguments are the most germane for our purposes, in light of her charge that the 'anti-essentialist critique [of feminism] is overblown, over-valued and largely invalid' (1995: 275). Anti-essentialists must provide concrete support for the claim that non-Western women are excluded from liberal feminist theory and, 'if possible, should show how their inclusion would affect the theory' (1995: 276). The slogan 'We're all Different!' is too often used, she believes, as a substitute for any argument or evidence demonstrating why the specificity of a culture mars a feminist analysis of a problem. Whilst she concedes Harris's (1990) claim that African American women have a different experience of rape than white women (Okin 1995: 27), she denies that the problems affecting minority women differ qualitatively from those in her own culture. Rather, since they differ only in quantitative terms (1995: 28), there is no reason to retreat from campaigns to apply general laws to women in all cultural contexts.

Many writers (see, for example, Bhabha 1999; Parekh 1999) have taken issue with Okin's claims, with one thinker calling her account 'militantly insensitive' (Benhabib 2002: 100). To a degree, this allegation misunderstands Okin's position, since she does not reject multiculturalism completely (Reitman 2005b: 221). However, while she believes that multiculturalism could conceivably override a concern for gender equality when groups have suffered grave injustice, she assumes these cases to be infrequent exceptions to a normally valid rule (1999b: 23). Therefore, liberal states should generally mandate assimilation or cultural reform, and restrictive family codes should be abolished (Okin 1999b: 23). However, when the issues raised by religious divorce laws are examined, problems with Okin's account emerge. Since these difficulties do not undermine the justifiability of liberal rights, but question their interpretation and priority, they imply the need to recognise the particularity of women's rights, while retaining a commitment to some interests that unify diverse women (Steans 2007: 11). The arguments below suggest that recognising cultural particularity represents an appropriate starting-point for ensuring gender justice, as this recognition responds to the problem of substitutionalism in feminist theory and acknowledges the insights of Young's account of gender as seriality. Treating people fairly involves being aware of how culture positively *and* negatively informs their lives. While this claim in itself amounts to a certain form of universalism, it differs from that defended by Okin in an important way.

The first objection to Okin's account acknowledges what we may call the *pragmatic trade-offs* that human beings often make in the real world. For instance, in postcolonial movements or campaigns for national independence, they often decide to forsake the dominant society's values and commit wholeheartedly to communities that have suffered discrimination, poverty and racism (Hirschmann 2003: 154–70). A person's decision to trade off liberal goods may be rational; and, if so, out of regard for her freedom of conscience, justice would mandate respect for her decisions, other things being equal. While it would, of course, be unrealistic to believe that women explicitly consent to disadvantageous divorce rules, it is not unreasonable to assume that some do consent to the normative order in which these rules are embedded. Cultural membership often involves an adherence to a network of practices, some of which individuals may value and others they may regard with ambivalence or distaste.

A person in any culture could, then, decide to endure non-ideal conditions and to accept what Narayan (2002) calls the 'mixed bundles of goods' that her way of life offers. She may go along with the unequal property distributions mandated by the Jewish *get*, for instance, if she believes that maintaining community support is important after family breakdown or if she wishes to ensure that her children retain their religious ties. Her decision not to challenge community rules would occur under far from ideal circumstances; and I am not suggesting that gender-discriminatory rules should go unchallenged. However, women often have reason to believe that enduring their existing basket of advantages and disadvantages is preferable to opting for those that they would encounter in the wider society. While one could argue that this point does not reflect any defect in liberal values, and only highlights the imperfect circumstances in which all principles are pursued, nonetheless an uncompromising pursuit of liberal ideals, irrespective of the social and political circumstances under which actual human beings live, is liable to hinder a meaningful under-standing of their interests. Feminists should not reject ideals such as equality and freedom, but would do well to recognise that they can be interpreted in non-liberal ways. Ascertaining the meaning of freedom and equality involves acknowledging that the imperfections in any society cannot be assessed objectively and that the content of gender justice cannot be articulated abstractly. Many women choose to wear the veil, for instance, as a mark of resistance to Westernised elites (Bulbeck 1998: 30–1), just as they sometimes see female genital mutilation (FGM) as affirming their traditional identity in the face of Western economic and cultural penetra-tion (Toubia 1995: 37). Whether their views represent deviations from a Platonic ideal of gender justice is contestable. In a non-ideal world, in which values are plural and inequalities of power are cross-cutting, ascertaining women's rights is not simply a matter of 'reading them off' a charter. For the list could include entitlements to adhere to conventions that conflict with liberal interpretations of the good.

Okin does not consider this possibility, even though she does raise the connected point that some women who are prohibited by apparently non-liberal religious and cultural customs from working outside their home are 'divided in their own minds' about the contradiction that they face between norms of female respectability and their potential to survive independently (Okin 1995: 292). While this is undoubtedly true, it is equally possible that people could reject liberal values without viewing their decision with regret. Supporting this point of view need not involve ignoring the fact that the oppressed, as we noted in Chapter 1, can often internalise their oppression so well that they fail to recognise their own needs and rights (ibid.).

Closely related this objection is the issue of '*moral standing*'. In light of the unequal historical relations between groups in many societies, male and female members of minority groups often resist the state's authority to demand internal reform. Even though the elderly woman in our central case approached the state to challenge her community's rules, for instance, both she and her community might be suspicious of state intervention in the name of 'justice', on the grounds that the state's actions may signal a hidden agenda of injustice (Spinner-Halev 2001b: 97). While this objection would not invalidate intervention into egregiously violent practices (Perez 2002: 58–9), it is likely to be important in more complex cases where state policies are inconsistent. Consider the Pueblo, an indigenous band at the US-Mexican border, which does not permit the children of female members who marry outside the group to receive community benefits such as healthcare, but which accords these goods to the children of male members, irrespective of whom they marry (Aks 2004). In *Santa Clara* v. *Martinez*,[5] the US government contended that the Pueblos' interest in cultural autonomy overrode the state's interest in ensuring sex equality. While some have rightly contested this judgement for feminist reasons (for example, Eisenberg 2005), a basis for limiting state intervention in this situation could be that the demand that the Pueblos adhere to normally applicable sex equality norms expresses a double standard, given that, in history, the state indirectly supported the development of gender-discriminatory laws which had previously not existed in this group. To make this point is not to say that any government that has perpetrated past injustices lacks the moral standing to pursue its ideals in the present. However, it does indicate the importance of attending to history (Carens 2000: 8). If the wrongs suffered by a community are compounded by the double standard sometimes implicit in state efforts to ensure compliance with its norms, male and female group-members may have rights to resist the state's demands. To say so need not involve sacrificing gender justice but it does involve recognising that gender interests may be best realised through women's own intra-community campaigns.

This objection to Okin's account deepens when we consider a controversial issue arising in our central case – namely the proposal in India to implement a Uniform Civil Code in lieu of different communities' religious laws (Mahajan 2005). Such campaigns may be deemed contestable in view of the government's failure to provide comprehensive assistance to women of the wider Indian society who suffer stigma and financial hardship after divorce (Roy 1996; Amato 1994). Here, the point is not that the majority society must 'put its own house in order' before complaining about injustice in minority groups (Phillips 2002) but only that the issue of who initiates change can be as important as change itself. While it would be misguided to accuse Okin herself of inconsistency, as she argues for the reform of the sexual division of labour wherever it occurs (Okin 1989), she does not confront the difficulty of holding minorities to a standard of justice that is not, in reality, enforced in the wider society, or which is coercively imposed by an 'oppressor-state' (Spinner-Halev 2001b). Moreover, while women do have interests in gender justice, they do not necessarily have an investment in achieving a liberal conception of it that prioritises negative freedom or individualistic goods. Therefore, a fair concern is that Okin does not engage with the implications of Kymlicka's point that, while Indian tribes, for instance, often do not object to being the subject of external review by international courts, they do object to being subject to the formal constitution of their former conquerors (Kymlicka 1999b: 119).

A final and connected worry about Okin's universalistic perspective relates to its failure to consider the *value pluralism* that characterises modern societies. Value pluralism, the view that the harmonious realisation of all goods is unlikely or impossible, is related to liberalism in a complex way. For while Berlin (1969) highlighted the plurality of values *within* the liberal tradition, writers such as Gray (1995) recognise different levels of value pluralism, including a type that is exemplified by thick cultural diversity. On either account, Okin's approach oversimplifies the nature of gender justice by failing to acknowledge that the human condition is such that people cannot realise all human goods in a single life, and that no single culture is ever likely to express all that is valuable. If this is the case, women could often have moral, rather than purely pragmatic, reasons for de-emphasising individual rights to autonomy and for preferring collective goods. An adequate interest theory of rights would need to recognise that the aspirations of some Jewish women, for example, who rebel against their tradition's exclusion of women from formal prayer cannot be perfectly aligned with the campaigns of American women who typically lobby for greater political presence and opportunities to succeed in the market economy. Defenders of value pluralism usually deny that the incommensurability that their accounts tend to engender amounts to relativism (compare Strauss 1989). If they are correct, accepting value pluralism would not involve denying that ideals such as gender justice are rationally justifiable; but it would support the assumption that there are different ways of interpreting this ideal.

Accepting these points establishes a preliminary case against Okin's claim that pursuing gender justice is simply a matter of redoubling efforts to enforce uniform rights and laws in all contexts. For Putnam (1995: 315) rightly argues against Okin that attending to the value pluralism associated with cultural diversity would yield insights into the issues around which women organise in different contexts. Feminists would acknowledge that, 'while for many American women, the chief obstacles to economic security lie in the gender structure of the market and the family, in contrast for . . . upper caste Hindu widows the chief barrier [may be] occupational *purdah*' (ibid.: 314). While Okin might reply that all such problems equally represent obstacles to achieving the same objective (that is, gender equality), attention should be paid to these culturally particular contexts in order to become aware of the specific benefits and burdens confronting women, and to appreciate the different ways that human values can be interpreted. Women's objectives differ, as do the forms of their vulnerability. Recognising this point leads to the plausible assumption that attention to cultural particularity would continually reconfigure a collective understanding of justice. It would encourage the view that the commitment to multiculturalism, conceived as the equitable accommodation of cultural, religious and ethnic groups, should not be seen as intrinsically bad for women.

While Okin insists that she does not reject multiculturalism (1999c: 131) but seeks a form of it that 'gives issues of gender . . . their due' (2005: 69), by this she appears to mean that multiculturalism is desirable only if it is synonymous with the pursuit of liberal values. However, contesting this assumption is only the beginning of the discussion. To support the cultural particularity of women's interests we must show how doing so would not, in fact, undermine feminist justice. While it is plausible to believe that dialogue with women would have constituted an important means of responding to crucial issues arising in cases such as Shah Bano, much depends, as I indicated at the outset, on the form that deliberation takes. Whilst Okin advocates listening to minority women in order to 'recognise unmet needs and unrecognised rights' (Okin 1998a: 48), she views dialogue primarily as a means to enable governments to uncover the full extent of the incompatibility between feminism and multiculturalism (Reitman 2000: 302–3). In this chapter, we shall challenge this view.

III JOINT GOVERNANCE: INTEGRATING THE UNIVERSALISM AND PARTICULARISM OF HUMAN INTERESTS?

Ayelet Shachar's theory of transformative accommodation presents an imaginative challenge to Okin's universalistic account, by combining a respect for minority groups' self-determination with a defence of women's rights in terms of a scheme of power sharing. While she concurs with Okin that multicultural policies can have harmful effects on women, she is critical of the 'secular absolutist' model as practised in France and the Netherlands, which guarantees uniform rights for all women regardless of their group affiliation, whilst also questioning the 'religious particularist' model, ex-emplified historically by the Ottoman Empire's *millet* system and practised today in Kenya, India and Israel, under which each community governs its own matters of family law (Shachar 2000: 214). Both systems are flawed, she argues, since each ultimately demands that women choose between their culture and their rights. Her awareness that women have multiple alle-giances motivates her to propose a 'brave new blueprint' for multicultur-alism (Shachar 2001: 7). While she emphasises that no magic formula can fully overcome the obstacles involved in making groups responsive to women's interests, she defends an arrangement according to which neither states nor communities possess exclusive control over any area of law. In brief, her scheme is designed to 'alter the incentive-structure operating in a minority group, so that female members' indispensable contribution to the group can serve as a source of [their] empowerment' (Shachar 2000: 221). However, while her approach addresses the first two objections raised against Okin's account, it does not respond to the issue of *value pluralism*. While Shachar rightly emphasises the need for a 'transformative' multi-culturalism that ultimately paves the way for my own account, she is wedded to a liberal universalism that does not recognise sufficient diversity to conceptualise women's rights as multicultural claims.

In order to reach this conclusion, consider first Shachar's account of Jewish law in Israel (2001: 45–9) and, in particular, her critique of the *agunah*, or 'anchored woman', as depicted in the biblical Book of Deuter-onomy. According to this convention, a husband can hold his wife to marriage even if the union has been terminated by state laws. Not only are children born from later marriages of anchored women denied inheritance rights, but men have been able to blackmail *agunahs* when the latter petition them for a *get*, or traditional divorce (Radoszkowicz 1991). The injustices of this system have deepened on account of pressures on Orthodox Jews to assimilate to the wider society, which have led to rigid readings of *Halakhic* law. Jewish women now frequently face ostracism if they appeal to the state (Shachar 2001: 45–8). Yet Shachar refuses to respond to this problem by making a contentious and seemingly arbitrary choice between feminism and multiculturalism. Rather, by recognising the 'paradox of multicultural vulnerability', or the tendency of liberal policies of multiculturalism covertly to sanction the abuse of women and other at-risk group members, she contends that power sharing should 'hinge' cultural accommodation on reducing intra-group oppression (2001: 89).

Importantly, Shachar intends to respond not just to Okin's 're-universalised citizenship' model but also to Will Kymlicka's influential theory of group rights (1989; 1995a). Specifically, she proposes to transcend the difficulties with Kymlicka's distinction between 'internal restrictions' (that is, group rights which serve to limit the freedom and equality of individuals within a group), and 'external protections' (that is, group rights which protect the community from the assimilative policies of the wider society). Kymlicka regards the former as inadmissible in a liberal state, and the latter as legitimate.[6] Shachar believes that Kymlicka's distinction is unviable and self-defeating because external protections can be used to impose internal restrictions on group members (2001: 44). One difficulty with her account is, admittedly, that it does not acknowledge Kymlicka's own recognition of the instability of this distinction (1999b: 112, 27, n.7). She does not note his retreat from it, even in the case of immigrant groups, on the grounds that, if there is a consensus within a community with respect to the legitimacy of informal internal restrictions, it might not be appropriate for governments to intervene (1995a: 176). Yet, as it is fair to suppose that the important distinction that Kymlicka wishes to draw here between the *defence* of liberal values and their *enforcement* leaves the thorniest questions about gender and culture unresolved, she usefully addresses the problems with this approach by recommending interaction between state and communities in defining the terms of accommodation (Shachar 2001: 111). The approach promises a degree of engagement with non-liberal cultural diversity which would not be considered productive in Okin's view and which is not explicitly considered by Kymlicka.

In brief, Shachar addresses the *pragmatic trade-off* objection to Okin's account by acknowledging that, while aspects of the *get* may be unjust, Jewish women's desire to retain their traditional identity must be seen as partly a matter of resistance to cultural 'pollution' that plays an important role in minority struggles (Shachar 2001: 167–70). Resistance to secularisation explains why insisting on religious and cultural uniformity and proceeding according to the absolutist model is neither realistic nor desirable in most multicultural societies. Moreover, by granting minorities a greater slice of the jurisdictional pie (ibid.: 120), Shachar addresses the issue of 'moral standing'. The question of multicultural justice, she argues, must often give way to that of multicultural *jurisdiction*. Given the imbalance of power between state and minority groups, the question is often not whether a demand is just in an abstract sense but where decision-making authority is located. Transformative accommodation assumes that decisions to challenge gender-discriminatory community rules must lie with women who occupy a 'dynamic new space for meaningful participatory membership' under her scheme (ibid.: 15). While the state must provide incentives for communities to respond to women's interests, it should not simply impose its own schedule of rights upon them (ibid.: 56–8). In order to avoid a backlash against women or 'reactively culturalist' policies (ibid.: 96–109), transformative accommodation recognises the validity of religious and cultural conventions, but provides exit options that enable women to choose state jurisdiction in certain situations (ibid.: 67). The policy aims to pressurise communities to reform the most contentious aspects of their customary codes and to encourage what Shachar sees as the natural evolution of minorities in ways that are hampered by liberal group rights. These rights can arrest 'organic change' (ibid.: 85), by requiring communities to adhere to rigid understandings of their identities as a condition of recognition. While Shachar's assumption that 'all cultures naturally evolve in a linear, and uniquely progressive, fashion' (Mitnick 2003: 1657) is doubtful, she rightly seeks to avoid the Scylla of vesting too much power in the state and the Charybdis of leaving women with no state protection at all.

For all its advantages, Shachar's proposal is problematic, however, as, like Okin's account, it does not respond fully to the value pluralism prevalent in modern societies. The problem arises from the fact that her central distinction between 'distribution' and 'demarcation' is open to two objections that expose her adherence to an over-idealised account of gender justice, rather than a commitment to discovering the meaning and entailments of gender justice through deliberation with various groups. Specifically, she encounters difficulties by holding that, within each area of law, minority groups acquire compulsory control over 'demarcatory' issues which are pertinent to securing group membership, such as, in family law, the conditions under which divorce is granted (Shachar 2001: Chapter 6); and by claiming that ancillary 'distributive' issues regarding maintenance and property inheritance should, in contrast, be subject to exit options imposed by the state. Shachar supports this policy on the grounds that distributive issues relate to material needs with which the state should be concerned and because these issues are not crucial to ensuring group identity (ibid.: 142–4).

However, this is a questionable claim. One problem is that most identity-related practices have distributive implications, if not in terms of tangible goods, then in terms of the good of self-respect or freedom to worship. Shachar's defence of exit options in the contexts that she outlines fails to acknowledge the fact that cultures often disagree over a host of distributive issues, broadly defined, and that they could regard their rules concerning maintenance as central to their identity, if these norms are premised on their beliefs about the distribution of freedom between the sexes. Indeed, this was a salient problem in Shah Bano's case. It is therefore unclear why a powerful state should be entitled to assert its own views without taking those of minorities into account (Parekh 2002b: 811). One might reply that Shachar does not defend the state's prerogative to impose its values coercively, since she merely offers women a right to decide whether to opt for state jurisdiction on specific issues. However, in view of the state's greater power, the line between encouraging a community to reform through making such options available and using coercive power to bring about reform is unstable. If the state indirectly supports women's rights to challenge their communities' norms on issues such as property inheritance, this process might exert – and, in a sense, *intends* to exert – pressure on these groups to reform other identity-related practices over time. Thus, if the *get* is justified according to Judaism's conception of a sexually differentiated humanity and restricts women's freedoms on grounds of their reproductive power (Hyman 1995; Miller-McLemore 1997: 30–44; Spinner-Halev 2001b: 104–5),[7] one might ask how it can reform the resource-distributive aspects of its divorce code without weakening others. One might ask how it can accept secular egalitarianism on some issues and still retain its doctrinal consistency. While it could be argued that minority groups are likely to be robust enough to withstand a great deal of reformist pressure in practice, there is a case for believing that women and men within these groups would ultimately regard Shachar's policy as excessively burdensome. This is not to say that cultural reform is impossible without cultural destruction, but only that how this process should proceed is more contestable than Shachar assumes. It is therefore significant that she concedes, albeit in a footnote, that her approach supports the indirect enforcement of liberal values in the private affairs of minority groups, by sanctioning 'a multicultural state acting *ultra vires*' (Shachar 2001: 126, n. 20).

Shachar might reply by conceding this objection but insisting nonetheless that the line has to be drawn somewhere; and that the state is justified in offering women formal protection on economic issues, as material well-being is a universal human need and an area in which they experience disproportionate vulnerability. However, the assumption that ensuring basic justice is primarily a matter of securing material goods betrays what Sen (1982) calls 'commodity fetishism', or a prioritisation of a person's success in the market economy at the expense of attending to other spiritual or social dimensions of human well-being. The emphasis on resource allocation leaves her account unresponsive in the short term to cultural conventions which undermine women's status rather than their access to tangible goods. Thus, the problem is not only that, following the first objection, Shachar ultimately assumes the priority of the same universal rights as Okin and thus dismisses the costs that her policy visits over time on women who wish to remain in traditions that regard family law as a uniform code that governs their 'global faith community' (Baumeister 2006: 400). In addition, if she offers immediate legal protection only on economic issues, her approach would fail to respond to the status-oriented problems affecting women at the *current* time. This narrow account of justice would not address the fact that *agunahs* would still depend on their husbands to obtain a divorce or the deepest issue confronting Shah Bano, whose predicament arose as a result of her husband's unilateral power to divorce her under sharia law. Shachar might reply that her proposed exit options would weaken the strategic advantages that men hold over women in the context of divorce, such that women's *overall* power would increase, promoting their 'voice' in the long run. However, the short-term threat posed by women's limited right to exit on financial matters could, in fact, induce male elites to maintain the status quo by rigidly enforcing those aspects of community codes over which they have control (Reitman 2005a). Song similarly emphasises the paradoxes of adhering to transformative accommodation in *Santa Clara v. Martinez*. Imposing exit options in relation to healthcare, she observes, would mean that female members 'would receive the [material] benefits associated with tribal membership, but must live with their outcast status' (Song 2007a: 133). This outcome 'suggests the arbitrariness of the . . . division of jurisdictional authority that Shachar proposes' (ibid.). This arbitrariness is the outcome of her eagerness to assert a uniform understanding of basic rights, without engaging with thick conflicts over conceptions of justice in a multicultural society.

Shachar's failure then to respond to the issue of 'value pluralism' entails that she does not recognise the complicated interplay between cultural particularity and universality in a feminist account of justice. Relatedly, she does not suggest a way of recognising the disparity of power between groups, since her proposals do not challenge the state's prerogative to define the content of women's basic rights. Mitnick (2003: 1658) rightly observes that Shachar hardly discusses the process of intercultural negotiation that she initially proposed as one of the advantages of her approach. While she contends that her approach would adapt the power-structures of the community and the state (Shachar 2001: 117) and that minorities must not be 'denied voice' (ibid.: 129, n. 22), apart from some passing references to 'incentives' for authorities to 'engage in constructive dialogue' (ibid.: 130), and to the idea that 'generosity' is required from the state 'as the stronger party' (ibid.: 130), it is unclear whether substantively neutral processes would be used to resolve disputes or whether the state would prevail in virtue of its greater power (Mitnick 2003: 1659). Therefore, her account fails to address the issue how an interest theory of rights could recognise the fact that a polity's knowledge of women's interests is likely always to be mediated through different cultural conceptions of value.

Yet, in spite of its paradoxes, Shachar's approach does draw crucial attention, like the theorists of recognition in Chapter 1, to the *need* for deliberation to alter the power imbalance between groups in the course of bringing about gender justice. Moreover, she could be right to propose exit options as one means through which these objectives could be met. However, a transformative multiculturalism requires a sustained and inter-active dialogue about substantive values in order to ascertain whether supporting particular conventions or options for exit would genuinely support women's rights in particular times and in particular contexts. While Shachar is clearly in favour of dialogue, the kind that she recommends would not necessarily be productive since, as Reitman observes, the distributive function of the family law is 'off the agenda' (2005b: 235). The discussion would be limited by the fact that Shachar rules out debate about substantive values and recommends only a bargaining procedure in what one writer calls a state of 'moral cold war' (Benhabib, 2002: 212). In the following sections, I therefore jettison her distinction between demarcation and distribution but retain her aspiration to defend a transformative multiculturalism. The cultural particularity of interests brought to light through my proposed approach responds to the complex issues confronted by Shah Bano.

IV TAKING VALUE PLURALISM SERIOUSLY – THE RIGHT TO MEDIATION

Central to my defence of a transformative multiculturalism is a 'right to mediation', a right that would be exercised by minorities with corporate interests in the survival of their value systems. This is to say that groups are understood as entities with interests that are not reducible to the sum of the interests that individual members might have in their culture; and that there is a need to promote the civic inclusion of minority groups through deliberation. While this account does not assume that groups are timelessly committed to discrete sets of values, it recognises the civic benefits of providing their members with opportunities to defend their values when disputes about their practices arise.[8] Focusing on the expression of community values is important in terms of equal citizenship, not least in view of the instability of Kymlicka's distinction between a culture's 'structure' and its 'character'. Kymlicka takes the former to be essential to a culture's survival and to consist in its history and language, and the latter to include particular norms and practices, which change over time and which can, thus, be assumed to be peripheral to the issue of survival (1989: 167–8, 172;

1995a: 104–5). This distinction lacks clarity, however, since 'what is deemed a part of the "cultural structure" is itself the result of a community's struggles over meaning and power' (Song 2005: 475). Kymlicka's distinction is also unsettled by his definition of a cultural structure in terms of the concept of 'societal culture', which is a 'meaningful way of life' based on a common language and values (1989: 135, 165).

If, then, the distinction between a culture's structure and its values is vague and fluctuating, there is reason to believe that recognising a community's values is important in debates about the egalitarian accommodation of religious or cultural conventions. Here, the right to mediation assumes that intercultural conversation should be 'bifocal', in the sense proposed by Parekh (2000a: 271). That is, the discussion should be directed inwards – by encouraging the community to scrutinise its own practices – and outwards – by prompting debate about whether public standards of justification unfairly exclude minority ways of life. Characterised by a split-level interactive dialogue, then, the right to mediation would provide groups with a high-priority entitlement to deliberate with the state on substantive questions of value, in a way that promises to address women's interests in retaining cultural identity *and* in avoiding the vulnerabilities that arise on account of their particular affiliations. As we shall see, the approach makes available equitable responses to cases such as Shah Bano, by engaging with the thick value pluralism characterising modern societies.

In particular, this approach to multicultural justice differs from the liberal strategy of assuming 'status quo neutrality' (Sunstein 2001), or the idea that the public language of reason is impartial. While even committed liberals have conceded that status quo neutrality does not guarantee fairness (see, for example, Raz 1986: 113–14), it is nonetheless generally true that liberals tend to see prior agreement on abstract principles as the condition of political legitimacy (Rawls 1993: 212–14). Rawls, for instance, claims that '[n]o sensible view can possibly get by without the reasonable and the rational *as I use them*' (Rawls 1995: 118, my emphasis); and is usually taken to require that citizens' non-public reasons play only the limited role of sustaining the conception of public reason antecedently fixed by the public conception of justice (Rawls 1993: Lecture I). On this account, while one might invoke non-public reasons in exceptional situations, 'it will be usually desirable' to refrain from 'going beyond the political' on issues relating to constitutional essentials or basic rights (ibid.: 215). Thus, the strong interpretation of Rawlsian theory holds that citizens must agree not only on the content of public values, but also on their weight and priority (Freeman, 2000: 403–4). Rawls notably supports this perspective by contending that, if the parties to a dispute about, say, abortion disagree about whether women's freedom and equality should be given great weight, 'their conceptions of justice are different'. Meaningful debate about the issue is therefore impeded (Rawls 1971: 36–7).

However, this strongly consensual version of Rawlsian liberalism has been challenged by Peter Jones, who rightly argues that the appeal on Rawls's part to a stable distinction between the reasonable and the not reasonable 'leaves everything still to be argued' from the perspective of adherents of diverse cultural traditions (Jones 1996: 195).[9] Moreover, Rawls himself vacillates considerably on the issue of whether non-public reasons have ever counted as public reasons. For instance, he equivocates about the legitimacy of Martin Luther King's invocation of religious doctrine in his defence of civil rights (Rawls 1993: 250–4); and ultimately concludes that King's action was legitimate in so far as it contributed to establishing the ideal of public reason (ibid.: 254). Rawls also acknowledges the plurality of conceptions of reasonableness (ibid.: 226) in a manner that unsettles the criticism that liberalism is inevitably committed to 'sterilizing' deliberation of all expressions of non-public identity (Laden 2001: 116–18; McCarthy 1994). The right to mediation builds on efforts to theorise this pluralistic strain in Rawlsian theory by writers such as Laden (2001), Ivison (2002) and Song (2007a), who recognise that, while minorities may not reject liberal values tout court, they may sometimes prioritise collective over individualistic goods in a way that liberalism has been historically ill-disposed to recognise. They acknowledge that this point is germane to the equitable negotiation of the interests of internal minorities too. In general, they challenge Barry's (2001) conviction that the special claims of minorities are usually hard to justify. For Barry, the key issue is whether general laws serve a legitimate purpose and, to his mind, it is 'absurd' to suppose that general laws do not visit uneven burdens on diverse citizens. The right to mediation emphasises that, while Barry is right to say that uniform rules inevitably impact on citizens differently, and that this situation alone does not establish an injustice, it is too swift to assume that these differential outcomes should very seldom be called unfair. Song explains why this is so by invoking the idea of the 'state establishment of culture' (2007a: 61). While the state can avoid having an established church, it cannot avoid having one language for public schooling and other state services; and the cultural disadvantages to which this situation gives rise can translate into wider economic disadvantages. Moreover, the predominant culture of a liberal society can generate burdens on a person's capacity to pursue her way of life, which cannot be quantified in material terms, since they relate to psychological goods such as self-respect.

Thus, to appreciate the nature of the burden involved in particular cases, expanded practices of political deliberation are required. To make this point is not to jettison all standards of reasonableness, but it is to recognise that an important source of unjustified disadvantage in liberal societies lies in the dominance of certain cultural values, such as the priority attributed to participating in a market economy or the sanctity of individualistic means-end reasoning. To clarify, my point is not that demands for accommodation can be settled purely by appealing to cultural or religious values, since the civic legitimacy of accommodation always depends on a broader assessment of what is at stake (Laden 2001: 170). The right to mediation, however, recognises that those who adhere to minority values are not necessarily unreasonable, but may 'demand not to give reasons that are grounded in a particular conception of public reason' (Ivison 2002: 72). While Rawls once argued that there is 'but one public reason' (1993: 220), even he later conceded that a liberal conception need not be accepted 'down to the last details' (ibid.: 226; see also Estlund 1996: 71–3) and that 'the forms of . . . public reason *are always several*' (Rawls 1997: 769, my emphasis). While pluralising public reason anticipates the difficult issue of how any non-public views could be deemed unreasonable, the right to mediation has the advantage of locating cultural diversity at the centre of a debate about women's rights, whilst still seeking to challenge the iniquities of gender subordination across different communities.

One might point out, however, that the standard purpose of insisting on the ideal of public reason is that it frees citizens from local prejudices and encourages them to think in terms of the common good (Galeotti 2002: 64). In response to this criticism, while the dangers involved in encouraging the public expression of cultural and religious values cannot be dismissed, a strategy of inclusion would achieve greater civic cohesion in many cases, as it would provide minority citizens symbolic recognition that is lacking if their claims are evaluated solely on the basis of their conformity to liberal priorities. It would therefore be unwarranted to implement 'gag rules' that keep religious and cultural discourses entirely out of political debate (Holmes 1995). One reason for this is that the religion–state separation in most liberal societies was the historical outcome of governments' desires to guarantee non-discrimination; yet this, precisely, might be compromised by prohibiting the expression of cultural and religious diversity today (Laborde, 2005). Moreover, while the threats posed by radical groups is a contextual matter (Rajan 2003), in the case of moderate religious groups 'we are . . . talking about bodies with very little power' (Modood 2005: 146). As 'mixed' forms of politics are the norm in multicultural societies, it is unduly purist to wish for a public sphere devoid of identity-related discourses (Kymlicka 1999b: 121).

Of course, the deeper objection to my account may be that the norm of public reason requires *mutual acceptability*. It assumes that I must offer you an intelligible reason, even if you do not accept its religious or philosophical basis. Public reasons must be shareable 'in the sense that they are reasons for each, in virtue of being reasons for all' (Ivison 1997: 130; D'Agostino 1991: 392). Thus, the question is how far down cultural differences can go in a multicultural society without undermining the degree of unity needed to motivate all to engage in debate fairly, and without rendering all settlements perennially unstable. I turn, in Chapters 4 and 5, to the potential motivational deficit caused by the commitment to the right to mediation. However, I address this concern for the present by emphasising that the dialogues of the right to mediation enhance civic unity in the sense of encouraging the wider society's recognition of the normality of non-liberal values, even if it does not guarantee consensus between all citizens regarding their priority. By jettisoning the demand for agreement on the weight and interpretation of goods imposed by the strong interpretation of liberal public reason, the approach stipulates only that minorities have an enforceable right to express their value commitments in the public sphere as the precondition for meaningful debate. To be sure, the approach demands more of the liberal state than Kymlicka's and Shachar's accounts. Aside from Kymlicka's concession that self-governing national minorities that have suffered historical injustice should only be held to account if they justify systemic violations of human rights such as slavery, genocide or mass torture (Kymlicka 1995b: 167–9), these approaches assume, as we have seen, all groups' acceptance of liberal priorities on constitutional essentials. The right to mediation challenges this view, and acknowledges that, as gender inequality exists in all sectors of society, the state must guard against assuming swiftly that a group's failure to comply with liberal values renders it excep-tionally discriminatory towards women. As Song argues, an inclusive ap-proach would recognise that the 'problem for feminists is not so much "multiculturalism versus gender equality" as "patriarchy versus gender equal-ity"' (Song 2005: 486). Assuming, then, that the right to mediation could support civic unity in many cases, and drawing critically on recent deliberative approaches to these issues (for example, Deveaux 2006; Eisenberg 2006; Song 2007a), I propose that the dialogues of the right to mediation be structured according to the following considerations, which are broad but sufficiently normative to lead to just outcomes.

IV (i) The 'Expression of Values' Consideration

Discovering a convention's normative meaning is essential, as it would not suffice if the representatives of minority groups simply assert that a failure to accommodate them burdens their community, or that a practice is 'central' to their culture (compare Eisenberg 2003: 52). This is because ascertaining why a practice is central would give rise to deeper questions about the community's values. In addition, many practices could conceivably be called central to a way of life; and the fact that courts refrain from questioning communities' self-definitions on this issue (Rosenblum 1998: 89–90) makes it hard to see how an assertion of centrality represents a contribution to debate rather than a non-negotiable demand. In contrast, because community survival is seldom likely to hinge entirely on the perpetuation of a single practice, claims about centrality would be only too easy to refute. The normative focus of the right to mediation is more attractive, therefore, because it challenges the assumption that minority practices are adhered to irrationally. It assists the wider society to appreciate that, while destruction of an entire community may not follow from the failure to accommodate a practice, the policy could still visit serious burdens on individuals within that group. This stage of deliberation recognises that, while cultures are undoubtedly constituted to some degree through mutual interpenetration, assertions of 'hybridity' often obscure the sense in which they can exist as distinctive systems of meaning which have sometimes been marginalised by dominant ideologies. Cultures often represent ways of 'looking at the world that require an account of . . . why meanings generate action, and why actions produce meanings when they do' (Wedeen 2002: 720). This approach does not betray a naively essentialist understanding of cultures as hermetically sealed wholes. I defer my full response to this charge in Chapter 3, but support this conception of groups for the moment by referring to Parekh's idea of cultures as systems of meaning, in terms of which individuals organise their collective lives, which cannot be dismissed as mere anthropological fictions (2000a: 143). While it could be argued that explaining particular practices in cultural terms would not be appropriate because culture is pervasive and, thus, lacks explanatory power, particularly in relation to gender subordination (Phillips 2006: 15), when practices differ from the mainstream, it is vital to provide the communities that defend them with an opportunity to explain their meaning.

These opportunities should not be seen as unfairly intrusive since, with the exception of isolationist religious groups, most communities are likely to favour greater political inclusion. The strategy also enables the larger society to appreciate the goods that women gain through preserving cultural identity in the course of an engaged debate about the applicability of sex equality laws in particular contexts. As cultures are partly constituted through dialogue, intercultural communication is usually possible (Parekh 2000b: 114–16); and, while cross-cultural understanding is not guaranteed, there is potential for conversation. The ensuing dialogue would enable Orthodox Jews, for instance, to explain the *get* in terms of an ideal of gender identity that focuses on women's reproductive power. While this conception might be thought to differ from a liberal norm, intercultural debate would enable the state to gain an understanding of the community's beliefs about gender roles, and, in turn, the community would gain symbolic recognition. The importance of such a policy is exemplified by North American debates about indigenous land claims that arise on the basis of communal understandings of property that had long been rejected as inconsistent with liberal commitments to self-ownership and possessive individualism (Tully 1995: 78).

One might initially worry that this approach would allow few constraints on public reason, and that states would be enjoined to accept even the extreme conception of gender advocated by, say, the Taliban. However, invoking a cultural or religious reason publicly establishes only whether the community has a normative basis for its claim. The state need not find these reasons compelling but it should, as Larmore insists, use a person's 'having a perspective on the world as a reason for discussing the merits of a [practice] with her' (1986: 175–6). Of course, sometimes the cultural reasons invoked by certain sectors of communities may turn out to be unsupportable, or intensely contested by some members, and I shall say more about such situations shortly. Yet, generally, the state should at least acknowledge that members of a community can, in principle, offer cultural reasons in good faith as a means of explaining why civic belonging is more burdensome to them without particular forms of accommodation. In this context, determining what is sufficiently burdensome must be left somewhat open as it involves assessing what else is at stake (Laden 2001: 175). The flexibility of this approach enables the state to gain insight into an 'insider's perspective' (Mullally 2004), in a process that is supported indirectly by Deveaux (2005: 357). She argues that, in evaluating the issue of bride price (*lobolo*) in South Africa, adhering to liberal priorities would not enable the state to acknowledge that the received interpretation of African customary law as discriminatory obscures the fact that *lobolo* signifies women's power to negotiate their children's marriages and, thus, that the practice constitutes an effective source of female influence in the family. While we shall see shortly that Deveaux does not view this justification as *normative*, the advantages that African women gain through this custom could be taken to confer on them a certain moral status within their community on account of their gender, which may go unrecognised by liberal public reason alone.

However, even if we accept the advantages of this process, the obvious question is how the dialogue would avoid domination by community elites, who could use the consultation as a means to shore up their power. In this context, the 'bifocal' nature of the dialogue is crucial – intra-cultural dialogue would be necessary in order to render an insider's perspective credible. Difficult judgements would have to be made with respect to the degree of intra-community controversy that would undermine a unified cultural perspective on a practice. Moreover, there is frequently a contested relationship between values and practices and, indeed, the entire matter of defining a community's values is often fruaght with difficulty. Thus, this inward-looking feature of the dialogue would respond to the concern that it is often unfair to associate particular practices with certain communities when, as in the case of sati, most group-members reject them (see Phillips 2005: 123). Gaining insight into an insider's perspective must involve achieving as comprehensive an account as possible of the contestation that exists over the meaning of a practice. In this context, Eisenberg (2005) points to a useful paradigm found in US cases such as *Reynolds* v. *United States* and *People of the State of California* v. *Kong Pheng Moua*.[10] Involving marriage by capture and polygamy in Hmong and Mormon communities, the courts attempted to discover the meaning of practices through documentary sources and anthropological evidence. These strategies are important if the right to mediation is not to become a vehicle for supporting the agendas of community elites, or a means through which the state simply chooses the most liberal interpretation of a convention.

What, however, of the concern that it would be counterproductive to insist that participants convey their views in terms of normative public reasons, because the existence of intra-cultural conflicts suggests that many cultural claims are primarily strategic in character (Deveaux 2005: 346)? To jettison the requirement for normative public reasons, it seems to me, would be to assume too swiftly that such reasons are unavailable. This assumption would fail to treat members of minority groups with civic equality, or to appreciate that normative differences often do exist between groups' conceptions of gender identity. Cultural claims are likely to be both normative *and* interest based; while they often do involve the abusive deployment of community rules, it is important not to overstate the sense in which they merely represent struggles over power or material interests rather than embodying real divergences in values (Song 2007a: 74; Bader 2005). In this context, focusing on the historical relations through which liberal priorities have prevailed over minority value-systems suggests how difficult it is to separate normative issues from the question of power. Of course, all deliberative approaches give rise to a serious question about the audibility of women's voices in debate, and I address this problem presently. My claim for now is that, if significant intra-community dissent is detected in relation to a convention, it would be hard to establish a prima facie justification for it in terms of public reason. The right to mediation cannot, however, impose on minority groups a duty to comply fully with liberal norms of sex equality, as this requirement would risk undermining the engagement with non-liberal diversity. However, all democratic approaches confront the problem of not being perfectly inclusive (Phillips 2002).[11] States can encourage the inclusiveness of dialogue and, as strategies exist, as we shall see, for revealing intra-community dissent, it is fair to assume that an insider's perspective on cultural practices can at least sometimes be articulated to the end of providing valid, if not always indefeasible, public reasons.

IV (ii) The 'Grave Risks' Consideration

The consultation must also consider what else is at stake in granting accommodation. It must therefore appraise the rationale behind the general laws in question, consider the non-right risks arising from accommodation, such as threats to the economy or political stability, and evaluate the potential grave effects of the convention on what we may call the 'cultural participation' of individuals. By this I mean that the state and community would need to assess the vulnerabilities to which the convention gives rise in terms of a person's ability to attain the goods that she values. This approach acknowledges that the value horizon of most cultures is likely to contain influences by other cultures and reformist strands that tend to emerge in any group's 'hermeneutical struggle' for meaning (Parekh 2000a: 174–5). Thus, an interactive dialogue is important in this context because it is rarely the case that hermeneutical inquiry is a purely internal affair (Walzer, 1994: 10ff.). Parekh illustrates this point by referring to the growth of Islamic feminism, observing how Muslim women, influenced by Western notions of equality, began to reinterpret their religious mandates (2000a: 175).

In brief, the 'grave risks' debate emphasises the need for public reasoning that is persuasive to all, and particularly to those affected by the conventions in question. It acknowledges that the deepest problem confronting Kymlicka's distinction between external protections and internal restrictions is the normative standard according to which the latter are deemed unacceptable. In the dialogues of the right to mediation, communities would be prompted to discuss the range of goods to which their members aspire, and their shifting meaning through the community's interaction with the state. At the same time, the state would be enjoined not simply to impose its own conceptions of harm or coercion on a minority community.

Assessing the grounds for accommodation, then, requires a contextual investigation that recognises the difficulties involved in weighing the seriousness of a risk to community integrity against the gravity of threats to individual freedoms, especially in cases where the minority group may contest the dominant society's interpretations of core human values. The assessment undertaken here cannot be an abstract matter but must depend on 'immersing oneself in the details of the case' (Carens 2000: 14). Hard-case situations may indeed arise, such as communities that justify extreme practices such as slavery, in relation to which little or no intra-community dissent emerges. I shall say more about these cases shortly. For now, my contention is that issues of administrative inconvenience, public resources, state security, the safety of other citizens and the cultural goods prioritised by group members would have to be considered in formulating public reasons that would lead to mutually acceptable outcomes.

One key question, however, is whether, given the limited impact of many minority practices on non-right objectives such as preserving a thriving economy, this strategy ultimately implies that all practices should be tolerated so long as they do not involve brutalising individuals. This extreme view can be countered by the plausible assumption that a form of meaningful agency is likely to be advocated by all enduring communities, even if its form cannot be defined in the abstract. We need not accept Kukathas's (1995; 2003) 'right of exit' thesis, which holds that communities should be left alone so long as their traditions are not cruel and degrading, and in so far as their members have the right to leave. While I elaborate on Kukathas's approach in Chapter 3, it is worth noting here that, against his account, the consultative process should assume that human life in any context involves more than a struggle to avoid extreme cruelty. Middle ground exists between accepting all conceivable infractions on freedom as reasons for refusing a claim; and assuming that, so long as individuals are not facing imminent death, cultural freedoms must have priority. It is plausible to defend women's rights to enjoy the goods that they value and not reason deductively from a comprehensively liberal notion of what freedom must involve. I shall elaborate on this claim in Chapter 3.

If this is right, we can appreciate the insights that stand to be revealed through dialogue in Shah Bano's case. Here, it would be important to recognise that, according to Muslim law in India, husbands can issue a talaq unilaterally, without approaching a court, whilst women must petition religious courts in order to obtain a divorce and can only do so in the event of their husband's cruelty or sexual impotence (Ahmad 2003). Dialogue could reveal the pressure that this convention might place on Muslim women to remain with partners who could ban them from work or study, or who might be unfaithful. These pressures would not necessarily be discerned through a simple assertion of universal liberal rights, which might construe women as formally able to obtain a divorce and, thus, not evidently at a disadvantage. Conversely, the dialogue could bring to light the dangers of assuming that the inequalities arising from Muslim maintenance conventions are best addressed by demanding cultural reform. While Muslim women are indeed disadvantaged by these rules, deliberation could reveal that to demand their repeal might only divert attention from problems confronting divorced women in the wider society and, therefore, might obscure the state's responsibility to provide social care for all citizens. This point is exemplified well by Song's (2007a: 145) account of twentieth-century anti-polygamy movements in the USA that arose in opposition to Mormons' demands for accommodation. As some feminists observed, polygamy was no more exploitative in certain respects than the larger society's family structures. Here the state's opposition to Mormon practices seemed to deflect attention from the structural inequalities experienced by women generally. Such 'diversionary effects' are significant to ascertaining how to combine requests for cultural reform with the state's efforts to redress the burdens experienced by women generally. In light of this point, it is plausible to suggest that, in Shah Bano, the state could 'ensure that divorced women . . . are cared for, either directly or by funding community organisations to do so' (Spinner-Halev 2001b: 111; Parekh 1993: 171).

While it would be naive to underestimate the difficulties involved in ensuring social security for women in complex and densely populated societies such as India, these suggestions should be taken seriously, not least because it would be counterproductive and rather chauvinistic to assume that empowering women always involves mandating reform of their communities. Here, Deveaux points to evidence that state economic initiatives targeting women, such as micro-credit programmes, can increase female bargaining power within the family (2006: 109; see also Rahman 1999); and Bader defends an individualized basic income on the grounds that, if core human needs are met by the state, the efficacy of gender-discriminatory conventions would be weakened (2005: 335). Of course, we need to resist the assumption that securing economic freedom for women ipso facto ensures gender justice. However, if the hardships confronting individuals such as Shah Bano could be addressed without visiting impossible costs on the state, the right to mediation would have acknowledged the importance that many women attach to their communal identities and the dangers of sensationalising gender inequalities in different cultural contexts. It would have located gender subordination in minority groups in the larger context of the structural inequalities that pervade society at large, and would have attempted to address these problems fairly. In the course of dialogue, moreover, the Muslim community would have received a symbolically important opportunity to explain the role of its maintenance conventions in its way of life, perhaps by emphasising that the talaq should be understood in the light of the Qur'an's prohibition of divorce without just cause (Mashour 2005: 563). In the event, the judge simply pronounced a clash between minority values and human rights (J. Chandrachud, in *Shah Bano*: 252, para. 22). This response was at best short-sighted for, as Phillips rightly explains, Shah Bano raised not 'just a question of what is right and wrong, but of how best to intervene in a context where sex equality issues are employed to promote hatred between different communities' (Phillips 2002: 128).

My point is to articulate the issues that would need to be considered within an interactive dialogue, rather than to put forward definitive solutions. I am not claiming that a universalised basic income, for instance, could be the sole remedy for women in countries in which the talaq is practised. While this approach cannot avoid the use of state power to compel communities to enact limited reforms, the symbolic recognition that groups would gain from civic inclusion would be likely to increase their tendency to cooperate. While real-world deliberation often does depend on extra-political contingencies, such as the willingness of the group to deliberate, communities on this approach would be motivated to work with the state towards gender justice, once they recognised the latter's emphasis on hermeneutical inquiry and the fact that no group is deemed solely accountable for gender injustice. Thus, while it could be objected that this proposal does not provide objective normative criteria for assessing particular claims, the give and take of deliberation enables liberal states to identify areas where reform should be encouraged without making falsely universalistic judgements about women's rights. The fairness of the process would encourage a feminist form of multiculturalism, which considers the particularity of women's situations and their serial position in their cultures.

IV (iii) The 'Minimal Future Argument' Consideration

At the final stage of the inquiry, all parties would be enjoined to affirm that the decision reached must be open to future contestation. The provisional nature of settlements in a society characterised by thick diversity would help minorities to view political decisions with greater equanimity. Deveaux defends a similar 'revisability' condition, on the basis that change is often gradual and dependent on extra-legal measures (2006: 114–17). While she appears correct on this point, the 'future argument' consideration accepts more non-liberal diversity than her account. For Deveaux argues that one of the entailments of her revisability condition is that a claim would not be legitimate if allowing it undermines the capacity of individuals to engage in future political debate. Thus, a rule that prohibits women from involvement in politics would not be permissible (ibid.: 117). The difficulty with this view is that many campaigns for cultural and religious recognition involve conventions that do not encourage equal political participation between male and female members. Therefore, to insist that women not be denied an equal political voice is likely to inhibit deliberation from getting underway in a wide range of cases. While the state can enact measures to encourage both sexes to participate, as we shall see in later chapters, the 'future argument' consideration accepts the non-ideal circumstances of political deliberation and assumes that future consultations could arise between groups even with respect to very restrictive community rules. However, this is not to say that women's apparent consent to absolutely all conventions should be viewed with equanimity. Hard-case situations do arise where no dissent on women's part is detected even in seemingly coercive situations that would appear highly dubious even on a culture-sensitive view. These situations indicate a significant limit to the capacity of any form of deliberation to protect women's interests in the most extreme cases. As our analysis of harmful internalisation indicated in Chapter 1, risks to human interests cannot always be ascertained through intercultural deliberation, if some individuals are precluded from participating, and lack the capacity to contest pernicious interpretations of community conventions.

V THREE CHALLENGES TO MEDIATION

A number of pressing concerns about the right to mediation need to be addressed before turning fully the issue of individual agency raised above. Consider, first of all, the worry that dialogue would be impeded because the arguments advanced in debate may not conform to any recognisable standard of reason. While mediation makes the public sphere more amenable to what Fraser (1997) calls the 'counter-discourses' of minority groups, to justify practices simply by means of a direct appeal to God's word, for instance, is not likely to be persuasive to a secular polity (Quong 2002: 307). While I address this problem in later chapters too, to allay worries about it at present, it is plausible to expect that the middle ground can be found between full conformity to liberal standards of reasonableness and demands that are unintelligible to anyone outside a given community. This middle ground is significant, because the purpose of the dialogue is to enable marginalised communities to demonstrate why existing public reasons fail to reveal the burdens that they experience on account of general laws. The idea is not that minorities should compel others to accept their doctrinal beliefs, but to draw attention to the fact that citizens of the majority society do not face similar difficulties in expressing their normative commitments, as they are generally embedded and taken for granted in the prevailing public culture. Moreover, the fact that the basic claims of the world's religions and cultures are unlikely to be obscure to secular citizens (Swaine 2001) suggests that the state could, in principle, come to appreciate why existing standards of reasonableness can be unduly restrictive for citizens of non-mainstream cultures and faiths. To reiterate, while many liberals follow the standard Rawlsian requirement that a condition for invoking non-public discourses in deliberation is that citizens are prepared to give public reasons in due course (Rawls 1997; compare Reidy 2000), it is not implausible to go beyond the political when doing so is a matter of fairness. Cultural reasons are not, of course, indefeasible and I have distinguished between making a public reason argument and having a winning one. Whether all minorities would be satisfied with an approach that does not guarantee the success of their reasons presents a thorny problem; but this approach at least conceptualises these reasons as contributions to discussion rather than as incontrovertible assertions.

But, even if this is so, the concern persists that the focus on cultural or religious values misses the point, as the real issue is the structural domination of women which renders their voices inaudible in political debate (MacKinnon 1987). Focusing on value disagreement may thus be interesting but largely irrelevant to the issue at hand, particularly if the guiding conventions of the dialogue do not specifically demand the equal participation and non-domination of all sectors of a given community. For these reasons, Phillips and Deveaux, as we have seen, contend that debates about gendered cultural practices should be seen as primarily 'political' or 'strategic'. Similarly, Galeotti argues that, while the idea was crucial in Reformation Europe, when persecution by religious sects was rife, today the 'idea that [group claims] can be reduced to the most philosophically intriguing conflict, namely religious, moral and metaphysical conflict', leads to a failure to recognise inequalities of power (Galeotti 2002: 66). Therefore, these authors argue for the salience of interests, which they take to allow for compromise, imperfect settlements and the emergence of a plurality of voices *within* a group, in a way that claims expressed in terms of values often do not. Deveaux, for her part, is sensitive to the argument that to conceptualise campaigns to assert cultural identity as struggles over benefits and resources could be thought to demote the moral dimensions of deliberation which would, in turn, fail to live up to democracy's ideal of

representing parties to deliberation as rational, uncoerced and equal participants. However, she contends nonetheless that certain kinds of reasons, such as the desire to shore up one's power or to further one's financial gain, should not be deemed illegitimate in democratic deliberation, as these considerations inevitably *do* impact on political debate in the real world (Deveaux 2006: 105). Focusing on the non-ideal conditions of political deliberation, she argues, militates against requiring normative arguments and cultural reasons, which 'may or may not speak to the crux of the issue' (ibid.: 105). This point is supported by Weinstock's contention that 'arguments that appeal strictly to group cultural identity may serve as impediments to compromises in political deliberation' (Weinstock 2006).

In response to this objection, while we can concede that focusing on cultural values in political debate does not resolve the dilemma of how the plurality of voices that exist within any particular tradition might be rendered audible, it is not evident that the open admission that strategic interests end up figuring in real-world deliberation speaks fully to the problem either. It would not necessarily address, as Deveaux hopes, the 'epistemological inequalities' that marginalised groups confront in terms of access to information and the means of expression, which impede idealised models of deliberation based on moral consensus (see Deveaux 2006: 106; Valadez, 2001). This is because the concession that minorities' contributions to public debate are *not* normatively grounded could perpetuate their 'otherness' in relation to the state and wider society, in a context in which inequalities of power often relate closely to the dominance of certain materialistic or possessive individualistic values. These inequalities may be experienced by male and female group-members alike. Moreover, while it is true that women might gain strategic advantages from adhering to non-liberal practices, there is no guarantee that explicitly permitting reasons based on power and interest would deconstruct the balance of existing power relations with a group. While Deveaux believes that accommodating strategic interests would enable the perspectives of women to be heard, the problem is that, in her own example of bride-price, male community elites are also likely to have 'strategic' interests in maintaining the convention, if it contributes to sustaining the group's underlying sexual division of labour. If this is so, the weight that is finally attached in political debate to the increased status that women gain through this practice calls for normative argument about gender roles, which ultimately cannot be avoided.

Moreover, while it is contentious to assume that Shah Bano, for instance, involved value-disagreement simpliciter, it is equally difficult to deny that values were an issue, when the injustice that Muslims felt with regard to the misrecognition of their belief system explains their reactionary response to the state, and when there evidently was an issue concerning the compatibility of Muslim divorce conventions with the state's commitment to human rights. This point emphasises again the difficulty of separating normative from strategic issues – a point that Deveaux herself concedes in observing that persons who share a strategic interest in maintaining male-only inheritance or succession probably come to believe that this is the natural, fitting and morally *correct* arrangement (Deveaux 2006: 101). Thus, what is considered normative in any context (for instance, which interpretations of human rights prevail or which interpretation of sharia law is adopted) cannot be distanced from the issue of power. My point is that, when we consider issues ranging from the Muslim talaq to the Catholic Church's rejection of women from the priesthood, it is hard not to consider the relevance of women's cultural and religious commitments, qua normative commitments, in assessing their interests. The right to mediation does not deny the centrality of structural inequality to gender subordination. On the contrary, it focuses on non-public values in part as a means of responding better to *all* structural disadvantages – those based on gender *and* culture. This is because the complexity of women's interests often requires a differentiated, rather than a universalistic, response.

Related to this issue, however, is the anxiety that mediation would nonetheless simply entrench the power base of community elites, as I have stressed that it would not always be productive to demand that minorities comply with liberal norms of sex equality in every case. Yet the potential domination of the consultative process by these elites would be mitigated in practice in a number of ways. First, to recap, the inclusiveness of the process would entail that communities would tend to experience a sufficient degree of trust in the state, which would, in turn, promote a sense of 'healing' in wounded communities that would restore their sense of wholeness (Eisenberg 2005). To this degree, they would be less likely to tighten controls over vulnerable group-members, and might even be better disposed to encouraging them to participate in deliberation. Furthermore, the extent to which elites would monopolise the dialogue for the purposes of sustaining misogynistic practices should not be exaggerated. Their interpretations of religious scriptures, for instance, would not be taken as self-validating since historical records would be adduced, which could reveal internal dissent about practices that impact on women negatively (Eisenberg 2005). Finally, to reiterate, to have a cultural reason is not to have an indefeasible reason. While these points provide important grounds to characterise the dialogues of the right to mediation as a feminist form of multiculturalism, in the final analysis it should be conceded that any deliberative approach must confront situations where no evidence of women's resistance to seemingly coercive arrangements comes to light through dialogue; and in the context of which the community offers a weighty reason for protecting its conventions. In these situations, any transformative policy of multiculturalism that seeks to address the inequalities associated with gender subordination should be supplemented by a range of protective measures, not least of which is a universal individual right. This is a right to freedom of thought and decision that would support the inclusiveness of the process of deliberation defended here.

VI CULTURAL PARTICULARITY AND ITS INTERPLAY WITH THE UNIVERSAL

We are now in a position to see that the right to mediation responds to the three concerns raised against Okin's universalistic account. Our approach engages not just with the *pragmatic trade-off* and *moral standing* issues but with that of *value pluralism* too. However, even if adhering to this right could have reconfigured the Indian state's response to the plight of Shah Bano, we must, however, confront the hard-case situations mentioned above. Mitnick (2003: 1659) voices concern about them vis-à-vis Shachar's account, arguing that, while state–community negotiations are vital in bringing about gender justice, protecting individuals requires a focus on individual capacities to transform cultures, as well as on the procedural question of group interaction.[12] For this reason, a feminist form of multiculturalism must appeal to a universal right that should be understood to underlie and support the inclusiveness of the right to mediation, namely a culturally-sensitive individual right to freedom of thought and decision. While this right is clearly not the only entitlement that liberal states ought to protect universally under conditions of diversity, it is one of the highest priority and merits special attention in a feminist and multicultural theory. Measures to protect it would involve ensuring that women enjoy substantive capacities and, crucially, it would also provide a critical standard against which direct intervention to assist women at risk of abuse in extreme cases could be justified. Yet the key question is what *form* this right could take. As our examination of the capabilities approach indicated, the substantive capacities that underwrite a schedule of rights are likely to involve some form of choice or an ability to exercise independent thought. However, our critique of Nussbaum's perfectionism alerts us to the risk of asserting the universality of capacities that are controversial from the point of view of cultures and religions which advocate the seclusion of women or which limit their freedoms in various other ways. Thus, defining this universal right presents a difficulty on which I elaborate briefly in concluding this chapter.

At one extreme, much liberal political theory is characterised by a strong conception of freedom of choice which is permeated by assumptions about the objective priority of individualistic ideals of rational self-direction. This approach is exemplified by Nussbaum's capabilities perspective and the 'objective interests' account of Susan Babbitt (1993), who insists on the need to distinguish real from apparent desires and authentic values from spurious ones. Babbitt places stringent constraints on how agency can be exercised or the goods that people can choose. She contends that the 'ideological oppression' inflicted by certain communities can instil desires in a person that do not reflect her interest in her own flourishing and which prevent her from pursuing her interests (ibid.: 246–7). While a person in a highly restrictive culture may have 'nonpropositional knowledge' about her basic interests (in the form of intuitions that imply some understanding of her personal worth), that knowledge may be inexpressible within her 'ideological regime' (ibid.: 477). Babbitt illustrates this point by considering the character of Celie in Alice Walker's novel, *The Color Purple*. When taunted by Mister – '[Y]ou nothing at all' – Celie simply replies, 'I'm pore, I'm black, I may be ugly and can't cook . . . but I'm here' (Walker 1998: 125–8). Babbitt's worry is that the racial hierarchies of the deep southern states of 1930s America do not provide Celie with a vocabulary through which to assert her moral status, and that it is therefore impossible for her to express her convictions and aspirations (Babbitt 1993: 253).

However, Meyers responds convincingly that the exchange between Mister and Celie reveals how meaningful self-expression is possible even in the most restrictive circumstances (Meyers 2000: 478). Celie's retort, her insistent affirmation of her presence, shows that she does have an adequate sense of personhood through which to engage in what Meyers calls 'poignant self-assertion' (ibid.: 482). 'Objective interests' accounts are, according to Meyers, too ready to universalise the necessary conditions of human agency (ibid.: 485). In doing so, they risk characterising women in conservative cultures too swiftly as alienated and dominated. In this context, Paul Benson's value-saturated theory of autonomy is also contentious, as it suggests that inferior socialisation in some circumstances can be so extreme that individuals are literally disabled from discerning reasons not to submit to self-harm (see Benson 1991). Meyers again responds that it is not self-evident that even seriously restrictive socialisation necessarily inhibits a person's capacities to discern coercion, even if it might impede her ability to respond effectively to her situation. Meyers' responses indicate that the 'objective interests' account of human agency would not support the value pluralism that the right to mediation seeks to acknowledge.

However, any deliberative account needs, at the same time, to react critically to Shah Bano's renunciation of the court's decision in her favour. The elderly woman's action raises questions about the effect of community pressure on individuals' capacities to decide for themselves, and to act in defence of their own wellbeing. Clearly, when confronted with the complexities of this case, it would be contentious to attempt to support the inclusiveness of the right to mediation by appealing to a form of agency that assumes that people are free when they are able to show even a minor sign of resistance. The difficulties with such a broad conception of agency can be illustrated by returning to Deveaux's account. Drawing from Foucault's account of power as 'governing conduct', and his assumption that 'power is exercised only over free subjects, and only insofar as they are free' (Foucault 1983), Deveaux claims that, in evaluating women's effective freedom, multicultural states should consider the subtle ways in which individuals negotiate domestic and other micro-level arrangements. While the analogy that Deveaux recurrently draws between women's agency and the rebellion of peasants against their colonial masters, as exemplified by the peasant's subversive methods of 'foot dragging, false compliance and feigned ignorance' (Deveaux 2006: 124), emphasises her awareness that such non-ideal strategies may be of limited efficacy in altering the overall status quo within particular communities, she insists that women's ability to react creatively in an imperfect world, even one containing gross disparities of power, indicates a degree of agency that unsettles the idea that restrictive gender codes render women victims.

Using Kandiyoti's term 'bargaining with patriarchy' (1988), Deveaux follows Narayan (2002) in focusing, for instance, on the way that upper-class Indian women make pragmatic decisions to conform to cultural expectations, in spite of having misgivings about doing so. While they do not make a free choice in the liberal sense, they often engage in verbal and nonverbal displays of discontent or temporarily abdicate household duties in order to gain control over their situation (Deveaux 2006: 181; see also Menon 2000). Moreover, by drawing attention to the recognition of polygyny in South Africa to emphasise the advantages of her wide view of agency, Deveaux contends that the conclusions reached through her account of agency differ productively from those achieved through narrowly liberal approaches. For, while polygyny might be thought to transgress liberal commitments to sex equality and individual autonomy, taking a broader view of women's agency establishes how the political recognition of this practice could, in fact, empower women in their lived contexts by providing them crucial legal protection. In other words, women in de facto polygynous marriages would be worse off if the legal status of their unions were not recognised. 'Agency, construed broadly,' she therefore argues, 'illuminates the evaluative and transformative activities of group-members vis-à-vis social customs in flux' (Deveaux 2006: 185).

While these claims are attractive, it is not clear how persuasive they are in practice. As we have seen, Deveaux's approach provides an instructive means of supporting the right to mediation's recognition of the value of non-liberal practices; and her focus on informal sites of contestation as relevant spaces of democratic activity is illuminating. However, her wide view of human agency risks conflating an individual's attainment of meaning through cultural practices with what might ultimately be, in some situations, a basic struggle for survival. She rightly avoids setting the bar for freedom too high by refusing to hold minority women to a normative standard of critically reflective decision making that would seldom be applied to members of the wider society. However, the fact that a person is capable of transgressing community codes in limited ways does not entail that they are free from illegitimate coercion. For instance, it is unclear whether the women whose interests Deveaux supports by endorsing the recognition of polygyny have any real prospect of altering existing power relations, given that the entire matrix of practices in this context, including polygyny, *lobolo*, the levirate and child betrothal, are ultimately related to an ideology of patrilineage, to women's lack of proprietary capacity and the inequalities that they confront in living independently (Hellum, 1999). Although it was by means of direct consultation with women that the preference for the (at least temporary) continuation of polygyny was revealed and understood in post-apartheid South Africa, Okin legitimately asks whether the views that the women expressed were their *authentic* opinions about the practice, and what ascertaining women's freedom to voice an undominated view would involve in practice (2005: 84). Moreover, the substantive conditions that Deveaux sets for democratic negotiation, such as 'non-domination' and 'non-intimidation' (2006: 34, 117), together with her underlying commitment to equality and human rights (2006: Chapter 3), might provide reasons to contest practices such as *lobolo* on her own account. Finally, Deveaux insists that efforts should be made to prevent endogenous forms of influence, such as wealth, power and pre-existing inequalities, from impacting on deliberative outcomes (2006: 118). However, if this is so, her broad account of personal agency is likely to play a residual role in practice, as it would not support the inclusiveness of the deliberation that she recommends at the formal political level.

The difficulty arises in part from Deveaux's insistence that resistance to injustice is likely to be a human universal (2006: 170). Resistance, she claims, is 'any activity or expression that signals a response to a prevailing social norm, custom, role or arrangement' (ibid.: 173). However, even if it could be true that the tendency to resist injustice constitutes an important feature of the human condition, normative questions still remain with respect to the effective capacities of particular agents in their lived social contexts. Thus, it would be misguided to adhere to a value-saturated 'objective interests' account of agency to support the inclusiveness of the right to mediation; but we also need not believe that even the most minor and ineffectual sign of agency amounts to meaningful freedom that should be endorsed as proof that a group-member does not experience coercion. A feminist and multicultural theory of rights requires not only a project of discovering meanings through the right to mediation but also additional rights to actualise substantive capacities – rights that would, if violated, justify remedial and protective action by the state. Responding, then, to women's serialised position in culture involves more detailed inquiries into culture, agency and autonomy, to which we shall turn fully in the following chapter.

VII CONCLUSION

Attending to the cultural particularity of women's interests represents, I have argued, the first stage in configuring women's rights as multicultural claims. I have contended that: (a) women's positive interests, goals and priorities are not always synonymous with liberal interests; and (b) the vulnerabilities that they experience can also often depend on the specificities of their cultures. Therefore, contextual responses to women's rights are required in contemporary multicultural states, which recognise the interplay between the universal and the particular in an account of justice that is concerned with redressing hierarchical group relations and prompting civic equality. I have argued that the right to mediation would assist in reconfiguring multicultural policy in a feminist way, by supporting group rights to engage directly with the state in a debate regulated by three culture-sensitive guidelines. While this approach contains resources for responding to intra-group oppression and for guarding against the abusive deployment of cultural rules, the hard-case situations that beset any deliberative account indicate the need to supplement the right to mediation with the commitment to at least one crucial individual right. While deliberation alone does not afford a panacea in all instances of the so-called multicultural paradox, it is, however, a crucial precondition for ensuring a feminist form of multicultural justice that deconstructs the liberal dilemma in important ways. Formulated as a high-priority entitlement of marginalised groups to engage with the state on substantive questions of value, it responds meaningfully to the standard assumption that gender

justice and cultural autonomy are inevitably opposed, or that multiculturalism is usually bad for women.

NOTES

1. My claim is not, of course, that cultural difference is the only difference that
   matters. Recognising the issue of *multiple* differences is important if we are to
   avoid a 'fruitless game of hierarchies of oppression' (Rich 1984: 289).
2. The Indian Constitution of 1949 explicitly recognises religious 'personal' laws
   of Muslims, Hindus, Christians and Parsis. However, the framers of the
   Constitution also declared their commitment to bring about a Uniform Civil
   Code (Article 44), an objective that has not been realised. Women are
   understood to be vulnerable to both state and religious community exploitation under current arrangements. Personal law pronounces on marriage,
   divorce, maintenance, adoption, child custody and inheritance (Mahajan
   1988). One disadvantage of this system lies in the confusion that it generates
   with respect to justice for women. For instance, while the Indian government
   usually provides some form of public assistance to single mothers in urban
   areas, this service is not fully taken advantage of because many women are
   unaware of its existence, or are inhibited for social and customary reasons from
   doing so.
3. *Mohammed Ahmed Khan v. Shah Bano Begum and others* [1985] (see Engineer
   1985).
4. It is worth emphasising that religious and cultural claims are not easy to
   separate in debates about multiculturalism. As Parekh notes, '[T]here is hardly
   any culture in whose creation, constitution and continuation religion has not
   played an important part, so much that we have few, if any, examples of a
   wholly secular or humanistic culture'(2000a: 46–7). Sagar similarly argues that
   the 'normative distance between culture and religion may not be so very great'
   (2000: 195–6). Moreover, it is difficult to 'disaggregate' religious from cultural
   claims, by suggesting that the former may raise issues of freedom of conscience
   and the latter claims about historical injustice (Song 2007b). The problem is
   that the two types of claim are likely to intersect. Freedom of conscience is
   likely to become an issue for those whose ways of life have been historically
   marginalised.
5. *Santa Clara v. Martinez* 436 US/49 [1978] 436 US.
6. I examine Kymlicka's (1989) influential arguments over the next chapters.
7. Note Miller-McLemore's argument that the celebration of women's maternal
   power in Judaism overlaps significantly with Western feminist discourses on
   'mothering' and the ethics of care (Miller-McLemore 1997).
8. Here I broadly accept Shachar's broad account of a 'nomoi' or customary
   group, which takes groups to 'share a unique history and collective memory, a
   distinct culture, a set of social norms, customs and traditions, or perhaps an
   experience of maltreatment by mainstream society or oppression by the state'

(2001: 2, n 5). However, in my view, not all these conditions need necessarily obtain for a group to be classified as such.

9. Many left-wing critics and feminists such as MacKinnon (1987) also express frustration with the liberal rhetoric of reasonableness that, arguably, pushes demands for change off the agenda.

10. *Reynolds v. United States* [98], US 145 (1878); and *People of the State of California v. Kong Pheng Moua*, No. 315972-0, Frezno County Superior Court (7 February 1985).

11. I do not use the term mediation to refer to the diplomatic resolution of disputes in international law (see Dodson 1996). Also, I do not use it in the sense found in family law that refers to legal assistance for reconciling an estranged husband and wife (Merry, 2006). The latter kind of mediation is rightly deemed highly problematic, as it has resulted in increased violence against women (Greatbatch and Dingwall, 1999). Mediation (in this sense) has been particularly damaging in cases where women are encouraged, through processes of family law mediation, to return to a coercive marriage or family situation. I am indebted to Samia Bano for her insights into this issue, and for her recommendation that I distinguish my own use of the term 'mediation' from that used in UK family law.

12. Mitnick reacts to Shachar's approach as follows:

> Imagine the following paradigm: In a local jurisdiction government governed according to a strict interpretation of cultural law, one woman, call her Amina, has given birth to a child outside wedlock . . . Tribal authorities sentence Amina, after allowing her one year to wean her child, to death by stoning . . . How might this woman have exercised an exit option to switch to a public source of authority? (Mitnick 2003: 1160)

CHAPTER 3

Plural Autonomy – Force, Endorsement and Cultural Diversity

I INTRODUCTION

A crucial limitation, then, of deliberative democratic strategies that aim to respond to conflicts of culture is that women, as a historically vulnerable internal minority, might often struggle to voice their needs in the public sphere. In light of this problem, a theory that responds equitably to the interplay between the universal and the particular should supplement the defence of group rights to deliberation with a commitment to enhancing women's capacities to participate in their communities and in democratic consultations over time. While liberal democracy's commitment to treating people as equals requires that individuals have a voice in governing collective affairs, bringing this situation about involves equipping them with certain capacities for self-direction, even if traditional sectors of minority groups might often prioritise collectivist goods over the ability of individuals to decide for themselves. In this chapter, I defend a universal normative commitment to individual self-direction which I frame in terms of a right to *autonomy*. I contend that a commitment to this universal right sometimes justifies special protective measures for women of non-liberal cultures, for reasons that stand free of the deliberative process, but which support its inclusive nature in the long term. This approach to protecting women's interests, as will be demonstrated, is consistent with Young's awareness of women's serialised location in different cultures.

One might initially resist this claim on grounds that, while the idea of autonomy has been widely praised by political theorists and has been called the 'lodestar of much modern liberalism' (Mendus 2000a: 127), its meaning is highly contested and elusive (Dworkin 1989: 54–5). Moreover, feminists such as Code are suspicious of this value on grounds that it has long been the preserve of male elites and emphasises a masculine ideal of self-mastery (see Code 2000: 181). Farley similarly contends that autonomy is too often associated with 'exaggerated individualism, detached spectatorship and Faustian desires for control' (Farley 1993: 182). Furthermore, multicultur-alists, for their part, often dispute the priority that liberals accord to this value, insisting that it is not the 'obsessional core' of non-Western societies (Hirschmann 1988: 348). Louis Dumont's anthropological writings suggest that the separatist notion of the individual on which this value is based is absent from many non-Western world views (see Dumont 1980). Yet it seems contradictory to reject autonomy on the basis that it is not of great value *and* to complain of the unfairness of restricting it to privileged sections of society (Friedman 2003: 50). Given that a certain form of self-determina-tion is likely to be crucial to the well-being of all human beings, it is plausible to retain a focus on autonomy in a feminist and multicultural theory of rights, even if our conception of it must respond to the charge that it would be self-defeating to defend the interests of the historically marginalised by invoking apparently elitist concepts, or what Lorde calls the 'master's tools' (1984).

I define a suitable conception of autonomy in this chapter by engaging with the debate about arranged and forced marriage in the UK. Arranged marriage is a longstanding tradition in many cultures[1] which entails that parents make decisions about marriage partners for their children, or that young people make their selection from a list approved by their parents (Phillips 2007: 119).[2] The issue came under scrutiny in the 1990s following reports of high rates of self-harm amongst women of South Asian cultures (Bhardwaj 2001). Several cases of criminal violence also heightened public anxiety at this time, amongst the most widely publicised of which were the murders of two British Pakistani women. Tasleem Begum, a supermarket worker, was crushed to death by her brother-in-law, who ran his car over her in 1995. She had allegedly compromised her family's honour (izzat) on account of her infidelity to her Pakistani husband, to whom she had been married at sixteen against her will (Burke 2000). In a similar vein, following a marriage to a Pakistani man at the age of fifteen, Rukshana Naz became pregnant by her boyfriend and, as a consequence, was murdered by her mother and brother in 1998 (Donnelly 1999: 13; Deveaux 2006: 165). The Home Office subsequently undertook an investigation of forced marriage. Its report estimated that, annually, ten per cent of the ten thousand arranged marriages in Britain were likely to be forced, even though only about three hundred cases were reported per year (Home Office 2000). Later, the government mooted the introduction of a criminal offence of 'forcing someone to marry' (Home Office 2005: 3). While the law was not implemented, the Forced Marriage (Civil Protection) Act was passed in 2007, increasing family law protection for women who face pressures to marry (Hickley 2006; Hundal 2007).

It should be recognised that using any form of law to intervene in unions that involve physical force, such as drugging, torture and abduction, is likely to be more straightforward than in cases involving psychological pressure.[3] This is on account of the invisibility of the harm in the latter cases and the possible disagreement between communities over the legitimacy of parental pressure. A reason for assisting women in these situations, the justification for which stands free of the deliberative strategy defended in Chapter 2, should be specified without 'infantilising' women by assuming that they are incapable in principle of deciding for themselves. This issue is crucial to a theory that demonstrates how attention to women's cultural particularities interacts with universal concerns for gender justice. For, although forced marriage can occur in any culture, and cannot be fully understood in isolation from domestic violence in all societies, it is likely to occur most readily in cultures where marriages are typically arranged (Home Office 2005: 13). Thus, in the context of diaspora on which I focus in this chapter, forced marriage is likely to constitute a specific cultural vulnerability which, nonetheless, calls for a universalistic response.

This chapter focuses on the British debate on forced marriage in order to defend a distinctive conception of the right to autonomy. As before, I intend my argument to apply to the broader issue at stake – in this instance, the extreme psychological pressures that might be experienced by individuals within their communities. Specifically, the ideal of *plural autonomy* is defended, or self-determination conceived not as a single concept but as a culturally variable family of skills. While I argue that adhering to this account would assist authorities that seek to protect women under the new forced marriage law, assessing a person's state of mind in legal contexts is notoriously difficult. Thus, protecting women's rights should involve, inter alia, education that equips them with long-term abilities to exercise their independent judgement in important life decisions, by attempting to redress the structural inequalities that make intra-community coercion of this kind possible. In sum, my approach recognises that, while attitudes to arranged marriage differ between generations, with many young Asians opting not to adhere to it (Phillips and Dustin 2004: 538; Modood et al. 1997: 317), many view it as a crucial marker of cultural and ethnic identity (Goodwin and Cramer 2000). Intervening in the issue of forced marriage should therefore involve enhancing autonomy through policies that empower women within their lived contexts. In supporting this view, I do not explain forced marriage in 'culturalist' terms; and do not claim that any community's values justify it. Nonetheless, this approach supports my central claims that contextual responses are needed to respond to women's vulnerabilities; and that attention to the particularity of a culture should influence and shape a feminist understanding of women's universal rights.

My discussion proceeds as follows. In Sections II and III, I ask whether liberal conceptions of autonomy permit a meaningful distinction between forced and arranged marriage. After outlining the difficulties with these accounts, Section IV introduces the idea of plural autonomy. The first dimension of this approach highlights the way in which women often negotiate traditions such as arranged marriage in creative ways, without making free choices in a liberal sense. Hence, the concept indicates that liberals do not have a monopoly on the capacity for autonomy. Section V outlines the 'endorsement' dimension of this concept, demonstrating how coercion, or a lack of autonomy, should be ascertained. Section VI concludes that the difficulties involved in ascertaining the issue of endorsement for legal purposes indicates the need for a range of policies through which women's rights to autonomy can be supported, without incurring the costs of cultural alienation that would arise from imposing liberal values on them comprehensively.

II PERFECTIONIST LIBERALISM – A SUBSTANTIVE CONCEPTION OF FREE CHOICE

Do liberal conceptions of autonomy respond critically to the coercion of individuals whilst recognising the worth of practices such as arranged marriage? This question is important if we take seriously the view that a government that fails to act on knowledge of a forced marriage risks failing to meet its obligations to protect its citizens' human rights (Home Office 2000: 3). While the relevant right at stake might initially seem to be an entitlement to choose one's marriage partner freely, the British government has sought to distinguish forced from arranged marriage, and to emphasise the different degrees of independent judgement involved in varying forms of marriage (Foner 1997). It is therefore reasonable to assume that all parties to this debate are concerned to protect young people's capacities to avoid coercion rather than their rights to absolute free choice. The key question with which I begin, then, is whether rights to avoid coercion could be defended by appealing to liberal perfectionist ideals of autonomy that emphasise independent judgement in public and private life. While our critique in Chapter 1 of the perfectionist conception of choice underlying Nussbaum's account of basic capabilities alerts us immediately to problems with such an approach, the perfectionism defended by Joseph Raz appears more promising in light of his open acknowledgement of the pervasiveness of thick value pluralism (see Raz 1986 and 1994). However, while Raz's awareness of the ubiquity of cultural diversity in modern societies is compelling, his account does not clarify the distinction between forced and arranged marriage for reasons that relate to those that we raised against the 'objective interests' account of agency in Chapter 2.

Raz's defence of autonomy is situated, then, in the context of a keen awareness of the pervasiveness of cultural membership. The common character of cultural groups is 'one of the prime facts by which people are identified' (Raz 1994: 116), as cultures determine horizons and facilitate relationships. In his words, '[O]nly through being socialised in a culture can one tap the conditions which give life meaning' (ibid.: 178). However, Raz's awareness that a multiplicity of values contributes to human well-being stands in tension with the priority that he accords to a strong liberal notion of autonomy. While he holds that culture and autonomy can both be respected in a liberal state, since cultural groups 'are the precondition for, and are a factor which gives shape and content to, individual freedom' (ibid.: 178), a person is not autonomous on his account unless their choices satisfy the following conditions: first, their decisions should be 'unmanipulated'; second, they should be deliberate and based on a careful assessment of reasons; third, choices should relate to important matters such as marriage, occupation and long-term projects; and, last, they should be 'genuine' in the sense of being made between significantly different and equally valuable options (ibid.: 179). Cultures that do not protect their members' autonomy so defined do not warrant special protection by liberal states. Each culture should educate its members for autonomy (Raz 1986: 198) and, if they do not, they can be deemed 'inferior', since they do not prepare their members for success in modern societies in which autonomy is generally prized (ibid.: 432).

Thus, according to Raz, '[t]he picture that this pluralistic and autonomy-based liberalism suggests is one in which the community and its institutions foster and encourage a wide range of diverse forms of life' (Raz 1994: 119). Since all subgroups in a liberal order share an economic environment and a political sphere, citizens have an equal need to become autonomous. While an autonomy-suppressing culture might enable a person to lead a satisfying life, it will not enable her to thrive. While he concedes that his argument 'does not apply to enclaves of traditional pre-modern communities' (ibid.: 124, n. 30) and, thus, implies that groups such as the Amish and the Roma would be exempted from this account, the practices of all other autonomy-suppressing subgroups would be subject to assimilation (Baumeister, 2000: 122).

Yet Raz's belief about the inferiority of cultures that do not support this particular conception of autonomy is contentious. As Parekh (2000a: 93) observes, immigrant communities typically do prepare their members for success in the modern world and liberal autonomy should therefore not be considered the sole means through which a person can flourish in industrialised societies. By drawing on the resources of a tightly knit community, British Asians have achieved remarkable success in the national economy (Werbner 2000). While Parekh invokes this example in order to claim that human beings can prosper without valuing autonomy, his point could also be taken to emphasise the cultural particularity of Raz's account of this capacity. Asian communities might indeed encourage a certain form of self-direction in their young members, but this capacity might not usually involve making the nonconformist choices that Raz identifies with autonomy. While I shall return to this crucial point later, it is worth considering for now that the thickness of Raz's account of autonomy is also challenged by Spinner-Halev, who complains that it is hard to see how the society that Raz recommends 'will be made of different cultural groups' (Spinner-Halev 2001a: 48). In particular, he takes issue with Raz's assertion that communities that do not subscribe to his strong definition of autonomy are simply 'unviable' (Raz 1986: 43-4). Parekh, too, finds this claim circular, as the viability of a minority culture always depends in part on the state's attitude to it (2000a: 94). In sum, then, Raz's concession that a culture need not be liberal so long as it embodies values the point of which we can appreciate stands in considerable tension with his claim that, if cultures do not encourage liberal autonomy, they should be deemed unsupportable.

The implications of Raz's view for the debate about arranged and forced marriage emerge on considering Robert Young's similarly perfectionist ideal of 'making a conscious commitment to [one's projects] or a deliberate rejection of them' (Young 1986: 13). His emphasis on potential nonconformity evokes Berlin's ideal of negative freedom, according to which 'my decisions . . . depend on myself, *not on external forces of any kind*' (Berlin 1969: 131, my emphasis). In adhering to such strong conceptions of autonomy, Raz and Young leave, paradoxically, little room to recognise that autonomous choices are generally made in the context of adhering to commitments to one's communities and personal relationships. Consequently, the recognition of value pluralism ultimately plays a residual and conditional role in Raz's account, and he risks accepting the caricature of autonomy as self-sufficiency or as a 'retreat to one's inner citadel' (ibid. 1969: 135). For, while, in his understanding, cultural commitments provide a range of 'significantly different' (Raz 1986: 43) options from which individuals choose, it is important to note that the only value worthy of being pursued autonomously seems to be autonomy itself. However, while it is undoubtedly worthy at times to 'choose choice', as existentialists would say, autonomy is valued by human beings because our decisions express our commitments to values that originate *outside* the self. If we do not direct our freedom towards any commitment stronger than what we subjectively desire, towards a concern grounded in a 'strong evaluation' in Taylor's sense (see Taylor 1979), then our lives risk lacking meaning. Raz keenly acknowledges this point, as we have seen. Yet the paradoxical result of following his account is that one would not only struggle to accommodate arranged marriage, but would also misdiagnose how people make important life decisions in liberal societies. Mendus therefore rightly argues that autonomy, if understood as a strong form of 'self-authorship', trivialises personal commitments and is of doubtful merit in any society (2000a: 127).

These concerns intensify when we consider how authorities would test for Raz's idealised form of autonomy in hard-case situations. Inquiring whether a person has a range of alternatives from which to choose would be problematic, because the fact of having alternatives does not, in itself, show that a person exercised control over her situation. It would therefore be more reliable to ask whether the content of her decision maintains her in an autonomous condition, or whether she has reflected on her actions 'and [has made] choices that . . . avoid conflicting in their content with the ideal of autonomy' (Friedman 2003: 20). However, this test does not help to distinguish between forced and arranged marriage because, again, the perspective fails to acknowledge fully that marriage in any culture is a convention that involves giving up one's right to unlimited sexual partners and, arguably, 'consent[ing] to an unalterable and hierarchical . . . status' (Mendus 2000b: 95). Failing to recognise this point fully, Raz's substantive account risks classifying as non-autonomous sexual and marital commitments that demonstrate reasonable levels of agency. While it would be worrying if our choices diminished our future autonomy drastically, we may sometimes have good autonomy-related reasons to alienate some future autonomy. As Lindley explains, in the case of marriage, 'a strong belief in autonomy [could legitimately] motivate the autonomy-restricting behaviour' (Lindley 1986: 91).

Although one might object to this interpretation of Raz's account on the grounds that it is very unlikely indeed that he would oppose marriage tout court, this analysis emphasises that the substantive approach to autonomy that he recommends amounts to a high ideal which justifies a deal of paternalism to protect individuals from making conformist choices. The dangers of this approach are weighty enough to lead us to seek a more modest account that recognises that 'full autonomy is a chimera, not something that operates in the real world' (Mendus 1986: 108) and that, as Raz himself concedes, 'full autonomy is an impossibility' (Raz 1986: 155). In recognising this point, we would accept that human beings make valid decisions while being strongly influenced by restrictive cultural codes (Mahoney 1994: 96; Deveaux 2006: 161); and that they are constituted by factors that lie beyond their reflective control but that nonetheless structure their thoughts and motivations (Taylor 1991: 33). This account would acknowledge that some arranged marriages may not be agreed to freely but that, apart from in egregious instances involving torture or abduction, it is difficult to determine abstractly which unions are forced. This point is crucial for the social and political recognition of arranged marriage in liberal states, as, arguably, the practice does not involve the free choice of individuals so much as their renunciation of freedom to choose or their decision to trust in the wisdom of others (Ballard 1994: 14). Since the substantive account maintains that a person is not self-governing unless she chooses so as not to undermine this value (Benson 1990; Kristinsson 2000), it risks failing to acknowledge the normative structure of meaningful agency in any cultural context.

III CONTENT-NEUTRAL AUTONOMY – NON-DECEPTION AND NON-MANIPULATION

A suitable alternative to the substantive account appears to lie in Fried-man's 2003 content-neutral conception of autonomy – an approach that may be allied with 'political', rather than perfectionist, liberalism (Rawls 1993). As a political conception, content-neutral autonomy does not require that individuals prioritise autonomy in their private decisions. It holds only that a person's decision be regarded as supportable so long as it coheres with her life perspective, whatever that happens to be. This seemingly modest approach has a problem too, however. While Friedman assumes that acting in accordance with non-liberal reasons can be *consistent* with autonomy, she does not explain the role that cultural or religious commitments play in *constituting* this capacity. The indeterminate relation between culture and autonomy in her account entails that it can be pushed towards two different standpoints, each of which poses difficulties in the debate about arranged and forced marriage. This conception of autonomy therefore fails to make sense of the hard-case situations that motivated our search for a universal account of women's rights, and does not acknowledge how the universal interacts with the particular in a feminist and multicultural account of justice.

In order to appreciate why, let us first concede the advantages of

Friedman's approach. It is plausible to hold that a person's decision to live a domestically servile life or to join a religious order could be minimally autonomous if it is congruent with her deepest commitments. She could agree to an arranged marriage or, as Friedman says, to female genital cutting if she is an adult 'who may . . . prefer it to the alternative of not having the surgery . . . and may have reached that conclusion through careful reflection' (Friedman 2003: 190). By avoiding controversial views about the content of human choices, Friedman rightly accepts that people of all ways of life are susceptible to social pressures; but she counsels against rushing to conclusions about the need for state intervention, so long as the persons in question have defining values to which they are genuinely committed. While one might ask whether this perspective makes light of the potentially profound effects of socialisation, which need not be as direct as manipulation in the form of brainwashing to have deep effects (Mackenzie 2000: 143), it correctly recognises that cultural pressures are ubiquitous and, thus, lowers the bar for autonomy to a realistic point.

However, the problem lies in Friedman's reliance on the terms 'non-manipulation' and 'non-deception' as key conditions for autonomy. These terms are too ambiguous to explain why cultural values matter positively to and, indeed, constitute a person's autonomy. While Friedman indicates that practising autonomy is consistent with holding a range of different normative outlooks, her failure to explain the relationship between culture and human agency leads her to support contradictory perspectives on specific practices. On one interpretation, her account recalls our earlier worries about the substantive conception of autonomy. For, when Friedman attempts to define the conditions that persons need to develop content-neutral autonomy, she argues against educational exemptions that conservative religious parents frequently demand for their children in liberal states (Friedman 2003: 172). For the sake of consistency, she would probably also have to reject many non-liberal group claims, including campaigns for the recognition of arranged marriages, on grounds that these practices undermine substantive autonomy (Deveaux 2006: 175). In this context, Okin rightly observes that Friedman's conditions for autonomy turn out to be unexpectedly high. After all, how many people 'are . . . capable of reflecting on their cultural practices – or even knowing that their practices are "cultural" ones?' (Okin 2005: 79). This worry deepens when we consider Friedman's view that women need a range of meaningful options in order to be autonomous and, hence, her agreement with a key aspect of Raz's perfectionist account. It would not suffice, Friedman believes, if exiting from the community is a person's only alternative when faced with pressures to comply with cultural expectations (Friedman 2003: 197). 'The conditions [of autonomy] *must include the presence of genuine alternatives*' (ibid.: 201, my emphasis).

However, it is too demanding to assume that meaningful decision making must involve contemplating a range of significantly different alternatives. After all, many cultural practices are viewed by their adherents as part of a natural course of events, to which no alternatives are entertained. The fact that this is so should not lead to the assumption that the people in question lack a certain degree of control over their lives, or that they do not pursue a path that they value. Freedom is often exercised in limited ways in relation to practices that constitute one's identity. This point can be illustrated by the testimonies of the Asian women in London interviewed by Kalwant Bhopal, most of whom were either in or about to enter arranged marriages (Bhopal 1991: 21, cited in Phillips and Dustin 2004: 540). The statements that they made, such as 'if a girl says no, it's really considered a bad thing' and 'you just have to go along with it', suggest that they do not believe that they have a realistic opportunity to reject arranged marriages. Whilst the pressures on these young women should not be underestimated, the 'negotiated consensus' that Asian women often forge with their parents on marital issues should also be considered (Eckert 1993). Moreover, the fact that the women interviewed by Bhopal evidently have a reflective and critical awareness of their situation[4] should lead us to question the coherence of the liberal demand that all persons have 'significantly different and equally valuable options' in Raz's sense. For, if a person believes that one course of action represents the right way to live, it is hard to see how she could view the alternatives as equally valuable; and, if she does not think that one course of action has more value, one might question its meaningfulness for her. While people can undoubtedly be torn between two or more options, or be mistaken about the relation between their proposed actions and their well-being, it would be superficial to argue that actions can generally be assigned universal value. In this context, Friedman's adherence to the 'non-deception' condition for autonomy is arguably very strong as it seems to suggest, counter-intuitively, that a person has been deceived if they are led to believe a given action is the one right path, and that other options have significantly less value. In light of these worries, this strong interpretation of Friedman's perspective appears ill considered.

Moreover, a different but equally problematic interpretation of content-neutral autonomy arises from the fact that, if Friedman retreats from these demanding conditions and simply adheres to a minimal understanding of non-manipulation and non-deception, she could accept that even those in highly restrictive situations are capable of autonomy (Friedman 2003: 26), so long as they have not been directly brainwashed or indoctrinated. For instance, she accepts that even a reticent German official under the Nazi regime, who is under enormous pressure to follow orders, can make an independent decision. This is because autonomy is 'not only about choosing a luxurious life from among a range of prosperous options' (ibid.: 26). Yet the concerns that we raised in Chapter 2 against Deveaux's expansive view of agency indicate that the thin interpretation of content-neutral autonomy is likely to be as contentious as the thick version. While it is true, as Narayan (2002) argues, that the imperfections of a restrictive life do not necessarily preclude meaningful action, this perspective risks failing to explain why anyone but an abject torture victim could be said to suffer coercion (Narayan (2002). The only provisos specified by Narayan are that people should not have 'serious cognitive impairments' and should not be subject to 'literal' or 'outright' coercion (ibid.: 429). However, again, much depends on what these terms are taken to mean. To be sure, Asian women do often resist family pressures by insisting, say, on a university education before getting married (Deveaux 2006: 171). However, it would be crucial to investigate the degree of control that a woman has in making her decision and to ask whether she 'authorises' her eventual acceptance of community norms. It is not that human beings need, metaphorically, to write their life script from scratch but that they should at least be able to take responsibility for their decisions, and view them as having sense in the ongoing narrative of their lives (see Mendus 2000a).

This point can be illustrated usefully by considering the voice that Ralph Ellison constructs for his protagonist in his 1952 novel, *Invisible Man*. Against the backdrop of post-war racial divisions in America, the eponymous protagonist remarks that others refuse to see him as anything but a figure in their nightmares. His resentment towards a society that refuses him positive recognition leads him to a criminal life: 'To whom can I be responsible,' he asks, 'and why should I be, when you refuse to see me?' (Ellison 1952: 45). The invisible man emphasises that certain acts, such as the decision to relinquish responsibility for oneself, does not amount to autonomy, and that we should not place the bar for autonomy so low that it performs very little normative work. Christman therefore criticises content-neutral accounts for accepting choices such as voluntary slavery (Christman 2004: 149); and Mackenzie observes that, for Friedman, 'just about any practice short of physical abuse would be tolerated so long as women who are affected by it consent to it' (Mackenzie 2006: 113). Specifically, she takes issue with Friedman's readiness to accept anthropological findings that certain Egyptian women consent to FGM (see Friedman 2003: 197). She objects that Friedman does not ask whether the women would have consented to these surgeries if they were not interwoven with symbolic meanings of marriageability or whether they have considered the possibility that their decisions could be 'oppressive for women as a group'. Against these points, it seems too extreme to hold that practising autonomy has to entail contemplating remote counterfactual situations or having an in-depth understanding of the social implications of one's choices. However, Mackenzie's criticisms do encourage us to ask whether a person can genuinely be autonomous if they do not have the psychological freedom, material conditions or information to contest arrangements that might restrict their agency in the long term in a number of basic ways.

Moreover, the key issue for our purposes is this. The fact that such different perspectives issue from Friedman's account indicates its arbitrariness with respect to evaluating the situation of diverse women. As I indicated earlier, the problem lies in Friedman's failure to explain the *constitutive* connection between cultural values and autonomous agency. This failure leads her to make the apparently contradictory claims that FGM is permissible in some situations but that 'forced childhood marriage' undermines autonomy (ibid.: 191). These claims appear to conflict because, in supporting FGM, she implies that the Egyptian women consent as adults to surgeries that they presumably underwent at the onset of puberty and, thus, before full adulthood. However, if women can consent to FGM retrospectively, it is not clear why childhood marriage should be assumed to be forced. Rather, one would have to wait until the children have reached adulthood to ask whether they consent.

Since doing so would give rise to the concerns about oppressive socialisation to which ideals of autonomy are supposed to respond, however, it is tempting to agree with Okin that focusing on reflective consent in the debate about gender and culture is misconceived, as one of the problems associated with trying to ensure that consent is free is that, in many of the cases where it is in doubt, the people involved are young (Okin 2005: 78). Thus, the validity of their consent will often be debatable, as young people are frequently initiated into rites without their consent. Moreover, how many people are free from manipulative interferences such as parental pressures, religious education or capitalist advertising? Finally, if a person demands your money at gunpoint, the key issue is ultimately not whether you agree, but the legitimacy of the situation. Yet while Okin's reasoning is compelling in extreme cases, a feminist and multicultural theory of rights should retain a focus on reflective consent in a wide range of cases. This is because there is so much controversy over the meaning of harm in multicultural societies that authorities cannot but ask whether people willingly adhere to their practices. As our examination of sati in Chapter 1 demonstrated, it is reasonable to believe that, apart from in egregious cases of violence, over which there is likely to be a significant degree of cross-cultural agreement, a view from which to determine what counts as harm is difficult to locate.

However, even if this is so, it nonetheless appears that Friedman fails to consider the fact that commitments to cultural goods, such as marriage-ability and solidarity, influence what people think of as consent and coercion. She does not consider that there is likely to be a constitutive relation between cultural values and one's conception of freedom. While she contends that FGM should sometimes be tolerated on the grounds that it 'constitutes a tradition in the honorific sense of the term' (Friedman 2003: 200), the relationship between culture and autonomy still remains ambig-uous on this account. For, on the one hand, the substantive interpretation of her account holds that any marriage in which a woman does not have an extensive range of options should be assumed to be forced. Yet the weaker view holds that any marriages, bar those involving egregious violence or direct psychological manipulation in the form of drugging, would be acceptable. In response to this problem, the following sections of this chapter elaborate on the constitutive relationship between culture and autonomy. While the relationship between the self and its surrounding culture has been defended by a number of communitarian thinkers (see, for example, Margalit and Raz 1990; Tamir 1993), I concentrate on the link between culture and autonomy specifically. In doing so, my claim is not that autonomy is the only worthwhile value or that it need be prioritised by those whose lives are embedded in communitarian groups. However, the commitment to autonomy, suitably conceived, nonetheless plays a special role in protecting the interests of potentially vulnerable individuals. It should, therefore, be defended centrally as a basic entitlement in a feminist and multicultural theory of rights. To this extent, my account reveals that the disadvantaged should indeed sometimes invoke what at first appear to be the 'master's tools' to overcome their subordinate position.

IV PLURAL AUTONOMY AND ITS 'CULTURE-CONSTITUTING' COMPONENT

Given the deep contestation over definitions of autonomy in political philosophy (see Dworkin 1989: 59), it is plausible to suppose that self-determination can vary according to historical and cultural location. I therefore understand this 'essentially contested' concept (Gallie 1968) as a capacity that comprises a culturally variable family of skills. Let us call this idea *plural autonomy*. This idea entails that, while agency must involve a mental ability to reflect on one's situation free from extreme domination, non-liberal cultures often avail their members of skills such as empathy and psychological resilience which are frequently subordinated to the individualistic, means-end reasoning typically prized in Western societies (Meyers 1993). This is not to say that cultural groups can be separated perfectly in terms of the behavioural patterns that they promote. This claim would fail to reflect the realities of many immigrant women, who often experience a high degree of overlap between their culture and that of the majority society. It would also risk reviving undesirable claims about absolute cultural differences reminiscent of colonial times. Our conception of autonomy takes account of sociological insights into the 'new ethnicities' that portray group membership not in terms of shared behavioural patterns but of a shared experience of oppression. Yet a 1997 British survey showed that minorities typically subscribe *both* to the new account of ethnicity and the older one that assumed continuity in terms of customs and behaviour (Modood et al. 1997: 334–8). Responsive to both accounts, plural autonomy denies that cultures have a Platonic form or essence, but insists nonetheless that historical continuities do exist, which hold groups together, as I argued in Chapter 2, in a Wittgensteinian sense (Modood 2007: 99; Wittgenstein 1968). For instance, Tariq Modood rightly argues that one need not be an essentialist in order to believe that some ways of thinking and acting have coherence within a community (Modood 2007: 98; Wittgenstein 1968). It is not therefore contradictory to claim that group-members might share broadly a sense of the appropriateness of certain actions and a conception of which reasons for action matter, even if there is much internal contestation within any cultural group with regard to what should be interpreted as 'appropriate' in a particular sphere of life. If this is true, one can defend the reality of cultural differences whilst rejecting the idea that groups to which they relate are eternal and unchanging (see also Squires 2002: 116). A good illustration of this point lies in the practice of arranged marriage itself, as we shall see.

To support this point further, consider that anti-essentialist critiques of cultural difference often fall short because, as Modood explains, their claim that cultures change over time is a truism which most defenders of cultural diversity do not reject. Furthermore, the paradox is that this criticism presumes the reality of distinct cultures. This is because, for change to be an identifiable process, there must be a subject of change – that is, a cultural group (Modood 2007: 104). If these claims are plausible, it makes sense to conceive of autonomy as a capacity that could vary across groups in accordance with a loose and internally contested consensus within the group as regards reasons that motivate action, and by a shared view of the areas of life in which individual judgement should be exercised. This idea serves to challenge stereotyped characterisations of Asian women as passive 'victims of cultural practices that oppress them' (Shain 2003: 41); and it encourages what Phillips rightly sees as the readiness to 'finesse free will and determinism' that has become part of common sense in debates about gender and class but that has been, she claims, less salient in debates about culture (Phillips 2007: 131). The commitment to plural autonomy entails that motivations are likely to differ according to cultural value systems, as might the practical form that autonomy takes.

This account has the added advantage of addressing the difficulties with Kymlicka's account of this capacity. Kymlicka assumes a triadic relationship between autonomy, dignity and cultural membership, which seems initially similar to my account. However, consider his claim that a modest form of autonomy provides individuals with a primary good (see Rawls 1971), or one of the necessary conditions for a good life – namely, a social basis of self-respect (Kymlicka 1989: 23).[5] According to Kymlicka, as long as groups encourage in their members the capacity to 'rationally revise or reject' their inherited values (ibid.: 69), their practices should be tolerated. In his words, 'no particular task is set for us by society, and no particular cultural practice has authority that is beyond individual judgement and possible rejection' (ibid.: 50). If immigrant groups fail to foster their members' autonomy so understood, the state often has a 'right and responsibility' to pressurise them to reform (Kymlicka 1995: 168). This is so in spite of Kymlicka's distinction, as noted in Chapter 2, between the defence of liberal values and their enforcement. In essence, his account appears similar to mine in denying that autonomy need involve ambitious goals such as self-authorship or that it expresses our moral nature (see Parekh 2000a: 99). It suggests only that a person's culture should be viewed as an option, which contributes to their sense of dignity. However, the difficulty with this account lies in its ultimate distinction between the inner self and external cultural influences (ibid.: 106), which advocates of arranged marriage would be unlikely to accept. They would most likely reject the claim that culture is always encountered as an option, as it is often experienced as the source of a demand to do certain acts because they please God or because parental authority is paramount (ibid. : 107).

In contrast, the idea of plural autonomy accepts that human action can be motivated by non-liberal beliefs, and that culture is often not experienced as a repository of choice. Rather, it is the necessary condition through which an individual ascertains when and for what reasons individual judgement should be exercised. While the claim that cultures generally support autonomy would be resisted by strong Kant-inspired liberals, who would view the particularities of culture as sources of heteronomy and even irrationality, the 'culture-constituting' component of autonomy can be defended by focusing on Parekh's claim that, while individuals have capacities for language which their culture never determines, 'no society can flourish without cultivating its members' powers of thought' (ibid.: 157). Some cultures clearly do de-emphasise autonomy in favour of, say, obedience to God, but only in the rarest cases would they not ensure capacities for judgement in some form. This is because even communities that prioritise the value of humility depend for their inter-generational preservation on their members' abilities to respond creatively to the evolving circumstances of human life. Thus, 'a culture that worked to impair capacities [for judgement] would be creating the conditions for its own demise' (Moody-Adams 1994: 291). This point entails, as Meyers argues, that 'culture cannot turn its adherents into indoctrinated automatons who cannot question cultural beliefs and who cannot instigate . . . change' (Meyers 1993: 17).

While cultures often ward off dangers of dissent by circumscribing the autonomy skills that their members develop (Meyers 2000: 484), it is plausible to think that groups nurture those skills that enable individuals to function in their environment. Of course, the claims that (a) all cultures allow scope for the capacity for autonomy; (b) each culture integrates autonomy into a distinctive hierarchy of values; and (c) each culture is likely to have a distinctive conception of the spheres of life in which autonomy should be exercised, do not logically entail the stronger claim that there are *different forms* of autonomy. However, my suggestion is that any plural autonomy more likely. This suggestion is supported by the example raised earlier against Raz concerning British Asians' success in industry. Over time, older generations in these communities have evidently encouraged decision-making capacities in their younger members; yet these skills may be thought to differ from a liberal capacity for rational revisability.[6] If this point is plausible, states should not assume the priority of *liberal* autonomy in the debate about forced and arranged marriage. Doing so would risk misunderstanding the priorities of women who see their marriage practices as a marker of ethnic identity that differentiates them from 'white society' (Pichler 2007). For this reason too, a criminal law against forced marriage would be unhelpful because it would probably not encourage members of the majority society to gain a realistic understanding of differing, but potentially plausible, conceptions of the borderline between consent and coercion in a plural society.[7] Moreover, this account of autonomy is supported by feminist thinkers who theorise this capacity in terms of social bonds (see Keller 1985). While few liberals would of course deny that autonomy is socially constituted, 'relational' theorists go further by holding that these bonds constitute a person's specific way of being free (Meyers 1989; Govier 1993; Huntingdon 1995; Code 2000).[8]

Yet a critic could insist that, even if this account avoids a Platonic-philosophical conception of groups, it cannot avoid encouraging essentialist assumptions at the political level. Governments would have to assume that different cultures have their own discrete standards of agency; and cross-cultural judgements about coercion would therefore be rendered highly unstable. Such concerns induce Phillips to defend 'multiculturalism without culture', an account that asks why culture should be employed in a more stereotypical way than gender or class (Phillips 2007: 131), especially given that these stereotypes are often used to support draconian policies such as general bans on head scarves or on marrying spouses from overseas (ibid.: 124). Yet, while Phillips and I focus on different aspects of the debate over gender and culture, we are both conscious of the risks involved in misrepresenting and pathologising cultural difference in an era of globalisation. We both seek to understand the ways in which women's lives are shaped positively and negatively by their particular identities. While Phillips rightly contests the political misuse of cultural explanations, she also argues that 'it ought to be possible to recognise the relevance of culture without concluding that it dictates everything' (ibid.: 126). Her point is important because, as Song aptly warns, care should be taken not to overstate the claim that cultures are radically contested and hybrid.[9] for, while some groups can be so characterised, others are comparatively closed (Song 2007a). Here she cites David Scott, who asks, 'For whom is culture partial, unbounded, heterogeneous . . . the anthropologist or the native? Whose claim is this, theory's or that of the discourse into which theory is inquiring?' (Scott 2003: 101–2, emphasis in the original). These points indicate that to reject the idea of plural autonomy out of political concerns about reification would be to renounce the quest to understand the specific issues that women confront in different contexts, even when specifying women's *universal* rights. Moreover, assertions of anti-essentialism are not always politically innocent (Modood 2007). They can be counterproductive when they are invoked to support the dubious assertion that cultures are so internally disputed that they lack any relevance to people's lives, or that late-modern societies are 'beyond' or 'after' multiculturalism (Alibhai-Brown 2000a).

Recognising culture-specific autonomy skills indicates a productive relation between the universal and the particular in our defence of women's rights. It responds to Phillips' worry about the claim that members of some groups are intrinsically less capable of autonomy than others (2007: 132). This claim emanates from an extreme interpretation of Parekh's characterisation of culture as the source of unchosen disadvantage (2002c) or 'brute bad luck' (Dworkin 1981). To be specific, Parekh responds to Barry's 2001 scepticism about multicultural claims by explaining why it might be difficult for a person of a minority culture or religion to comply with general laws. For instance, when a Sikh policeman requests to wear a turban rather than a helmet on his patrols, his claim should not be dismissed on grounds that it expresses a mere preference (compare Cohen 1999). This is because his conception of value renders him unable, in an important sense, to comply with the rule. However, Phillips aptly warns that the 'culture/religion as inability' thesis is often extended in problematic ways (Phillips 2007: 128–9); and, while Parekh evidently does not mean that culture and religion are intrinsically disabling, plural autonomy responds to that interpretation of his claim by contesting the idea that minority women lack autonomy simply as a result of their cultural membership. Moreover, the approach views those who violate their fellow group-members' interests as responsible agents who cannot claim 'affected ignorance' (Moody-Adams 1994). Finally, the claim that all cultures typically value autonomy in some form is supported by Sawitri Saharso, who focuses on studies that differentiate 'egocentric' cultures, which are usually associated with the West, and 'sociocentric' societies in which individuals are socialised to conform to strict honour codes. She rightly points to instances of 'autonomous individuality *within* sociocentrism' (Saharso 2006: 130; see also Wuff 1972), such as the Orthodox Brahman community of the Mimamsaka School, in which the Indian ideal of the autonomous person as the holy man, or the 'drop-out', prevails.

The sceptic may insist that these studies reveal that there is *one* universal ideal of autonomy but it is more likely that the various forms of this ability constitute a family united loosely by a capacity for mental freedom. This mental capacity is likely to differ cross-culturally and need not amount to Western ideal of self-definition, as it could be constituted by introspective abilities such as emotional resilience within highly conformist environment. Accepting this possibility enables us to question early anthropological studies (for example, Dumont 1980), which purported to show that Asian cultures deny the notion of 'selfhood' that is normally endorsed by Western cultures. Against these accounts, more recent studies show that members of these groups develop a self-identity shaped by interdependence in an emotional atmosphere of sensitivity to others' needs (Roland 1996: 32; Saharso, 2000: 234). Whilst this ideal type underestimates the complexity of personality development in individual cases, it supports the view that *intrapsychic autonomy*, or 'the ability to maintain enduring mental representations of sources of self-esteem', as a result of a person's childhood internalisation of positive memories of the parent–child bond (Ewing 1991: 132, cited in Saharso 2000: 235), may be central to a person's autonomy, particularly in certain insular Asian communities. Intrapsychic autonomy, Saharso argues, can be contrasted with 'interpersonal autonomy', or the Western conception based on the capacity to make idiosyncratic choice in the world. Not only, she contends, does their conformist environment deny Asian women interpersonal autonomy but it also encourages a high degree of intrapsychic autonomy that enables them to cope in their environment (2000: 236). In sum, Saharso rightly insists that autonomy is *'not just one capacity*, or rather that it . . . is not necessarily always tied up with a highly individualistic personality' (ibid.: 241, my emphasis). Concretely, the difference between the 'intrapsychic' and 'interpersonal' capacities for autonomy lies in the fact that the former involves the ability to retain a sense of one's separateness from any engagement in the world, whereas the latter conception, which we may associate with Kymlicka (1995a), involves the ability to act with dignity in the world (Mookherjee 2008b). To conceive autonomy in terms of these differences promises to free liberal states from the tendency to 'discipline' diversity by demanding that non-liberal communities subscribe to thick liberal ideals as a condition of recognition. It encourages the larger society to see that a practice such as arranged marriage typically does not involve free choice but rather a union between two families which confers honour on both (Kakar 1978: 145). Thus, the approach stresses that attention to the culturally particular is crucial to a defence of women's universal rights. In view of the complexity of autonomy, then, states should not assume that protecting women obviously involves reforming cultural practices that traditionally reject a liberal conception of this capacity (Razack 2004: 134–6).

However, we need to address the further objection that, if a woman belongs to a wife-beating culture, for instance, then her cultural context impedes her agency in a way that plural autonomy would not discern. While it must be conceded that not all cultures obviously do promote all their members' autonomy, a number of points should be made in reply. First, domestic violence is rife in Western societies but it would be contestable to describe them as 'wife-beating cultures'; and cultures in which honour crimes occur contain a large number of dissident voices that contest these practices (Baker et al. 1999). Of course, the problem is that cultures need not be overtly committed to gender inequality to contain informal norms that make domestic violence possible. Arguably, these informal norms are sustained precisely by encouraging women's autonomy only in spheres that ensure community stability (Meyers 2000: 488). Thus, if community elites can so effectively induce women to 'compartmentalise' their autonomy, surely a culture *can* sometimes impair their core capacities drastically? If this is so, our account so far does indeed risk failing to acknowledge the possibility that socialisation in some insular communities produces high risks of forced marriage, if young people do not find it thinkable to transgress family norms. Here, Meyers' point that 'a culture's ultimate defensive weapon is to make alternative ways of life . . . imaginable only as bizarre . . . specimens' (ibid.: 488) is highly relevant.

However, a level-headed view of this issue must be retained. Apart from the doubt that we have already cast on the idea that the fact of having alternatives need be a condition of autonomy, Phillips rightly points out that there is no evidence that Asian women who have been pressurised to marry simply cannot contemplate a different course of action (2007: 148). Moreover, as I argued in Chapter 1, when a person is faced with a dire predicament, even unsatisfactory alternatives are likely to appear thinkable. Thus, the argument that a person's cultural norms limit her imagination to this point is likely to be erroneous in all but the rarest cases. Finally, as indicated earlier, we need to bear in mind that most cultures suppress some of their members' autonomy skills. In Western societies, for instance, people are often brought up to choose their marriage partners independently but to adhere to tradition in relation to religion or political views (Parekh 2000a: 170). Arguably, a middle-class, liberal culture does provide better opportunities for autonomy than some closed communities. However, while liberal cultures typically encourage individuals' capacities to choose goals with a high personal-satisfaction yield, women are often encouraged to accentuate caring skills in the domestic sphere (Meyers 2000: 485). Whether or not one contests the justice of this aspect of liberal society, the gendered way in which it selectively nurtures autonomy suggests, at least, that 'moulding' this capacity is not synonymous with denying it.

Taken together, these points reinforce my claim that, if we are to resist treating minority women as cultural dupes, we cannot assume the priority of liberal understandings of the borderline between freedom and force. This point is crucial if we are to appreciate the significance of 'gender as seriality', and the way in which the particularities of culture bear on an understanding of universal rights. Plural autonomy acknowledges the fact that some communities adhere to values that differ from those in the larger society, such as the belief that marriage is 'joint undertaking between parents and young people' (Brah 1996: 77; see also Patel 2000). To accept this point does not commit us to the misguided belief that human beings always act effectively even under the most coercive circumstances. As we shall see next, while culture should not be deemed the 'villain that shanghais a person's entire life' (Meyers 2000: 478), human capacities for agency sometimes do break down.

V PLURAL AUTONOMY, APPARENT CONSENT AND THE 'ENDORSEMENT' COMPONENT

Remember that our motivation for searching for an account of women's rights to autonomy arose as a result of recognising the limitations of democratic deliberation as a means to protect women from intra-community harm. In order to address the crucial issue of whether plural autonomy responds to the hard-case situations noted in Chapter 2, let us return now to the recent British legislation on forced marriage. As mentioned previously, the Forced Marriage (Civil Protection) Act extends family law protection to persons who are under pressure to marry,[10] by enabling the young man or woman or concerned third parties to apply for non-harassment or non-molestation orders against family members. In this section, I contend that plural autonomy's *endorsement* dimension assists in determining when a person should be understood to lack autonomy and, thus, to require assistance under the new law. However, I also argue that, in spite of the advantages of this approach, the difficulties inherent in evaluating a person's endorsement in legal contexts are so acute that relying on the law would not provide the most trustworthy avenue through which to protect women's rights to autonomy.

The problems associated with ascertaining individuals' consent to social arrangements clearly do not only arise in the case of minority communities. Women who choose to remain in violent domestic situations in liberal society, for instance, present policy makers with the difficult question of whether to institute mandated criminal proceedings, irrespective of the desires of the women involved (Friedman 2003: Chapter 7). A battered woman may opt to stay with her partner for a number of reasons: while being aware of the risk of further abuse, she may fear being killed if she leaves (Hirschmann 2003: 134); or she may adhere to a 'salvation ethic', an outlook according to which she stays with her partner in order to redeem him (Friedman 2003: 113). Similarly, a person facing serious parental pressures to marry is likely to seek social acceptance and the goods of family life. While these reasons are all rational in their own terms, plural autonomy holds that a person's stated reasons do not always suffice to show that she endorsed her decision. This is not to contradict Friedman's point that, even in a coercive situation, the victim's stated reasons must be given due consideration (ibid.: 142); or Narayan's related observation that human lives typically contain mixed bundles of goods, with reference to which people exercise agency in an imperfect world (Narayan 2002). While these insights should be accepted by any feminist and multicultural theory of rights that is relevant to a world in which structural inequalities and value disagreements are pervasive, plural autonomy also suggests a basis for assisting women in the context of oppressive socialisation and in situations in which they may not be able to form the practical intention to resist community expectations. While there is no objective borderline between socialisation and coercion, certain guidelines can be articulated that assist in making the relevant evaluations. Friedman, for her part, hints at the need for such guidelines by stating that there is something 'amiss' about a person who fails to act to protect against harm to her basic interests, and that 'such a failure calls for some explanation' (Friedman 2003: 144).

Here, plural autonomy's endorsement dimension asks whether the person acted in order to secure important cultural goods that support her agency. While 'endorsement' seems at first glance to be a strong notion that is closely associated with liberal ways of life (Benson 2005), its responsiveness to non-liberal diversity can be clarified by emphasising that it need not involve strenuous self-reflective affirmation. Christman, for instance, equates endorsement with a modest notion of non-alienation from one's deepest projects (2004: 153–4). A person who makes their decisions when in an uncontrollable rage or while on hallucinogenic drugs would not qualify as self-endorsing. One advantage of inquiring whether a person lacked the capacity to endorse her decisions is that, while we can remain committed to the first ('culture-constituting') dimension of autonomy, and we therefore need not, in Leti Volpp's language, 'blame culture for bad behaviour' (Volpp 2000), we also respond to the fact that individuals in dire situations often strategise by invoking their cultural values precisely to deny that they are being abused. Saharso illustrates this phenomenon by referring to a British Asian woman who killed her husband after enduring a violent marriage for ten years. The woman explained why she had lived with the situation for so long in a testimony taped while she was in prison. 'My culture is like my blood – coursing through every vein in my body,' she claimed. '[In my culture, women are taught] to endure many kinds of . . . pain in silence' (cited by Sahgal 1992; see also Saharso 2000: 234). While rationalising one's situation by appealing to cultural ideals may be an effective survival strategy in the short term, those who do not identify with life decisions are likely to suffer 'alienation from self' (Meyers, 2000) which could ultimately cause them to break down. The endorsement component of plural autonomy therefore holds that, in certain spheres of life, one's second-order beliefs, or one's *evaluation* of one's beliefs (Frankfurt 1988), matter greatly.

In response to the concern that this claim brings our account dangerously close to Kymlicka's conception of rational revisability, it is worth observing that, if cultural groups usually seek to preserve themselves, it would be counterproductive if they placed their members under such psychological pressure that they risk self-alienation, and become incapable of playing their role in sustaining the community. Pressures that undermine the capacity for endorsement can thus be criticised, therefore, from the premises of plural autonomy. This approach therefore justifies a more cautious approach to determining coercion than Kymlicka, who might well support a deal of paternalistic intervention into arranged marriages where women do not view their decisions as 'optional'. For Kymlicka, these marriages may 'violate existing laws regarding informed consent' (1995a: 4). Moreover, our approach does not reinstate the reflective consent requirement of content-neutral autonomy, as it responds to the merely contingent relationship that that theory envisages between cultural norms and autonomy. Plural autonomy insists that the necessary condition of personal autonomy lies in one's cultural or other group-based values, but it contests the idea that these values suffice to show that one always acts autonomously. On this account, coercion is defined not as manipulation or deception abstractly conceived, but as the threat of being alienated from cultural goods that sustain one's capacity to act. As Calhoun argues, meaningful agency operates against a set of 'frames' that people normally take for granted (Calhoun 2008). These frames include a lack of alienation from one's normative outlook and an assumption of security from disastrous misfortune. When these frames are disrupted, it is not that our agency is utterly defeated but that we find it emptied of significance. In Calhoun's language, we risk 'losing ourselves' and, in the terminology of this chapter, we fail to exercise autonomy (ibid.).

However, given that a person might often undertake, but feel quite alienated from, a number of purposive actions (such as the act of filling in a tax return), we need to show why particular decisions such as marriage should be endorsed. Ronald Dworkin's conception of endorsement helps to clarify this point. While a person's well-being is culturally defined rather than 'transcendent' or universal, no aspect of well-being, he argues, 'may even so much as contribute to the value of a person's life without his endorsement' (Dworkin 2000: 248). Thus, while my culture defines the goods that I am likely to pursue, it is important that I identify with the decision to pursue them. The important issue is that, by well-being, Dworkin does not mean basic needs, such as for food, shelter or a degree of literacy, as these resources can be assumed to contribute to my well-being whether I endorse them or not. Endorsement matters in issues that require an element of subjective evaluation (ibid.: 249). The point enables us to count as autonomous many intentional but unendorsed actions (Benson, 2005: 115), whilst still contending that states ought to be concerned if a person's decisions in an area of life in which endorsement matters are driven by a fear of losing goods that support their decision-making capacities.

Drawing on Dworkin's insights, then, plural autonomy assumes that important commitments such as marriage should be endorsed. This assumption does not compromise the openness of this account to non-liberal diversity, once we emphasise its definition as a minimal requirement for non-alienation in a circumscribed range of situations. As I argued earlier, we do not have interests in achieving unfettered Promethean freedom; but we do have a psychological investment in exercising agency in contexts that matter to us. Of course, people often have mixed motivations, and their reasons for action are often unclear. Hence, in many situations, taking a person's stated preferences on trust evinces respect from them as rational beings. Yet the commitment to endorsement suggests that sometimes a person's stated reasons do not suffice to show that her act would improve her *critical* well-being (Dworkin 2000: 123). Here, defenders of arranged marriage might respond to my account by objecting that no affirmation is required in marriage but only a *failure to repudiate* the situation. Yet it is hard to differentiate clearly between non-alienation and a genuine failure to repudiate, even though the practical concern remains that community elites could simply regard the self-alienation of their group-members as less important than the pressures that the community experiences to survive in the disorienting circumstances of diaspora. Indeed, it may be that such pressures contribute to a situation in which an arranged marriage becomes forced. However, it is ultimately hard to see how an empirical observation about the beliefs of community elites undermines the normative claim that marriage should be endorsed.

Finally, it is worth emphasising that I am not making the impractical claim that authorities should be obliged to ascertain whether people endorse their decisions in every sphere of life. I suggest only that some undertakings warrant scrutiny because they are profoundly significant to human agency. While we need to be sensitive to different cultural understandings of marriage (Foner 1997), and although it would be naïve to claim that people should never marry out of obligation to their families or communities or out of financial need, it is as important not to feel alienated from one's marital decisions as it is in equally serious decisions concerning religion or politics. Of course, a religious believer does not view her commitment to God as a free choice in the strict sense; and her political convictions are not chosen in the way that her outfit for a party may be. Given the need, however, for *non-alienation* in these contexts, plural autonomy insists only that persons should affirm their life decisions in the minimal sense outlined here.

In turning now to the issue of how endorsement could be invoked as a critical standard to assist women through the law, I leave aside the objection that controlling the behaviour of family members by legal means may often be counterproductive (Wilson 2007). The key problem for our purposes is whether any strategy for testing endorsement under the new law would have to appeal to notions of an authentic self and thereby require the sort of second-guessing of individuals that Berlin feared and for which writers such as Rousseau are excoriated (Hirschmann 2003: 37). My suggestion is that we need not be committed to strong notions of a real self to pursue a contextual inquiry that considers the person's material situation and their culturally specific autonomy skills to ascertain whether not going along with the decision would involve renouncing goods that support their capacity to act meaningfully. The flexibility of this contextual inquiry is likely to be familiar to family lawyers, for whom the issue of whether a woman has been, or is being, forced to marry is ascertained by asking whether she was or is suffering 'duress' (Phillips and Dustin 2004: 534). While ascertaining this matter is not usually taken to involve asking whether consent was *reluctantly* or *resentfully* given (compare Phillips 2008, forthcoming), it does entail inquiring whether the person was motivated by the fear of paying a price that is too high for a reasonable person in her situation, to a point that her 'will was overborne'.[11]

One difficulty with the current law of duress, however, is that it seems to appeal to the assumption that the agent entirely lacked a capacity for rational agency in the putatively coercive situation (see Rodgers 2004: Section 3). The definition of duress in terms of 'restraint of danger which is sufficient in terms of severity or appreciation to deprive a person of free choice or destroy his volition',[12] misunderstands the mixed motivations that are likely to be experienced by a person involved in a forced marriage. This legal concept therefore has the curious effect of pathologising young people caught in these situations, by suggesting publicly that certain reasons for action are irrational. The test for endorsement is more attractive as it inquires whether the person had at least one way of negotiating her cultural traditions such that outcomes would be altered in her favour She need not view her cultural practices as optional; but must have more effective agency than on Deveaux's 'democratic agency' view considered in Chapter 2. By requiring that the victim's situation be evaluated by those familiar with her cultural values, nuanced judgements can be made. While the motives of a person caught in these circumstances may often be obscure, this method is preferable to ascertaining coercion by relying on hypothetical reasoning situations that inquire whether all possible persons would have agreed to the given state of affairs (see, for example, O'Neill, 1993). 'Possible consent' approaches, as Deveaux rightly points out, are too abstract to take account of cultural differences (Deveaux 2006: 178). Therefore, the flexibility of the endorsement test refines the intuitions implicit in British family law, where courts nullify marriage if the person's act appear to border on necessity.[13]

The approach has the added advantage of addressing the difficulties with Kukathas's right to exit thesis, which we first encountered in the previous chapter. While Kukathas is not committed to the protection of internal minorities' personal autonomy, his view of how intra-group coercion should be assessed bears comment at this stage because it highlights the benefits of my approach in a particularly vivid way. Kukathas proposes to limit state power over groups by emphasising a form of liberalism that is grounded not in autonomy but in toleration. He therefore defends the rights of all persons to free association, arguing that, in the absence of cruel and degrading treatment, authorities should not inquire into cultural groups' internal affairs. Partly, this is because a person's situation should only be deemed unjust if they have no way of leaving it – that is, if they have no right to exit. This approach is advantageous in that it accommodates much non-liberal diversity. It is, at one level, motivated by a concern for the vulnerable, as it opposes the state's power to grant group rights on the grounds that they would simply affirm present power relations (Kukathas 2003: 79). However, the key objection to this approach is its narrow definition of intra-community coercion. While Kukathas concedes that oppression can shape a person's preferences, the issue of preference formation is, in his view, different from that of freedom (ibid.: 109). While some people cannot contemplate leaving their community because they have been socialised in such a way that gives them 'no taste – or hunger – for exit' (ibid.), he insists that this does not mean they are unfree. They are only unfree if 'they have to live lives that they cannot, in good conscience, accept' (ibid.: 113) or if they cannot dissociate themselves from options that they 'cannot abide' (ibid.: 114). Kukathas premises this view on the ontological claim that cultures are not natural but 'always inescapably political' (ibid.: 90). As cultural groups are akin to voluntary associations, the main rights to be defended in culturally diverse liberal order are rights to associate with and exit from groups.

Numerous versions of the right of exit view have been proposed (see, for example, Rosenblum 1998; Benhabib 2002; Galston 1995; Spinner-Halev 2005). While some are more sensitive to issues of intra-community coercion than Kukathas, they all claim that minorities should be left alone so long as members could leave the community if they are dissatisfied with its conventions. However, even weaker formulations of the right to exit raise the question of how far down state intervention will have to go to ensure realistic rights of exit (Song 2007a: 16). Deciding whether a person had a realisable right to leave involves making controversial calculations about the costs of exit (Kukathas 2003: 110–11). The difficulties involved in this task lead Kukathas to hold that the only provision the state must make is to ensure the existence of a wider society that is open to individuals wishing to leave their groups (Kukathas 1995: 252). However, it is unconvincing to suppose that guaranteeing a receptive civil society is all that the state should do to protect a person's freedom to leave their community. But, if it should do more than this, the account is open to the objections raised by Barry, who argues that, while the state could ensure compensation for material costs of exit in some cases (say, by requiring that groups such as the Hutterites in the USA contribute to an 'exit fund' on which shunned members could draw), there is likely to be nothing the state could do to offset the emotional and existential costs of abandoning one's community (Barry 2001: 150–1).

Furthermore, for Kukathas, the attempt to do so would not be just, since he believes that, if one is free to do something, the opportunity costs involved are irrelevant. As Phillips and Dustin (2004: 541) explain:

> On [this] austere understanding of freedom, anyone who felt so over-whelmed by [the pressures of exit] that he or she 'preferred' to go along with the family's choice of spouse . . . could not be considered a victim of coercion. (Phillips and Dustin 2004: 541)

Yet it would surely be misguided to ignore the intrinsic costs of exit, such as the loss the person would suffer in terms of 'club goods' or goods that can only be enjoyed with specific others, such as friendship, love or communal worship. The price of losing these goods is hard to generalise, but it could potentially be life shattering. Even to attempt to quantify them in particular cases would necessitate inquiries that are not available to Kukathas, in view of his commitment to limiting state power. The exit approach seems therefore to depend on inquiries into women's values and culturally derived autonomy skills, which it cannot undertake. Not only does the approach presuppose substantive capacities to exit (Okin 2002: 216–22), these capacities are also likely to vary across cultures in a manner that the account would not acknowledge.

Moreover, the 'exit' strategy suffers a deeper problem. The issue of whether a person had a realistic opportunity to leave their culture is likely to be too extreme a question to be realistic to, or relevant from the perspective of, those experiencing coercion. To ask whether a woman in a highly insular community could leave when facing pressures to marry would be misconceived, if she believes strongly in the utmost value of her community's kinship structures and much else that she values in life is bound up with networks of social support and the shared understandings of her religious or cultural group. While one could reply that the issue of whether women subjectively perceive exit as meaningful is not germane to the issue of whether exit is a reasonable moral standard, this response is inadequate in a theory that responds to a world characterised by a plurality of imperfectly reconcilable modes of living. For this reason, coercion is best judged by focusing not on the costs of exit but on the cost of *staying*. We need to ask whether the persons in question act primarily in order to preserve cultural goods on which their agency depends. For instance, if someone is required to marry a person without any possibility of negotiating when the union takes place, and on pain of excommunication from the community, it is likely that the costs would be too high. Phillips rightly argues here that the 'point at issue is not whether people should have the right to leave their cultural community, but whether having this right can ever be enough protection against cultural pressures' (Phillips 2007: 137). While this point is true undoubtedly, it is also important to determine which pressures should be counted as excessive in specific contexts. Our approach provides further support for attending to the particularity of women's vulnerabilities across cultures in the context of defending universal rights. While family estrangement is likely to be distressing for any young person, there is reason to think that it would not cause the degree of shame and sense of failure that it might to some who have been brought up in insular communities, because the coping skills typically encouraged in such contexts could well presuppose communal networks. In contrast, the fact that mainstream liberal cultures typically encourage goal-oriented independence *may* make the intrinsic costs of family estrangement easier for women in this context to bear.

To reiterate, my aim is not to propagate unwarranted stereotypes; but it is to reinforce the claim that a contextual approach to ascertaining women's universal rights to autonomy involves retaining a critical view of injustices arising in all communities. As Mike O'Brien, the former Minister for Racial Equality, emphasised in the forced marriage debate, 'multicultural sensitivity is no excuse for moral blindness' (cited in Alibhai-Brown 2000b). Recognising the cultural particularity of women's vulnerabilities should not entail ignorance about the link between forced marriage and domestic violence in the wider society; but it does involve acknowledging that the zeal with which the Western media often reports on sensational instances of forced marriage can impede women who encounter psychological, rather than overtly physical, pressures to marry from voicing their concerns. Taking theoretical account of these issues exemplifies how attention to the particular can shed critical light on what is considered to be of universal or collective feminist concern. Also, by conceding that the pressures that some Western women confront to stay in abusive marriages out of fears of 'separation assault' may sometimes be graver than the pressures confronting some Asian women to accept an arranged marriage, the approach enables us to expose the difficulties with the claim that 'the problems of other women are similar to ours, only "more so"' (Okin 1994: 8). It encourages us to accept instead Song's apt point that the 'majority society is not always less, but rather differently, patriarchal than minority cultures' (Song 2007a: 4).

Yet an important question remains as to whether relying on plural autonomy's endorsement test constitutes an effective means of defending women's rights. Even if it could be in some cases, it is likely not to be the optimal route, given the ambiguity surrounding the motives of individuals in the confusing circumstances of family disputes. There are profound 'epistemological' difficulties involved in ascertaining a person's state of mind, since people differ widely as regards their ability to cope with the loss of community support. The danger in this context is that the endorsement test would empower states to generalise about people's behaviour in ways that would be insensitive to the potentially unlimited contextual factors that influence their actions. Moreover, relying on protection orders to restrain relatives in the context of a forced marriage treats the symptom rather than the cause of the problem. For this reason, it would be more productive to ensure, through non-legal means, that young women are equipped with knowledge of their rights and with the practical capacity to exercise them. To this issue we now turn.

VI PLURAL AUTONOMY – EDUCATION WITHOUT ETHICAL LOSS?

It is sensible to believe that a range of policies should supplement legislation to secure women's rights to autonomy and to ensure that they endorse their most important (marital and other) decisions. Deveaux usefully recommends the institution of a 'tangible social infrastructure' that ensures that laws against abduction, harassment and related offences are enforced (Deveaux 2006: 179). The state should also, she suggests, ensure that women at risk of forced marriage have access to outreach services, and should encourage an ongoing dialogue within communities to raise awareness of the problem (ibid.). While these recommendations are apposite, they raise the question of whether strategies that enhance awareness of forced marriage amongst young women and their communities would entail the state mandating a liberal form of education to ensure that all persons have information about alternative conceptions of gender relations and an awareness of their political entitlements, even if these conflict with communal or religious authority. This question is pressing not least because protecting women's rights through education has been favoured by women's groups in the debate about forced marriage. The Newham Asian Women's Project, for instance, argued for supplementary educational grants on the grounds that laws against forced marriage would not be effective if women are not able to survive independently. '[E]ducation,' they argued, 'might be the way to empowerment and an exit route from the cycle of abuse.'[14] These recommendations emphasise the need to investigate the concern that a liberal education would inevitably undermine cultural and religious diversity. While I present my perspective on this issue fully in Chapter 4, I close the present discussion by outlining the dilemma to which the imposition of liberal education gives rise in the context of addressing the evident harms of forced marriage.

On the one hand, a comprehensive liberal form of education that is associated historically with Kant and Mill seeks to inculcate in all persons the taste for liberty or the capacity for non-conformism and individuality (Mill [1864] 1978). This form of education is apparently endorsed by Okin, who demands that young people be 'thoroughly exposed' to 'other religious as well as secular beliefs held by people around the world' (1999b: 130), in a manner that she believes would inevitably unsettle the received view that 'their culture is the only right way to live' (ibid.: 129). This form of education is dubious from the point of view of protecting the culturally plural forms of autonomy, since its effect could be to undermine the integrity of minority cultures that de-emphasise, and even seek to suppress, idiosyncratic and arguably self-absorbed acts of choice. In contrast, a liberal education could take a more plausible, 'political' form that is typically associated with writers such as Rawls (see Rawls 1993). This form of education only encourages in young citizens a thin capacity for autonomy that pertains to the public realm. Young people would be left free to prioritise in the private realm values other than autonomy, and culturally specific autonomy skills as defended in this chapter, such as emotional resilience in the context of a highly conformist social world. They could, then, adhere to their non-public beliefs devotionally, even as they familiarise themselves with the ethical diversity characterising liberal societies. Of the two forms of liberal education, the 'political' variety would seem more appropriate in the context of addressing the issues raised by forced marriage, as it would encourage in all citizens some awareness of the different ways of conceiving human relations in a varied moral world, without unduly burdening conservative religious and cultural groups.

However, two problems may be thought to arise from a political liberal education in the debate we are considering. On the one hand, Callan holds that such education is liable to be self-defeating (Callan 1996: 19). In order to refrain from undermining any comprehensive way of life, it cannot provide any robust defence of the truth of its own commitments to tolerance and respect against those who deny these values. This form of education would arguably not encourage young people at risk of forced marriage to think critically about their rights in the context of ethical diversity. Since all controversial questions would be omitted from the educational agenda, young men within insular communities, for instance, may not be prompted to question traditional conceptions of gender relations and assumptions of masculine privilege. Moreover, if this form of education cannot teach young people the truth of any values, female members of insular communities would risk not forming the motivation to engage in fair-minded reasoning in the dialogues of the right to mediation, especially if their communities prioritise the seclusion of women and their uncritical obedience to a particular way of life. However, if those who are most acutely in need of empowerment fail to contribute to public debates about their entitlements, this form of education would not help to alter the structural disadvantages that make forced marriage possible, and would leave intact the perceptions and attitudes that underlie these acts.

In direct contrast, an equally worrying consequence of instituting a political liberal education might be that any effort to ensure that young citizens form the autonomous capacity to think critically about their rights (Rawls 1993: 164–5) would have inevitable 'spillover effects' (Gutmann and Thompson 1996: 55), in the sense of altering, perhaps irretrievably, how young people hold their private beliefs. The concern is that the emphasis placed by liberal educators on the capacity for critical rationality would not enable young citizens of conservative communities to hold their private beliefs in the absolute manner necessary to sustain a commitment to a transcendent God, or a belief in the idea that parental wisdom is paramount in marital issues. Moreover, a political liberal education aims to enable young people to appreciate what Rawls calls the 'burdens of judgement' (2001: 36). That is, it fosters their awareness of the evident disagreement in modern societies about fundamentally controversial questions, such as the nature of humanity and the meaning of life, and a consequent recognition that values are plural, conflicting, hard to weigh and interpreted differently under varying historical circumstances. Yet promoting this awareness would seem to involve teaching young citizens to accept the distinction between the 'self' and its beliefs (Baumeister 2000: 65) which many communities that support arranged marriage may find problematic. From their point of view, even a thin political liberal education may well amount to Okin's comprehensive conception. Indeed, some liberals agree that the journey from one form of education to the other may ultimately turn out to be a 'matter of running very hard to find oneself in the same place' (Callan1995: 325). Therefore, a serious question arises as to whether any form of liberal education must entail some 'ethical loss' or 'loss of diversity' (Callan 1996: 23). If it does, could it support women in retaining cultural identity as well as in their difficult choices to resist unwanted family pressures?

Some feminist writers eschew the need for exposure to diversity and contend that the most effective mode of empowering women lies in extending their existing cultural capacities for reflection to spheres that may not be traditionally seen by their communities as matters for individual judgement. Meyers highlights educational programmes for women in cultures where FGM is prevalent (Meyers 2000: 485). They have been most successful, she argues, when they have focused on capitalising on women's imaginative skills, using situations in which local women had died due to FGM to encourage empathy with the grief of their families and, through this means, to provoke critical thought about the practice. While such 'de-compartmentalisation' may appear to violate a culture's specific conception of autonomy, promoting changes within a culture need not be viewed as full-scale 'liberalisation' (see Mookherjee 2008b). Meyers' insight is that education for autonomy is unlikely to be successful it involves 'foisting a wholly new set of opportunities on people' (ibid.: 486).

While this is true, empowering young women at risk of forced marriage is likely to involve not only capitalising on the cultural bases of their autonomy but also making available new information and reasons for action. Some form of a liberal education appears vital to this end. If young women are often socialised to compartmentalise their autonomy skills in ways that ensure community stability rather than transgression, exposure to new information and points of view would be crucial to altering the perspectives of all within the community regarding the spheres in which individual judgement should be exercised. A certain form of liberal education would avail all young citizens of the opportunity to reflect on ethical diversity and gender equality. This is not in order to enable them, ultimately, to choose out of 'significantly different and equally valuable options', in Raz's sense. Rather, an awareness of diversity would enable them to think imaginatively about what their religious and cultural mandates mean in the context of their own lives. Whether they ultimately accept or reject arranged marriages, they would be in a better position to endorse their decisions, and would be better equipped in the long term to contribute to political debate about their entitlements. However, this form of education would also have to avoid Ackerman's strong conclusion in 1980 that, if parents are strongly opposed to liberal autonomy, then their claims should be summarily dismissed (cited in Callan 1996: 26). In sum, then, while education for autonomy is vital, the thorny issue is whether, from the perspective of conservative minorities, the endeavour to expose students to alternative 'images of worth and possibility', and, indeed, to alter men's perceptions of their roles in their families would have to undermine a commitment to cultural diversity (Nussbaum 2000: 288). Callan, for his part, believes that a truly liberal education would be incompatible with 'a comprehensively enforced ordering of values' (Callan 1997: 19; see also Enslin 2003: 85). Yet, given the mistrust evidently experienced by some non-liberal communities with respect to secular education in liberal democracies today, supporting the framework of rights defended in this book through civic education presents a troubling dilemma.

We shall examine this problem in greater detail in the next chapter. For now, it suffices to say that the urgency of addressing structural inequalities through non-coercive measures such as education is pressing in light of allegations that the new British law against forced marriage is counter-productive, because it is ultimately directed towards policing minorities rather than towards protecting women (Wilson 2007). While education for autonomy emerges as a key mode available to liberal states to protect women's rights, it remains to be seen how such education can genuinely respect the interplay between the universal and the particular. It remains to be explained, that is, how the approach proposed here would secure the rights of all persons to live the life that they value, free from 'autonomy-disabling cultural alienation' (Meyers 2000: 470).

VII CONCLUSION

We have now seen that women's rights not to be forced to marry should be defended without de-emphasising cultural differences, and that any defence of a universal right to autonomy must appreciate the pervasiveness of diversity. This point is central if liberals are to protect women from extreme pressure that might fail to emerge in the dialogue about 'grave risks' advocated in Chapter 2. It is, in addition, crucial if liberals are to protect women's abilities to advance their perspectives on cultural practices in the dialogues of the right to mediation. While it would be excessive to insist that all individuals take an actively self-critical view of all their cultural conventions in the non-ideal conditions of most contemporary societies, all young citizens require an understanding not only of their constitutional and civic rights, but also of the diverse ethical standpoints from which those rights are interpreted. Therefore, securing the framework of rights defended here requires the provision of a form of education that would empower young citizens in their private domestic decisions as well as in a public sense. More than strengthening the capacities of all to resist extreme forms of non-public harm, our framework should equip them to contribute to political debate about their entitlements in the long term.

NOTES

1. This chapter concentrates on South Asian rather than Middle Eastern communities, given the prevalence of the former in the British literature on forced marriages.
2. Brah conceptualises arranged marriage as a 'joint undertaking between parents and young people' which is also reflected in the terms 'assisted marriage' and 'assisted introduction' (Brah 1996: 77).
3. Important exceptions are the 'cultural' justifications given for honour crimes. (For an overview, see Baker et al. 1999.)
4. Pichler's study of young Bangladeshi girls in London's Tower Hamlets finds, significantly, that they were largely in favour of arranged marriages but opposed to marrying an unknown spouse from overseas (Pichler 2007).
5. Kymlicka's non-perfectionism is evidenced in his 'endorsement constraint' which holds that free citizens must support any (potentially non-liberal) value that they pursue (Kymlicka 1989: 9–13).
6. Veena Raleigh, an epidemiologist who studied suicide rates amongst South Asian women, points out that a typically close-knit culture 'has tremendous payoffs such as very low delinquency and very high educational achievement'. But she warns of that imposing rigid social roles on women can mean that they still lack 'self-identity' (cited in Burke 2000).
7. To be clear, my view is not that laws should not be enforced against crimes associated with forced marriage but that a *specific* offence against 'forcing someone to marry' would probably not be efficacious.
8. Some relational theorists (for example, Oshana 1988) are, however, wary of advocating any or all cultural arrangements and endorse a highly specific set of relations involving love and non-domination as the conditions for developing autonomy.
9. Also, the notion of 'hybridity' presupposes at least a fluid distinction between cultures since a hybrid is, by definition, an entity composed of elements of two or more *different* entities. Moreover, Kymlicka emphasises that there is a sense in which cultures, even in modernity, are discrete. Even a cosmopolitan Irish-American, who eats Chinese takeaways and reads her children *Grimm's Fairy Tales*, probably does not belong to a 'hybrid' culture in any meaningful sense (1995a: 85).

10. The Forced Marriage (Civil Protection) Act 2007 applies in England and Wales but not in Scotland. It inserts new provisions into the Family Law Act 1996 (FLA), by enabling courts to create a 'forced marriage protection order'. This order differs from general non-harassment orders that may be issued under the FLA, as it can be applied for by a third party as well as the person suffering the harm.

11. This phrase was used in the case of *Hirani* v. *Hirani* [1984 4 FLR 232 CA].

12. See the 'Lectric Law Library's 'Lexicon on Duress' at http://www.lectric. legal.com

13. In *Hirani* v. *Hirani*, a young Hindu woman had entered into marriage with a man previously unknown to her and then left the marriage unconsummated after six weeks. The court concluded that the crucial question was not whether she feared for her life but 'whether her mind was overborne, howsoever that was caused'. The court nullified the marriage in this case (Phillips and Dustin, 2004: 538).

14. Marilyn Mornington, the chair of the British Domestic Violence Working Group, identified education as a key issue in addressing forced marriage. See 'A Question of Honour', *The Independent on Sunday*, 10 February 2008.

CHAPTER 4

Ordering Souls without Intolerance – Towards a Constrained Presumption for Educational Accommodation

I INTRODUCTION

The pressing question raised by the previous chapter is whether women's rights to develop their culturally variable forms of autonomy can be supported by means of a uniform system of liberal education. On the one hand, in ensuring that all persons develop capacities for self-direction in a just political order, the state should not, as I have argued, undermine the cultural sources of their core capacities. However, we have also seen that cultural resources will not always suffice to ensure all persons' freedom from coercion; and securing different forms of autonomy should also involve encouraging young citizens' awareness of different ethical views and non-traditional gender relations to some extent. Taking my cue, then, from the dilemma highlighted previously, the question that I now address is whether a liberal educational policy can be formulated that avoids undermining cultural and religious diversity. In particular, would efforts to secure the rights that we have defended so far interfere with the conformist way that conservative groups often encourage their members to hold their beliefs? Or, in loftier terms, must liberal education 'order the souls' of those who adhere to non-liberal beliefs (Macedo 2000: 30)?[1]

To clarify the meaning of the term 'ordering souls' in this context, it is worth observing first that education in a liberal society is typically not neutral and, through its tolerance of alternative modes of living, levies a high tax on traditional cultures which often place priority on the transmission of faith between generations (Tomasi 2001: 25). In response to this concern, I concede that liberal education must involve 'ordering souls', in the sense of requiring that all citizens learn to appreciate the worth of refraining from asserting the truth of their private beliefs in the public sphere in some situations. However, to offset the effects of this process on the liberty of conscience and, thus, the autonomy of those who belong to non-mainstream communities, states must avoid alienating 'citizens of faith' (Rawls 1996: xlv) from state education. In brief, liberals should aim to lower the tax that civic education imposes on their ways of life (Tomasi 2001: 25). While political liberals do not generally intend to suppress non-liberal world views, consider their demise regrettable in some cases, and even advocate measures to encourage their 'vitality' (Rawls 1999: 62), they see their ultimate erosion as an inevitable or 'free' process (Rawls 1993: 145). This is because, inter alia, liberal education involves teaching children about their constitutional and civic rights, so that they know, for instance, that apostasy is not a legal crime (Rawls 1993: 199). Even if unintentionally, this process is likely to highlight the 'phenomenological' or individualistic character of religious belief over a vision of spirituality as a matter of revealed truth. For these reasons, evangelical and even moderately conservative religious and cultural groups risk being disadvantaged by liberal socialisation.

In response to this problem, I contend that a liberal system bears some remedial responsibility (Miller 2001) for its effect on non-mainstream world views. Liberals must be wary of the tendency of their political forms to impede the capacities of citizens to negotiate the relationship between their public and private beliefs and, in doing so, to undermine their capacities to lead self-directing lives. In light of the importance that liberals tend to place on personal conscience and integrity (Song 2006; Bou-Habib 2006), I argue that protecting the framework of rights defended in this book involves supporting a presumption for religious and cultural accommodation in education. The ongoing debate about the inclusion of evangelical Protestants in American public schools provides a useful reference point for an examination of this issue.[2] By turning to the American context, I continue to focus on intersecting concerns about gender justice and cultural and religious diversity by concentrating on a case that has been called 'the most highly polished touchstone of civic education theory' (Tomasi 2001: 91).[3]

Mozert v. *Hawkins* (1987) involved a group of 'born-again' Christian parents in Tennessee who objected to the readers used in the schools' civic classes. Bob Mozert and Vicki Frost, amongst others, complained that the Holt readers included positive depictions of different world views which did not privilege literal interpretations of the Bible and which, notably, contained favourable images of women who had been recognised for achievements outside the home. They argued that the exposure of their children to this material, which included a story about a boy making toast for a girl and a depiction of Leonardo da Vinci as the 'divine touch' of the Renaissance, violated their constitutional right to freedom of religion (O'Connor and Ivers 1988; Schimmel 1988).[4] Eventually, in 1987, a US Court of Appeal held that there were insufficient grounds to grant the parents' claim (Breyer 1991; Mawdsley and Mawdsley 1988). *Mozert* came at time when Allan Bloom's best-selling book, *The Closing of the American Mind*, had attacked the secular education system for failing to inculcate in students a passion for the truth and, allegedly, for encouraging in them only a soul-destroying materialism.[5] Later, in *Battleground* (1993), Stephen Bates sympathised with the religious right, arguing that *Mozert* had been wrongly decided.

Whilst the gender issues raised here are less direct than in the issues that we have considered in previous chapters, the controversy over the educational accommodation of citizens of faith bears deeply on our attempt to integrate commitments to gender justice and cultural diversity in a unified theoretical account. I have argued that states must not privilege a liberal world view when ascertaining women's interests and, following Young's account, must recognise their serialised location in different cultures. However, does this mean that liberal educators should support the freedom of parents to transmit to their children a non-liberal and possibly gender-inegalitarian world view? While this question raises wide issues concerning home-schooling and faith schools that lie outside the scope of this chapter, I respond to the problem by supporting a constrained policy of accommodation in state education that distinguishes between *manner* in which religious adherents purportedly hold their beliefs and the *subject matter* of their requests. To be specific, while liberals should respect religious diversity by acknowledging the weight of the truth claims proffered by diverse belief systems in a complex polity, the social consequences of accommodating specific beliefs in civic education should not undermine state objectives to ensure an ethos of non-discrimination that I take to be an important condition under which the autonomy of future citizens develops.[6] Whilst this approach ultimately assumes that female students of all denominations share certain universal interests in gender justice, it respects the fact that their lives may be embedded in life forms that warrant special protection in a liberal order. By configuring the universal and the particular in a distinctive way, then, I jettison political liberalism's commitment to a strong religion–state separation and maintain that liberals must ensure the capacity of future citizens to integrate their private and public commitments through equitable policies of religious and cultural accommodation. These policies are not, however, cost free. Liberals would still 'order souls', in the sense of requiring those committed to non-liberal doctrines to bracket their doctrines' truth claims in some contexts. Yet my approach accedes to a wide range of non-liberal demands, and does not summarily exclude those whose views of gender relations differ from a liberal norm, nor stigmatise their faith as 'unreasonable'. In cases such as *Mozert*, I advocate a search for compromises between educators and parents to offset the burdens imposed by apparently neutral education for citizenship.

My discussion is divided into three further sections. Section II considers the anti-accommodationist policy of political liberals in the sphere of civic education and questions their characterisation of religious devotion as a source of political unreasonableness. Section III jettisons this tradition's strong doctrine of separation and proposes a presumption to accommodate religious and cultural diversity in education. Section IV re-evaluates concerns about cases such as *Mozert* by shifting attention from the manner in which evangelical Christians (purportedly) hold their beliefs towards the subject matter of the accommodation that they demand. On the basis of this distinction between the 'manner' and the 'matter' of belief, I outline three issues that assist in determining when the presumption should be constrained, and in the context of which compromises between parents and schools should be sought. While this strategy indicates that liberal education cannot refrain entirely from shaping how religious citizens conceive their status as citizens, it also demonstrates how civic ends can be achieved without intolerance towards those who espouse beliefs that fall outside the mainstream.

II AUTONOMY, STABILITY AND THE PUTATIVE UNREASONABLENESS OF NON-PUBLIC BELIEFS

Political liberals typically reject the special provisions sought in cases such as *Mozert* on account of a concern to protect citizens' civic autonomy. They fear, in particular, that religious accommodation in education would discourage young people from cultivating the attitude of mind central to their awareness of their political status as citizens (Hare 1975: 36). Supporting religious children's apparent suspension of critical thought and their view of belief as a gift from God would risk subverting the state's commitment to encouraging in future citizens 'curiosity, imagination, and a broadened range of sympathies' (Baumeister 1998: 927). While political liberals highlight important concerns about tolerance and stability, their assumption that religious citizens are liable to hold their beliefs unreasonably is, however, contentious and, as we shall see, does not justify a general refusal to accommodate their concerns in the educational sphere.

To understand why, consider that, in the last decades, Stephen Macedo

(1995a, 1995b, 2000) and Amy Gutmann (1995b; 1999) have argued robustly that the purpose of liberal civic education is to familiarise children with the plurality of beliefs that characterise a diverse polity. Autonomy and civic virtue are symbiotic on their account, in the sense that the common realisation of these capacities enables future citizens to affirm their personal values whilst acting according to the common good. Macedo, for instance, presents his conception of autonomy as a purely political value, and envisages a triadic relation between this capacity, impartiality and tolerance (see also Raz 1986: Chapters 14 and 15). He is reluctant to prescribe a comprehensive conception of autonomy, since doing so would fail to respect those who privately prioritise values such as obedience or humility. Thus, he adheres to political liberalism's core idea that the state is obliged only to ensure that citizens develop the capacity to be reasonable and rational in their public interactions (Macedo 1995b; Rawls 1993: xliii. n.8, 26; Reich 2002: 124). Tolerance of diversity is not, however, limitless on Macedo's account. Securing civic virtue entails strict limits on the voices of conservative parents in shaping the curriculum. Political liberals cannot simply hope that a tolerant society will 'come about . . . by the deliverance of an invisible hand', but must plan for it by ensuring that children are taught core liberal values (Macedo 1995b: 304). Thus, liberals should commit not only to a negative rights-protecting constitutionalism but must engage in a transformative social project that ensures that the art of public reasonableness is learned by all young citizens.

This social project appears compelling, given our conclusion in Chapter 3 that public education constitutes an important means of empowering vulnerable individuals and addressing structural inequalities in various sectors of civil society. Macedo rightly holds that future citizens risk failing to develop core capacities if their parents insulate them from education for citizenship, either by exempting them from learning civic ideals or by allowing their sectarian beliefs to dominate the curriculum. Their children's potential failure to develop the (however elusive) virtue of reasonableness is relevant to the problem described in the previous chapter, as the intolerance and narrow-mindedness that typically arises from an ignorance of diversity would not enable future citizens to familiarise themselves with alternative accounts of gender relations and their civic entitlements in a way that would lead them to consider critically the meaning of their inherited religious and cultural mandates. At the same time, Macedo also seems right to distance his approach from Dewey's (1956) comprehensive commitment to secular humanism and its disparagement of all transcendental beliefs. He appears correct to seek instead to strike a balance between ensuring that all persons receive an education for citizenship, and leaving them free in principle to commit privately to their religious or other metaphysical beliefs, even if in dogmatic ways. Macedo's political form of liberalism, following that of Rawls (1993), depends on the requirement that all future citizens appreciate the worth of a religion–state separation, as expressed in the First Amendment's demand that the state 'shall make no law respecting the establishment of religion, or prohibiting the free exercise thereof'. Liberal education, thus, 'divides our lives' between shared political identities and divergent ethical convictions (Macedo 1995b: 308). In this context, the art of separation is essential to making a tolerant, and indeed multicultural, civil society attainable for all.

On this basis, Macedo echoes the misgivings expressed in *Mozert* about the possible failure of the children to develop critical rationality. Citing Judge Lively's disapproval of the parents' efforts to modify the curriculum in order to protect their literal beliefs (*Mozert* 1062), he warns that the parents would 'encourage [their children] to assert the truth of their own particular convictions . . . for political purposes' (Macedo 1995a: 471). This concern is plausible, as it is not unlikely that a Protestant evangelical would favour structuring political relations to conform to her private belief in, say, gender hierarchies. As Okin observes:

> It is difficult to see how one could both hold and practice the [private] belief that women or blacks, say, are naturally inferior, without its seriously affecting one's capacity to relate (politically) to such citizens as 'free and equal' with oneself. (Okin 1994: 21)

Moreover, if liberal education aims to assist all persons to appreciate that those whom they privately deem inferior must be respected publicly, exempting citizens from a humanistic curriculum could undermine the state's ability to achieve support of the majority of its members and, thus, to ensure the stability of the regime. For Macedo, a liberal civic education must refrain from teaching radical doubt or agnosticism. Educators must only expose young people to the historical and current fact of diversity and thereby encourage them to appreciate the importance of refraining from disparaging or persecuting those with whom they disagree (Macedo 1995b: 307). Because it seeks to inform students of ethical diversity without promoting or denigrating any particular creed, political liberalism does not encourage confusion with respect to moral truth, but only a capacity for 'epistemological restraint' (Nagel 1987; see also Quong 2007 and compare Barry 1995).

In spite of its attractions, the doctrine of restraint has significant problems in terms of protecting the framework of rights defended in this book. Macedo concedes that this process has unintended effects on citizens' private beliefs; that it is likely to promote indirectly 'ecumenical and even wishy-washy attitudes'; and that 'pressing hard on such civic virtues . . . may make many robust religious commitments seem problematic' (Macedo 1995b: 310). While he concedes that the protection of diversity is an 'honourable and important project' (Macedo 2000: 24), the erosion of devotional beliefs that could follow from his proposals threatens to undermine the goal of fostering peaceful coexistence. Apart from the doubt that must inevitably arise as to whether the corrosion of non-mainstream belief systems is entirely unintentional under political liberal policies, a significant problem is that the approach underestimates the existential dilemma that it creates not just for those who espouse 'fundamentalist' views but also for many ordinary citizens who are not necessarily opposed to liberal priorities, but who live according to a complex mixture of traditionalist beliefs and critical rationality. In upholding a strict distinction between religion and politics in civic education, this proposal risks being untenable for many ordinary citizens. This dilemma is exemplified well by the reservations expressed by some British Muslims about the non-prescriptive attitude that underpins the 'phenomenological' approach to education typically adopted in secular schools (Baumeister 2000: 64–5). While Macedo is correct to believe that the 'regime character' of any liberal society must have a 'transformative dimension' – one which seeks to inculcate in all young people values of tolerance, respect and impartiality – his concession that this process would undermine the diversity of private beliefs that liberalism claims to protect makes it difficult to see why it would gain the support of a large number of ordinary citizens.

Of course, it should be conceded that any form of liberal education inevitably circumscribes the manner in which beliefs about morality can be held, since its endeavour to encourage diverse citizens to view themselves as politically linked rules out the form of belief that is possible in a religious order. For instance, living as a devout Muslim in a liberal democracy may well involve an element of compromise that would not be necessary in an Islamic state – even though, as we shall see in the next chapter, the distinction between these two types of political order should not be overdrawn. Yet, for our current purposes, the difficulty lies in Macedo's assumption that 'no-one has a right to a level playing-field' in terms of how their beliefs fare under a liberal regime (Macedo 1995a: 473). It is not clear from the terms of his 'liberalism with spine' (Macedo 1990: 10) that a commitment to civic autonomy entails divesting the state of a responsibility to address some of the questions that conservative parents may raise about 'life at the interface of public and non-public values' (Tomasi 2001: 31).

Macedo is right to say that 'not every form of . . . diversity is to be celebrated' and that 'not all forms of what can be labelled "marginalisation" and "exclusion" are to be regretted' (Macedo 2000: 2), if by this he means that liberal educators should not support explicitly homophobic or racist views. However, attention should be paid to the disparity of power that makes tolerance easier for some citizens and to matters of religious conscience that bear on citizens' capacities for agency. Here Macedo observes that defenders of 'the politics of difference', such as, indeed, Iris Young (1995), are quick to champion the struggles of blacks, gays, women and the disabled, but do not pause to consider that their arguments would also apply to Nazis and fundamentalists, who would also qualify as 'oppressed' in the relevant sense. Defenders of the politics of difference thus often tacitly appeal to civic virtue without acknowledging the strong forms of socialisation needed to secure it (Macedo 2000: 25–6). While Macedo appears correct to emphasise that not all differences are benign, it is necessary to grasp the complexity of this issue. For instance, much ambiguity surrounds terms such as racism, sexism and homophobia. Does a person's antipathy to homosexuality, say, on grounds that it leads to the spiritual degradation of a person's soul, necessarily render her homophobic? As McKinnon points out, 'the tight connection between judgements of disapproval and action upon them . . . holds only for moral fanatics and fundamentalists' (McKinnon 2006: 27); and it is surely not the case that an opposition to homosexuality and the active denial of gay rights always go hand in hand. Moreover, cultural and religious beliefs are often edifying *and* potentially oppressive at the same time. If culture and religion can be simultaneously the source of vulnerability, prejudice *and* meaningful existence, the somewhat stigmatising language that political liberals often deploy with respect to religious belief should be avoided. In doing so, liberals should acknowledge that a general refusal to accommodate citizens of faith in the educational sphere would be to take a reductive view of the issues raised by the fact of pluralism.

Moreover, the problems with political liberalism's doctrine of separation are revealed by considering Gutmann's claim that, if children are to learn tolerance, the state should engage in 'conscious social reproduction' by prioritising an education which involves cultivating the virtues necessary for political participation (Gutmann 1999: 85). Democratic education must, she thinks, adhere to two principles that might thwart minority wishes. First is a principle of 'non-repression', which 'prevents the state, and any group within it, from using education to restrict rational deliberation of competing conceptions of the good life' (ibid.: 287). Second is the principle of 'non-discrimination', which holds that 'no child may be excluded from an education adequate to participating in the political processes that structure choice among good lives' (ibid.: 45). Gutmann takes these principles to support Judge Kennedy's opinion in *Mozert* that 'the education demanded by the plaintiff parents . . . is incompatible with teaching rational inquiry . . . in a religiously pluralistic society' (ibid.: 65). Whereas Macedo denies that his account amounts to comprehensive liberalism, Gutmann concedes that the distinction between the two forms of education often breaks down (Macedo 1995b; Gutmann 1995b). A political liberal education cannot offer any more accommodation than a comprehensive one to the kind of diversity represented by *Mozert* (ibid.: 173). Significantly, Gutmann's defence of religious toleration as one of the requirements of her proposed 'civic minimum' assumes that tolerance is inculcated through the exclusion of sectarian beliefs from civic education (Gutmann 1995b). While students must be made aware of the fact of diversity, they cannot appeal explicitly to the truth of any doctrinal premises when participating in civic education. As Stankiewicz (1991) explains, the Holt readers thus exposed students to a variety of values but could not, as a matter of liberal law, teach, promote or oppose any of them.

However, it is controversial to assume that the exclusion of religious beliefs enhances capacities for tolerance, or that all conceptions of the good are *equally* excluded in a secular school. This assumption is contested by Stolzenberg who argues that, by implication, promoting the value of toleration threatens evangelicals' ways of life and, thus, does not represent a tolerant stance towards them (Stolzenberg 1993). The evangelicals' argument, she claims, should be accepted 'on its own terms,' by showing that toleration and critical thinking are justifiable *if* they do not threaten evangelical ways of life (ibid. 1993). Now, this point is contentious, as it is surely not the case that *all* minority demands must be met on their own terms. Therefore, much hinges on what makes the evangelical demand plausible or justifiable. Moreover, the cogency of Stolzenberg's point seems to rest in key part on what constitutes 'threatening a way of life'. While we shall return to these issues, it is worth noting for now that her argument at least draws attention to the fact that the political liberal requirement that contestable metaphysical beliefs play no role in civic education does not necessarily guarantee fairness, as this policy prioritises by default a secular conception of the good.

Stolzenberg's argument thus draws attention to the fact that the *Mozert* parents were, on one interpretation, contesting the 'repression' of their own world view. They were claiming that the readers showed hostility to their beliefs by portraying a secular view with no discussion of the alternatives (Vojak 2003: 403). Although the International Reading Association warned that *Mozert* threatened to 'open the way for mass censorship of school textbooks' (Rowell 1987: 2), the American Civil Liberties Union had defended the parents on grounds that closeted censorship had already occurred. In Tomasi's understanding, the parents may therefore have been 'exactly the kinds of citizens for the accommodation of whom political liberalism was designed' (Tomasi 2001: 93). This point is important if we adhere to the plausible idea that civic education is a matter not of teaching future citizens abstractly about their rights, but of encouraging them to appreciate the meaning of rights and responsibilities in a way that is 'relevant to their own experience' (Baumeister 1998: 924). While young citizens need to learn to think in terms of the common good, and while the cultivation of civic autonomy clearly benefits the child, society and the state (Frazer 1999: 9), this interpretation of *Mozert* suggests that political liberalism's doctrine of separation tends to exclude religious children on account of the purportedly unreasonable manner in which they hold their beliefs. Yet liberals' frequent references to the elusive problem of unreasonableness are often unhelpful in ascertaining what is at issue in particular claims (Jones 1996; see also Horton 2009, forthcoming).

We shall return to this matter shortly. For now, it is important to see that such a strong doctrine of restraint is likely to be counterproductive in many multicultural and multifaith contexts. The concern to promote civic commitment in terms of nationalism, which is implicit in Gutmann's emphasis on an education that focuses on students' awareness of democratic and electoral procedures, would be alienating to many minority citizens, if accompanied by a strict obligation to refrain from expressing their religious or cultural identity. This policy is unlikely to achieve the sense of belonging across all sectors of society that is necessary to hold a complex polity together. Recognising this point, Modood writes of '*plural* Britishness' in the UK, or the need to emphasise hyphenated identities in a way that fosters citizenship through the inclusion of religious and cultural identities in social life (Modood 2005). Following his account, it is likely that civic education theorists exaggerate the extent of the 'legitimisation crisis' that would arise from the expression of sectarian loyalties in the educational sphere. For while, against the interpretation above, there is a case for claiming that *Mozert* parents did seek to shield their children from the fact of pluralism (Macedo 1995a: 485), they were not imposing their ideas on others and did not challenge the legitimacy of public education. Thus, even in the American context in which evangelicals have evident political ambitions (Kaplan 2005; Stephen 2008), considerations of stability do not clearly justify a refusal to accommodate their concerns. In fact, they may support the reverse.

Moreover, consider the forms of accommodation frequently sought in multicultural states, such as requests by parents that their children be allowed to pray during their religion's holy months or that they not be required to salute the national flag. Even if the threat of civic erosion to which these claims may give rise cannot be dismissed, this concern must be balanced against the need to safeguard liberty of conscience and the cultural bases of all persons' autonomy. One might object that political liberals would not wish to refuse the claims above but only those that impede children's access to knowledge of civic values. However, the commitment to teaching autonomy through a liberal education arguably cannot be restricted to certain aspects of the curriculum, as it pervades the entire ethos of a secular school (Baumeister 2000: 60). If this is so, the civic educational theorists' concerns would have to extend to most forms of religious accommodation in education and, if this is the case, they would be open to the charge that, in refusing to accommodate religious students on issues of minor inconvenience to the school, but which have profound importance to the student, their own policies would provoke political instability. To be sure, the claims of evangelicals in America raise historically explicable concerns about the church–state separation which have been fuelled by the 'religiously-inspired political zeitgeist' of recent years (McKinnon 2006: 48). However, if we take careful account of evangelical demands, as well as of wider minority struggles for accommodation, many such requests could be thought to raise issues of administrative inconvenience rather than a serious threat concerning social disintegration or the theocratic takeover of schools.

If it is not plausible, then, to believe that these claims would typically lead to grave social disorder, Justice Sandra Day's dissenting view in the case of *Smith* v. *Employment Division* should be considered. While *Smith* famously repealed the presumption to protect citizens' religious liberties in the sphere of employment, Day had insisted that 'the First Amendment was enacted . . . to protect the rights of those whose religious practices are not shared by the majority and may be viewed with hostility' (*Smith* 897). Of course, religious students cannot be accommodated with respect to every subject of instruction in state education because schools might then cease to function (Shachar 2001: 157). Nonetheless, the refusal to accommodate religious sensibilities would not enable political liberals to comply with their own promise to refrain from discriminating unduly against religious or communitarian conceptions of the good (Baumeister 1998: 930; Halstead 1995). In summary, then, our analysis suggests strongly that a general refusal to accommodate citizens of faith would not support the framework of rights that we have defended so far.

III PRESUMPTION FOR RELIGIOUS ACCOMMODATION

The doctrine of separation should be superseded, in my view, by a presumption for religious and cultural accommodation in the educational sphere. This presumption appeals to the idea that some future citizens risk being burdened considerably by apparently neutral educational policies, especially in relation to their ability to integrate the public and private sources of their autonomy. Without redressing these burdens, liberals would jeopardise their commitment to safeguarding the 'vitality' of what Rawls calls 'decent non-liberal' conceptions of the good (1999: 62). In defending a principle of respect for parental wishes (MacLeod 1997: 121–2), I challenge the assumption implicit in political liberalism that religious adherents typically adhere to their beliefs unreasonably. Yet, in doing so, I do not claim that parents' interests should take priority over children's. While a parent's interest in her child may be so deep that it could be interpreted as self-regarding, it may often be the case that a child's interests are at variance with her parents' desires to transmit their view of the world (Kach and DeFaveri 1987: 135; Tamir 1990: 163). By concentrating on the interests of future citizens, therefore, I argue that the stability of an order that respects the rights defended in this book could be enhanced through a form of education that does not alienate minority students. Here, our presumption for accommodation would be based firmly on a doctrine of *integration* rather than one of separation.

Initial support for this presumption can be found by going back to Parekh's 'culture/religion as inability' thesis, as considered in Chapter 3. A future citizen could be burdened by a school's failure to accommodate her beliefs, as these beliefs are matters of luck or chance for which she should not be held accountable. Macedo eventually concedes this point by drawing attention to a dissenting view in *Mozert*, which held that making the readers compulsory would be similar to requiring Catholics to read items on the Church's index of prohibited books on pain of giving up the right to free schooling (Macedo 1995a: 472, citing J. Boggs in *Mozert* 107). He thus concurs that the children's beliefs are not issues for which they can be held and yet that they give rise to responsible, unjustified disadvantages in the educational sphere. Of course, it could be argued that schools should be entirely secular precisely because future citizens should have the opportunity to make a choice about a matter as crucial as religious belief; and that, even if the assertion of religious independence may be questionable as a matter of fact, fostering a belief in it can help to bring about a society in which such independence is respected (Macedo 2000: 36). Yet political liberals generally abstain from the issue of whether religious belief is a matter of 'chance' or 'choice' (see Mendus 2002) and do not seek to ensure that cultural or religious beliefs are rationally chosen. Thus, the 'culture/religion as inability' thesis helps to explain why Macedo draws the judicious conclusion that the costs of refusing to accommodate religious children can be high; and that a 'second stage of public justification' that considers the non-neutral costs visited on them might need to be instituted (Macedo 1995a: 482–6).

Yet, if religious belief can be viewed partly as a matter of chance, and if liberals claim that luck-affected inequalities give rise to injustice (Arneson 1989: 85), there is a case for pressing harder on Macedo's point and supporting a general presumption in favour of accommodation.[7] This policy would not necessarily ignore liberal concerns about tolerance or stability. However, whether religious accommodation undermines these objectives depends on the nature of the claim and what accommodation involves. To be sure, it should not entail respecting parents' freedom to pursue any educational ideals, however idiosyncratic they may be. Yet, consider America's post-war self-image as a 'melting-pot', which has involved fostering an official commitment to neutrality through the assimilation of all identities within the purview of schools, in order to produce a public culture in which all have an equal stake (Levinson 1997: 344). In response to the sense of exclusion experienced by African Americans and indigenous peoples in relation to this ambitious ideal, histories of slavery and colonisation were later included in school curricula as a means of acknowledging, if not making amends for, historical injustice (Glazer 1997). While one might argue that there are important differences between evangelical communities and historically devalued racial groups, the commitment to representing differences equitably in education could, it seems to me, justify an inclusive and respectful discussion of religious diversity, including beliefs that are typically held devotionally, within a civics curriculum. States would of course face a logical challenge if equitable accommodation in this context were understood as the equal promotion of all values; and the risk is, as in our central case, that, if equitable accommodation is understood as the equal exposure of students to all conceptions of the good, then some groups would conceive this process as denigrating to their faith-based way of life (Levinson 1997: 345). In view of these difficulties, I conceive equitable accommodation as a matter of encouraging a respectful discussion that, through special measures, refrains from implying that beliefs should be viewed as a matter of indifference or that they necessarily have equal value. It would recognise the special care often needed with respect to the representation of minority beliefs in a common school. Three interrelated arguments support this policy.

The first argument may be labelled *the burden of certainty*. Public schools should be aware that citizens' commitments to public values such as tolerance and respect are often supported by beliefs that are held with a strong degree of certainty rather than critical doubt. Whilst early liberals such as Locke recognised this point, and although contemporary political liberals do not outwardly deny it, the latter's keen awareness of the historical experience of uncritical faith as a source of persecution leads them to construct a strong 'wall of separation' between religion and the public sphere, as we have seen. Yet, if liberals are to respond equitably to the depth of diversity in modern societies, they must recognise that people in a complex, pluralist world do not and cannot hold all their beliefs about the right and the good with an attitude of critical doubt; and the pervasiveness and normality of absolute belief should lead liberal educators to consider what sort of *existential* experience liberalism can offer its citizens (Tomasi 2001: 44). If the human point of liberalism is to enable all to live well in the context of a just state, then liberals should acknowledge the comprehensive concepts through which future citizens come to appreciate the meaning of their rights and responsibilities (Tomasi 2001: 45). While liberal educators cannot logically promote the truth of all moral sources, they should encourage discussion of young citizens' diverse conceptions of the good, not least because they provide many people with their only motivation for engaging with others with respect.

This point can be supported by a somewhat unconventional interpretation of *Mozert* which holds that the parents did not deny the need for reasonable discussion, but differed with the school only in terms of the moral source that 'would best equip the children to deal with the modern world' (Burtt 1994: 62). Moreover, arguably, the parents did not question the values of liberal citizenship but only disagreed on the 'process oriented' question of 'who decides how these lessons [in tolerance and respect] will be conveyed' (ibid.: 62). Admittedly, this reading of *Mozert* is at variance with the parents' statement that they simply did not wish their children 'to make critical judgements, to use their imaginations or to exercise choice' in areas where the Bible provides the answer (Tomasi 2001: 45). However, if process-oriented disagreements characterise at least some claims for educational accommodation, the point unsettles the assumption that strong certainty about moral sources and critical thought about the world are opposed (Schimmel 1988: 1051). To substantiate this point, consider Peshkin's study of Bethany Baptist Academy, which reveals that evangelical Christian students typically form 'personally crafted patchworks' of the meaning of religious beliefs in their lives (1986: 254); and Heilman's ethnography of ultra-Orthodox Jewish schools in Israel which, significantly, cites one informant's words: ' "We know much more about you than you know about us" ' (1992: 39). Finally, consider the fact that evangelical movements have seen vigorous debate for at least a century over what sacred texts require of women (Schrag 1998: 38; Bendroth 1993). Christel Manning's *God Gave Us the Right* (1999) highlights the fact that Protestant, Jewish and Catholic women routinely negotiate gender relations progressively. Thus, rather than construing religion as a mystically irrational and static institution (Bartkowski 1999), it is plausible to acknowledge that biblical dictates might offer evangelical women a 'dynamic toolkit' (Bartkowski and Read 2003: 72), which enables them to negotiate their entitlements in the world at large. Some women within these traditions, for instance, contest the Bible's 'doctrine of wifely submission' in terms of the more progressive conception of the family as an 'equilateral triangle' with spouses at the base and Jesus at the top (Gabriel 1993: 94).

While we shall return later in this chapter to examine the implications of these seemingly progressive discourses for the civic inclusion of young evangelical women, I raise the issue here only to suggest that the respect for diversity prized by political liberals would probably be enhanced through a robust policy of accommodation. Future citizens would be encouraged to recognise that secular views can be questioned by those who are not necessarily unreasonable or propagandist. The ways in which people become autonomous are plural, as we saw in Chapter 3; and, as defenders of differentiated citizenship contend, there are different ways of expressing one's commitment to a shared polity (Carens 2000; Modood 2005).[8] Liberal educators should thus encourage citizens to integrate their public and private beliefs. While it cannot be denied that many conservative religions contain beliefs that are opposed to the egalitarian tenets of liberal citizenship, they also typically contain basic moral precepts that justify treating others with humanity and respect.

Of course, those who see any exposure to diversity at all as corrupting present a dilemma for liberal education; and the *Mozert* demand is more troubling if the parents were indeed demanding that their children be shielded entirely from the attitudes of other students. In either case, however, the swift dismissal of their claim is contentious because, as Parekh (2000a: 225) argues, multicultural education that inspires intellectual curiosity about the world requires a practical, not merely theoretical, familiarity with the fact of both thick and thin ethical diversity. After all, the purpose of liberal education could not be to encourage future citizens to adopt an unrealistic view from nowhere, but to make available a 'cluster of mini Archimedean standpoints' from which they explore the strengths and weaknesses of their inherited perspectives (Parekh 1995: 9). In this context, a strong political liberal obligation of restraint would stifle the civic imagination, denying future citizens the possibility of appreciating the meaning of their rights and responsibilities in the context of their own lives. Grasping the complexity of the world in which rights are realised – that is to say, gaining a real sense of the burdens of judgement – can only arise from confronting the depth of value conflicts. As Damon argues, '[T]he capacity for constructive criticism is an essential requirement for civic education, but this capacity . . . must build on a sympathetic understanding of what is being criticised' (Damon 2001: 134). In addition, accommodation, conceived in terms of an inclusive discussion of comprehensive beliefs, would be beneficial because much religious teaching is concerned with exactly the questions about justice and human dignity that political theorists want citizens to be able to address (Burtt 1994: 69). Therefore, given that comprehensive conceptions of the good infuse citizens' understanding of their rights with a sense of meaning which the political liberal state cannot supply, religious accommodation would support Parekh's plausible claim that 'education is concerned with humanisation, not only socialisation, with helping students to become not just good citizens but also *integrated human beings*' (2000a: 227, my emphasis).

This argument depends, however, on the validity of a deeper one from equality of opportunity. Let us call this *the burden of cultural conformity*. Non-mainstream communities typically occupy an insecure position in relation to their wider society that threatens to undermine their members' autonomy. Initially, this claim may appear contestable because, as I argued in Chapter 3, cultures and religions should not be conceived primarily as repositories of choice. Furthermore, even if they are indeed *sometimes* viewed as such, the restriction of one option from a person's context of choice does not deny their autonomy tout court (Barry 2001: 37). However, against these criticisms, there are, as Kymlicka says, a number of psycho-social and even neurological reasons why a person might feel attached to their communities of birth (Kymlicka 1989). Thus, if she belongs to a minority group, her inherited beliefs are likely to merit special protection in the educational sphere precisely because of their tendency to be suppressed and marginalised in the wider society. As a result of uneven group relations in history, the survival of certain ideals and beliefs about justice is jeopardised by pressures emanating from a pervasively, even aggressively, secular culture (Burtt 1994: 63; 1996: 426). It would of course be superficial to suggest that liberal education only aims to instil in future citizens materialistic desires rather than introduce them to the arts, norms of political society and great ideas (Barry 2001: 245). However, even so, it is likely to be difficult for children of non-mainstream religions and cultures to view their inherited beliefs as plausible options in the marketplace of ideas. For one thing, they are likely to be aware of the high price they would pay in committing to them, not least in terms of the incomprehension and even ridicule of the wider society (Schrag 1998: 38). This argument recalls Kymlicka's case for external protections in terms of autonomy and assumes that one cannot choose something without first having deep knowledge of the content of one's choice. Spinner-Halev therefore calls for religious accommodation to equip young citizens to withstand the pressure to conform to secular values (2000: 76) and to encourage them to make a real choice about their beliefs (2001a: 126). Since the mainstream public culture is not neutral and since religious parents are aware that their children will have to navigate between their religion and the wider society's values at some point, 'the longer this navigation can be postponed, the better the chance the community has to survive' (ibid.: 117). While it is problematic to conceive equitable accommodation as a matter of shielding young people entirely from the fact of diversity, it may well involve special protection for non-mainstream beliefs. An equitable discussion of belief systems in a common school must be carefully structured, highlighting the religious and philosophical roots of developments in history, and refraining from the suggestion that what one believes is purely a matter of taste. These points are crucial because, if autonomy involves committing deeply to certain values, and if lots of different options are presented as being of equally little value, 'how', Spinner-Halev rightly asks, 'will [students] be able to choose?' (2000: 76).

The special protection of minority beliefs can be supported further by considering a case that is often deemed anomalous by civic education theorists, namely *Wisconsin* v. *Yoder*. This claim involved a demand by Amish parents to withdraw their children from school after the age of fourteen, two years below the normal minimum school-leaving age. In my view, the significance of this case lies in the connection that it supports between personal autonomy and the survival of a future citizen's inherited beliefs. This interpretation will initially appear questionable, since Amish communities do not typically prioritise the capacity for autonomy, and because the court was apparently concerned about the parents' freedom rather than the child's.[9] However, if we look more closely, the court was indeed concerned that requiring the child to remain at school would threaten his ability to commit to this particular way of life. While Galston predictably endorses this ruling in his Diversity State (1991: 45–9), Macedo also accepts it on the grounds that Amish children at fourteen had a 'real, if constrained' opportunity to exit from their community (1995a: 489).

Much debate about this case has turned on whether Macedo and other liberals are right to assume that socialisation in Amish communities prepares children for life in the wider society (Barry 2001: 243; compare Burtt, 1996). However, my point in focusing on this judgement is to suggest that, if the court was right to assume that the state should protect young citizens' opportunities to commit to their inherited beliefs in *Yoder*, it is hard to say why this argument does not support a general presumption for accommodation. In so far as the survival of any belief system depends to some degree on the capacity of its adherents to suspend critical judgement and to commit wholeheartedly to their way of life, *Yoder* appears unexceptional. According to the court, forced exposure to the different options in a secular culture could be taken to 'substantially interfere with the religious development of the Amish child and his integration into [that] way of life'.[10] If this is a credible argument, the *Mozert* court's view that 'no such threat exists in the present case' appears questionable.[11] The *Mozert* parents believed that the way in which diversity was presented in the readers interfered with their children's capacities to commit to their faith with integrity (Reich 2002: 452). The plausibility of their claim is substantiated by Baumeister's observation that one way of attacking a religion is to show that a variety of religions exist and to imply that one's choice between them is a matter of indifference (Baumeister 1998: 927, citing McIntyre 1981). While one could reply that it is difficult to see how ethical diversity could ever be presented in a way that would satisfy staunchly evangelical parents, it was not clearly justifiable of the court to decide for the parents whether the credibility of their belief system was under threat.

This is not to conclude that the *Mozert* demand should have been accepted, but only to emphasise the fact that the issue cannot be determined by drawing a contrast between groups such as the Amish as insular and born-again Christians as politically active. We can concede that the Amish are economically self-sufficient and take little part in public life except where the interests of their communities are involved and, thus, that their children *may* have lesser needs to learn the virtues of citizenship than evangelicals. However, it would be doubtful to distinguish these claims simply by characterising the Amish as 'partial citizens' (Spinner-Halev 2000). While the Amish are often exempted from medical taxes, and sometimes from social security if they are self-employed, they are nonetheless subject to federal income, property, sales and other county taxes (Huntingdon 1993). Moreover, while their discrete penal systems make them seem like semi-autonomous 'nations' (Barry 2001: 189), they are unlike indigenous peoples in the sense that their religion enjoins them not to exercise political power (Levy 1997: 51). Therefore, if the concept of partial citizenship does not explain why the claim of the Amish to the protection of their way of life is exceptional (see also Dagger 1997: 130), the argument from cultural or religious survival invoked in this case would apply broadly. At the very least, it would compel liberals to ask how they might address the burden that citizens of faith experience on account of the assimilative pressures exerted by the wider society.

Whilst liberals should be wary of accommodating harmful beliefs in the educational sphere, they should, as I have said, question their preconceptions of what should be classified as such. Furthermore, evangelicals might at least have a case for requesting that diversity be portrayed in a way that does not undermine their faith-based way of life. For instance, it could be necessary for educators to raise with students the existential comfort that is gained from religious belief, and the prevalence of religious world views in shaping human identities. Of course, the persistent objection to this claim is that, arguably, *no* form of respectful discussion would satisfy some traditionalist communities which fear that merely exposing a person to diversity leads to an awareness of ethical pluralism that undermines uncritical faith. This worry is seemingly borne out by Barry's claim that one can only accept the fact of pluralism if one accepts a degree of scepticism at the epistemological level (Barry 1995). This point, in turn, leads Baumeister to observe that, for the three major monotheistic religions, taking up even a moderately sceptical standpoint would amount to a serious crisis of faith (Baumeister 2000: 54). However, against this criticism, notice that political liberals do not typically believe that scepticism or agnosticism are the necessary psychological conditions for affirming the values of the liberal order (Quong 2007). One need not deny or even question the truth of one's own values in order to acknowledge the empirical fact that human beings disagree over moral sources. On this point at least, political liberals seem correct – two people could recognise that, without any epistemic failure on either person's part, they disagree about important beliefs. One might maintain that, while the other is not necessarily stupid or misinformed, her beliefs are nonetheless false. If this is right, the special protection recommended here through a policy of inclusive discussion responds to the charge that exposure to diversity per se substantially burdens evangelical students, and necessarily demands that they approach their beliefs with an attitude of doubt.

The final argument for favouring a presumption for accommodation may be called the *burden of exclusion*. Spinner-Halev argues that 'inclusion' bolsters citizenship and that 'a relentless insistence that religious students never be accommodated' harms it (Spinner-Halev 2001a: 136). Against the (unconventional) interpretation of *Mozert* considered above, he concedes that the parents did indeed object to key principles of liberal citizenship such as gender equality and equal respect. However, if, as seems likely, children would learn these values by participating in a common school, and if the refusal to accommodate them leads parents to put them in separate schools, refusing their demands would be counterproductive (ibid.: 37). If students see homosexual or female students being treated with respect within a school environment, then, irrespective of what their religion decrees, they will have a better chance of learning respect than if they are insulated within their communities. While it is unlikely that liberals can abstain from engaging with the content of minority world views when assessing the legitimacy of specific demands for accommodation, Spinner-Halev appears right once again to claim that a school that teaches tolerance should not exclude a child summarily because they adhere to an unorthodox value system (ibid.: 138), for the (apparent) reason that that they are likely to adhere to it unreasonably.

Yet, his ultimate reservations about *Mozert* prompt critical thought about when the general presumption for educational accommodation supported here should be constrained. Spinner-Halev observes that the gender-egalitarian and tolerant ideas to which the parents objected were taught in a number of classes, and that the parents finally admitted that they would have found all these classes objectionable too. '[W]hen parents . . . come to [this] conclusion,' he explains, 'they either enrol their children in private schools or try to force the public schools to change their curriculum' (Spinner-Halev 2001b: 140). While this reasoning appears to support our central idea of women's rights as multicultural claims, by conceiving cultural diversity and gender equality as equally valuable educational goals, the problem remains that those who object to one aspect of a secular education would probably find other aspects of it questionable. It is likely that they accept the general education system out of a need to secure basic goods for their children (Baumeister 2000: 63). In light of the fact such parents should not be dismissed summarily as unreasonable, a liberal state's reasons for constraining the presumption requires further analysis.

IV ORDERING SOULS WITHOUT INTOLERANCE – FROM THE UNREASONABLENESS OF BELIEVERS TO THE SOCIAL CONSEQUENCES OF ACCOMMODATING BELIEFS

Liberal educators cannot be entirely undiscriminating with respect to the beliefs that they accommodate in the educational sphere. Therefore, if, as I argued in Chapter 3, states have a duty to all future citizens to secure appropriate forms of their autonomy, the question is where the line should be drawn. Galston, for his part, believes that the *Mozert* parents had a constitutional right to accommodation, derived from their general right to the free exercise of religion (Galston 1991: 224–7). Yet, in view of the difficulties with granting such unlimited freedom, I shall contend that claims should be evaluated by shifting attention away from the (purportedly unreasonable) *manner* in which religious adherents hold their beliefs and towards the *subject matter* of the accommodation that they request. However, doing so entails that, if liberals are to ensure an educational culture in which all develop their capacities for autonomy equally, they must indeed order young citizens' souls, in the sense of ensuring that they are able to refrain from asserting their private truths in a manner that violates others' rights to equal concern in the public sphere. However, this capacity for restraint can be inculcated without the intolerance that political liberals often exhibit towards those whose beliefs fall outside the mainstream. Thus, the constraints on accommodation that I defend below differ from those defended under political liberalism, since they acknowledge centrally that the tendency of religious adherents to be politically unreasonable is a contingent matter. As we shall see, recognising this point enables us to explain how the presumption for accommodation is consistent with conceiving women's rights as multicultural claims.

The need for a shift of attention from the 'manner' to the 'matter' of belief can be supported by acknowledging that American Christian evangelicals are divided on a number of issues, including women's rights, and that the extent of their politicisation varies widely (Hoffman and Millar 1997). Moreover, cosmopolitan militant atheists, who hold their beliefs in a robustly self-critical manner, are likely to be concerned to see their views prosper publicly. In contrast, Catholics who oppose women's entrance to the priesthood often adhere to the tolerance prescribed by the doctrine of 'free faith', and therefore accept sex equality norms in the wider liberal society (Tomasi 2001). Finally, militant democratic atheists may have a keen understanding of the burdens of judgement but nonetheless hold that, in cases where they constitute the majority, the state should support their claims (Ingram 1996). Thus, while holding one's beliefs with certainty might make political intolerance or unreasonableness more likely, it does not make it inevitable. Attention should therefore be focused not on the reasonableness of the believer but on the specific content of the beliefs for which accommodation is sought.

One objection to this claim might be that the beliefs that typically raise liberal concerns about cultural or religious accommodation in education, such as beliefs about the inferiority of women or the evil of miscegenation, are usually held in an intransigent manner. Thus, the 'manner' and 'matter' of belief could be taken to be intimately related in this context. Protestant evangelicals, for instance, often make emotive appeal to theological premises to deny gay rights and to endorse creationism (Woodberry and Smith 1998; Deakin 1986). Holmes therefore contends that the prohibition of creationists tampering with textbooks does not turn solely on the content of these groups' beliefs but on the need to protect reason and rationality themselves (Holmes 1995: 55; compare Delaney 1979). Yet, while it is indeed often difficult to distinguish between the content of a belief from the manner in which it is held, particularly when the beliefs in question prescribe other-regarding conduct on the basis of intolerance, I seek to show that this distinction is germane to the evaluation of claims for minority accommodation.

This is especially important, in light of our underlying objective of configuring women's rights as multicultural claims. While this central issue has not been salient in this chapter so far, I shall now argue that, while liberals should accept a wide range of doctrinal beliefs as worthy of respectful discussion in the educational sphere, liberal states should not sanction gender or other discrimination in the curriculum, and must preserve the conditions under which all citizens can realise their rights to autonomy. The test I propose reveals that, rather than accepting the *Mozert* parents' demand, the school should have attempted to reach a compromise in terms of exposing children to diversity in ways that would not preclude their opportunities to commit to their inherited beliefs. While such compromises would probably not satisfy those who utterly fail to see their value, I support them by outlining three considerations that reveal why this educational proposal is consistent with the attempt to redress the structural inequalities arising from gender subordination *and* with recognising the cultural particularity of women's interests. Adhering to the balancing test proposed here entails the conclusion that a certain form of liberal education can indeed protect cultural diversity *and* the social conditions for gender justice. It therefore supports, in the final analysis, our configuration of women's rights as multicultural claims. While commentators on *Mozert* rarely focus on its gendered dimensions, this aspect of the case is significant, as we shall now see.

IV (i) Unjustified Intolerance

Is the subject matter of the demand one in relation to which the religious believer's intolerance of an apparently neutral rule is justified? Admittedly, minorities are not usually taken to tolerate the rules of the mainstream society, since the circumstances of toleration are generally thought to obtain where the tolerating group has the social power to act effectively on its antipathy or disapproval of others (Galeotti 2002; McKinnon 2006).

Moreover, the term 'justified' might appear contentious in this context, because the propositional content of most religions entails that a believer's intolerance of any rule that contradicts her beliefs would appear justifiable from her perspective. After all, '[t]o be a Muslim is to accept the truth of the Qur'an and to recognise it as qualitatively different from other world views' (Baumeister 1998: 927). However, since many groups often do tolerate one another, if only out of a pragmatic need to secure peace, by 'unjustified intolerance' I mean a believer's refusal to compromise on issues that are not necessary to maintaining a doctrinal commitment to her faith. Sunstein's 'asymmetry test' proceeds in this way by seeking to ascertain the burdens involved in requiring religious associations' compliance with sex equality laws (Sunstein 1999). This strategy acknowledges that most religions can tolerate contrary beliefs in the public square, except where the issue involves compromising on matters that relate to the individual's passage to redemption or salvation (Margalit 1996: 149). Thus, parents' requests to exempt their children from the timetable during Ramadan or Eid to allow them to pray, or for dietary provision such as halal meat, can be interpreted as justified intolerance of general rules (Denny 1994). This is because they arise vis-à-vis practices on which compromise would be profoundly difficult for the believer. While this test need not accept any subjective assertion, however contentious it may be, of what is 'central' to a person's belief system,[12] some assessment has to made of the inequitable effect of the rule from the believer's perspective, in a way that avoids the difficulties with the prevalent convention in American jurisprudence that inquires only whether the *purpose* of a law burdens a citizen's religious liberty (Song 2007a: 79). On that account, a student could not object if a rule that holds that students should eat together in the cafeteria at a set time incidentally, but substantially, burdens them.

If this test is plausible, it could be argued that the *Mozert* parents' intolerance of the readers was not justifiable. This is not because exposure to diversity never amounts to a violation of beliefs, for, as we have seen, certain forms of exposure could indeed undermine a faith-based way of life. However, because the *Mozert* children would have been exposed to similar beliefs and modes of reasoning in other classes, arguably it would have been hard for the parents to substantiate the claim that the accommodation that they sought was a matter of fundamental conscience. This test is, however, contentious once we recall that parents with wider concerns about a secular curriculum might be unable to reform it comprehensively for social and economic reasons. Since this test is not conclusive, it should be supplemented by further inquiries.

IV (ii) Subversion of Formal Rights

A surer ground on which to constrain the presumption lies in asking whether support for the beliefs for which accommodation is sought would interfere with the state's commitment to the formal rights that schools should protect to ensure the egalitarian conditions under which future citizens' capacities for autonomy can be nurtured. Thus, in some extreme cases, even compromises with religious parents should not be considered. While Macedo, for his part, rightly warns that a school should not use opposition to discrimination as a basis for directly prescribing the sort of religious convictions that people should hold (Macedo 1995b: 309), it is fair to suggest that the state should refuse a parent's request to exempt their child from learning basic literacy, on the grounds that literacy is spiritually corrupting; and that it should not allow their requests to exempt their children from sitting next to a black or Muslim schoolchild (Gutmann 1995b). The refusal to accommodate in these situations may indeed have the (albeit indirect) effect of circumscribing the content of the beliefs to which future citizens are likely to commit.

Nonetheless, it is worth emphasising how this approach differs from Gutmann's 'civic minimum' (1995a: 310), which seeks to ensure religious toleration and racial non-discrimination through a uniform educational curriculum. Rather than conceptualising religious accommodation and the pursuit of racial harmony as opposed, my approach assumes that the even-handed inclusion of religious sensibilities should not be seen as inconsistent with pursuing an educational culture in which other constitutional rights are duly respected. Many religions, such as Judaism and Methodism, admittedly could be considered sexist, homophobic and even racist in many ways; but adherents of belief systems, such as Islam, which view homosexuality with disdain, are able to tolerate those to whom they cannot extend equal respect (Modood and Ahmad 2007). I return to this issue in Chapter 5, but emphasise for now that most conservative creeds contain both the principles of other-regarding respect *and* a particular mode of distributing that respect. The difficulty is of course that a particular religion may impugn liberal commitments to *equal* respect; and, indeed, the concern that evangelicals deny the moral equality of all persons lies at the root of Gutmann's concerns about religious accommodation in the US since, in a liberal society, the premise of equal respect is the starting point from which reasonable discussion begins. However, if many conservative religions can indeed *tolerate* those whom they cannot, strictly speaking, respect, liberal states should not assume that compromises cannot be found with minority groups. While there are profound difficulties with the distinction between tolerance and respect, to which I shall turn in Chapter 5, it suffices to say for now that, on the formal rights test, it is likely that a school should not accede to religious parents' demands to exempt their children from, say, sex-education classes. For if the information that female students receive in these classes is very important to their comprehension of their reproductive rights, then there is reason to believe that the state would not treat them with equal concern by exempting them. However, in enforcing this rule, liberal educators should make efforts to accommodate the sensibilities of the students by presenting the information a non-coeducational setting, for instance, or without the use of potentially offensive images (Shachar 2001: 147).

IV (iii) Subversion of Informal Equality

The final test for constraining the presumption enables me to explain fully how this educational proposal supports our configuration of women's rights as multicultural claims. This constraint assumes that liberal educators have a duty to refrain from sanctioning informal inequality through the curriculum. Granting exemptions to children from egalitarian subject matter may not violate constitutional rights; but these exemptions would be liable to undermine the broad culture of equal respect for gender equality and ethical diversity necessary for children to realise their capacities for autonomy. This argument does not contradict our earlier claim that the way in which students are exposed to diversity might undermine their capacity to commit to their beliefs. If children are encouraged, even indirectly, to believe that scepticism or even nihilism are the only plausible responses to the diversity of beliefs that they confront, this form of education could indeed impede what Nussbaum calls their 'religious capabilities' (Nussbaum 1999b: 108). However, if children are exposed to the idea of women's success in the public sphere in the context of a serious discussion about the relationship of this idea to their traditional beliefs about gender, education can be respectful of non-mainstream ways of life whilst adhering to civic ideals. On this account, the *Mozert* parents were not justified in seeking to exempt their children from access to knowledge of alternative family structures and gender relations. As I argued at the end of Chapter 3, such exposure is likely to be an important means through which the liberal state challenges the structural inequalities associated with gender subordination in different sectors of society.

To voice concerns about *Mozert* for this reason could initially appear misconceived. But consider: critical of the privileged status of expressive individualism in America (Bellah et al. 1985), the *Mozert* parents wished their children to adhere to Biblical mandates such as the 'doctrine of wifely submission', to which we referred earlier.[13] While we should not under-estimate the fact that evangelical women often interpret this doctrine in unconventional ways – for instance, as a testimony to the 'soft' egos of men which are in constant need of women's deference – this does not mean that the state need not protect young evangelical students' *capacities* to under-take such progressive re-interpretations of religious mandates. As I argued in Chapter 3, it should not be assumed that the resources for developing autonomy within any tradition always suffice to provide young women with the psychological equipment or social conditions to resist male-centred readings of cultural or religious mandates. While defenders of indigenous feminist movements often understandably appeal to the fact that non-Western women reinterpret sacred texts and cultural mandates in order to challenge the paternalistic intervention of a state that seeks to 'emancipate' them, to view one's local struggle for gender justice as entirely disconnected from wider campaigns for justice, may well be, as Edward Said expressed the point, 'as exclusivist, as limited, as provisional and as discriminatory' as the paternalistic interference that many women contest (Said, cited in Attwood 1992). Moreover, it is important to acknowledge in the specific case we are considering how easily evangelical Protestant beliefs about gender conform to the sex inequality that has prevailed historically in mainstream liberal societies, informed, as they typically are, by a weak form of Protestantism. It is thus not unlikely that young evangelical students would confirm rather than question their religious doctrines in the context of a secular school, if the commitment to exposing students to alternative images of gender relations through a civics curriculum were not upheld. The state should thus aim to foster an educational culture in which young women are likely to form the capacity to reflect critically on their traditional doctrines, in a way that would support their rights to autonomy, as well as their potential to engage in the dialogues of the right to mediation in the long term.

Some would contend that this argument goes too far. For instance, Burtt distinguishes between a school's duty to protect constitutional rights to racial equality and 'informal' sex equality norms. As she writes:

> the state may wish to raise boys and girls to similar roles in society; but absent a constitutional affirmation that men and women are to be treated equally . . . schools cannot claim a right to impose this preference on children over the religious . . . objections of their parents. (Burtt 1994: 69)

However, this reasoning is difficult to support. To be sure, almost all laws in American society that have a discriminatory effect on women are upheld in practice, so long as their intention is not discriminatory (Sunstein 1995). However, not only is the pursuit of sex equality usually understood as a compelling state interest in liberal democracies (Sunstein 1999), but most states are signatories to the Convention on the Elimination of all Forms of Discrimination Against Women, article 2(e) of which requires states to take appropriate measures to eliminate gender discrimination and which enjoins them, in education, to 'modify the social and cultural patterns of conduct of men and women, with a view to achieving the elimination of prejudices and customs and all other practices which are based on . . . stereotyped roles for men and women' (cited in Bennoune 2007: 385). Even if general laws do not mandate the uniform treatment of the sexes pervasively in all arenas of civil society, it is unsatisfactory to conclude that public institutions have no responsibilities in this respect. To say so much is not to deny the difficult questions that arise with respect to the interpretation of gender justice – indeed, precisely the questions that have underwritten the case for recognising the cultural particularity of women's interests in previous chapters. However, the existence of these interpretive controversies does not justify shielding students from knowledge of alternative conceptions of gender relations in education. If these measures encouraged serious-minded discussion, liberal education would not substantially burden the abilities of religious students to integrate their private beliefs and public commitments. Indeed, this point is reflected, somewhat unexpectedly, in Nussbaum's educational ideal, which aims to foster capacities for 'world citizenship' through the inclusion of norms and traditions from different ways of life, whilst leaving room for a critical perspective on them (see Nussbaum 2000; Enslin and Tjiattas 2004).

Thus, the most serious objection to my argument is likely not to be that schools have no responsibilities with respect to gender issues; but whether this approach ultimately demands of religious students precisely the form of epistemological restraint advocated by political liberals. Does it make a difference to present diversity inclusively within the school, if the awareness of the burdens of judgement that this policy aims to cultivate reinstates the division of psychological labour that we found to be existentially untenable for many young citizens in a multicultural polity? In response to this objection, it should be conceded first that the balancing test that I propose does entail that future citizens must learn to separate their private beliefs from their public commitments to some extent. Their awareness of the depth of diversity in modern societies entails that they must exercise tolerance towards those whom they may privately consider inferior or deviant, at least when presenting their claims in the public sphere. There are times, therefore, when they must regard the theological truth that they cherish as one belief amongst others. However, the way in which the need for tolerance is inculcated in future citizens according to this approach would not be as costly as that proposed by political liberals. It can be achieved by encouraging all to view their membership in the state as potentially continuous with their non-public lives.

This proposal does not amount to advocating the inclusion of all sectarian beliefs in the civic curriculum in order to encourage the holders of these beliefs to liberalise. While non-liberal standpoints by definition evince values that are not perfectly reconcilable with a liberal way of life, they should not be considered, purely on that account, grossly unreasonable or unjust. While it may of course be impossible to establish continuities between public and private values in the case of extremist groups, and while this account would not command the support of those whose comprehensive beliefs entirely reject the value of respect, a zero-sum conflict between adherents of minority belief systems and the secular state should not be assumed. On the contrary, a wide variety of requests, such as those of Muslim parents to exempt their children to pray during Ramadan or Orthodox Jewish parents that their children follow a 'split-day' programme should be permitted. One must acknowledge the costs of religious restraint on non-mainstream communities, accord them symbolic recognition by protecting their 'vitality', and not summarily stigmatise them as unreasonable. A liberal education that secures the framework of rights defended in this book does indeed require that young citizens learn the arts of restraint to some degree. However, the costs of learning these arts are not as high those incurred through political liberal civic education.

In the final analysis, Tomasi rightly argues that an innovative compromise should have been struck with the *Mozert* parents in our central case (Tomasi 2001: 94). He recalls that, before the judgement, some schools had already reached an accommodation with the parents by 'specifically not[ing] on worksheets that the student was not required to believe the stories' about science fiction and Renaissance philosophy. While it is somewhat unlikely that this measure would have allayed the fears of evangelical parents, it is surely plausible that compromise would often realise the objectives of civic education better than outright refusal to negotiate. A more credible avenue would have been to encourage a non-trivialising discussion of biblical narratives alongside secular stories. Doing so would have conformed to the former American legal principle that the state should pursue its interests in the manner that is least restrictive to those who view their private beliefs as inerrant truths[14].

V CONCLUSION

This chapter has supported a constrained presumption for religious and cultural accommodation in education as a means of protecting the public and private dimensions of future citizens' autonomy. While the gender issues in this discussion were initially less direct than in previous chapters, I sought ultimately to emphasise the importance of educational accommodation in supporting our conception of women's rights as multicultural claims. Constraining the presumption through the 'subversion of informal inequality' objection and, thus, refusing the demands of parents who seek to shield their children from gender-egalitarian subject matter in civics classes does not undermine our acknowledgement that women often opt to live by non-liberal, and indeed sometimes gender-inegalitarian, values. Rather, the proposed test suggests that diversity can be supported while protecting the conditions under which gender justice can be achieved and structural disadvantages challenged in the long term. The form of education recommended here should therefore be viewed as a part of a 'minimum basket of social goods' that strategically secures for women the rights defended by this book. It would, as Subrahmanian argues in relation to education generally, assist young female citizens to 'assert voice and internalise a sense of entitlement' (Subrahmanian (2002: 229).

Of course, a hard question arising from this argument is whether the presumption for educational accommodation can be extended to practices which may appear inegalitarian from a liberal perspective, but which are interpreted in an empowering way by young minority women. Accordingly, in the next and final chapter we turn to an issue that has raised intense controversy in Europe – namely, Muslim women's campaigns to wear to the hijab to school. If the existential point of liberalism is to enable all to live well within a just state, the pressing question is whether this controversy can be understood and evaluated through our configuration of women's rights as multicultural claims.

NOTES

1. This title derives from Macedo's reference to the certain 'ordering of the soul', or the way of organising one's deepest beliefs, that Locke ([1689] 1955) ascribed to religious adherents who practised tolerance towards those of different faiths. While Macedo does not use this phrase in connection with liberal civic education, I contend that his account of such education does, metaphorically, demand a kind of 'ordering of the soul' too. Unlike for Locke, this 'ordering' involves the capacity to separate one's public from private beliefs in certain respects.

2. I refer to 'evangelicals' rather than to 'fundamentalists' owing to the pejorative connotations surrounding the latter term. While the term 'evangelical' is deeply contested, it is usually associated with (a) the need for personal conversion or being born-again and (b) a strong belief in biblical inerrancy.
3. For an examination of the differences between American, French and British educational systems, see Levinson, 1997.
4. *Mozert v. Hawkins County Board of Education* 827 F2d. 1058 (6th Cir. 1987).
5. This is not to say that Bloom would necessarily have supported *Mozert*. His preoccupation was largely with 'high culture' rather than religious truth.
6. Peter Jones's distinction between the 'manner' and the 'matter' of expression about belief in his discussion of the Rushdie Affair prompted me to frame the issue in this chapter in terms of this distinction (Jones 1990).
7. Macedo's and Gutmann's concerns about religious accommodation seem to be out of line with current practice in American schools which aims towards maximum accommodation. Macedo's and Gutmann's emphasis on civic commitment arguably evokes the pre-war vision of a nationalist ideal of 'true America', which played itself out in the classroom in the form of 'school pride' activities and the daily 'Pledge of Allegiance' (Levinson, 1997: 347).
8. Ironically, the political apathy of which civic education theorists are critical may be a greater problem within the mainstream citizenry than in some evangelical circles (Schrag 1998).
9. *Wisconsin v. Yoder* 406 US 205 (1972), p. 219.
10. *Wisconsin v. Yoder* 406 US 205 (1972), p. 218.
11. *Mozert v. Hawkins County Board of Education* 827 F2d. 1067 (6th Cir. 1987).
12. The debate has become salient in American jurisprudence over the years following the political firestorm set off by the abrogation of religious liberty in *Employment Division v. Smith* 494 US 872 (1990).
13. Protestant evangelicals frequently give interpretive primacy to the biblical passage, Ephesians 5:22: 'Wives, submit to your husbands as to the Lord. For the husband is the head of the wife as Christ is the head of the Church, his body, of which he is the saviour.'
14. The Religious Freedom Restoration Act 1993 in US law held that, where a claim is made that a general law substantially burdens a person's free exercise of a religion, the claim can be refused only if (a) the burden is in furtherance of a compelling government interest and (b) it is the least restrictive means of furthering that interest. This legislation was subsequently deemed unconstitutional and, since 1997, the government is not enjoined to adhere to the 'least restrictive means' requirement.

CHAPTER 5

Unveiling Mediation and Autonomy – Women's Rights as Citizenship and Reciprocity

I INTRODUCTION

In this chapter, I provide final support for conceiving women's rights as multicultural claims by engaging with the issues examined previously – namely, rights to mediation and autonomy and the presumption for educational accommodation. My analysis will also articulate the farthest-reaching implications of adhering to Young's notion of seriality in the debate about gender and culture in political philosophy. Specifically, I contend that the idea of *civic reciprocity* helps to demonstrate why the educational accommodation of some apparently non-liberal practices would support the framework of rights defended in this book. While liberals should not sanction gender inequality in education, accommodating certain minority gendered practices could sometimes lead to women's greater participation in the public sphere, and would thereby occasion a politically responsible dialogue between diverse women that responds to the complex and subtle social constraints that should concern feminists across the permeable boundaries of their cultural and religious differences. While these issues may not amount to the extreme pressures involved in, say, forced marriage, and might not warrant direct legal prohibition, they nonetheless deserve feminist attention. Therefore, this chapter establishes the final sense in which attention to cultural particularity serves to reconfigure universal judgements about gender justice in an interest theory of rights.

To clarify the role played by the notion of 'civic reciprocity' in supporting this argument, consider the standard liberal appeal to the special relationship that obtains between citizens of a political state (Dagger 1997: 46; Callan 1997: 99–102). Gutmann and Thompson (1996]: 64–5) follow Rawls in appealing to this crucial bond to support a liberal conception of 'reciprocity', which they define as a situation in which citizens mutually invoke arguments that cannot be reasonably rejected by their fellow citizens in the course of justifying the polity's laws. Thus, citizens' reciprocal justifications of the polity serve to affirm its legitimacy and to maintain its stability. Citizens listen to others' proposals sympathetically without necessarily agreeing comprehensively on a shared conception of the good (Callan 1997: 100). While I do not repudiate this conception of reciprocity, I emphasise what may be seen as its precondition – namely what I call *reciprocity in justification*. This account maintains that mutual reciprocity is dependent on all citizens having the capacity to justify the political order from the perspective of their non-public moral or religious beliefs. Bringing this situation about involves ensuring a minimal degree of non-alienation between a citizen's private values and public commitments. A commitment to reciprocity so conceived sometimes justifies accommodating non-liberal gendered practices in the educational sphere, as we shall see.

I support this claim by focusing on the debate about the Muslim veil (hijab). This issue has become contentious all over Europe (Shahid & von Koningsveld 1995); and the French government in 2004 controversially banned 'conspicuous' religious symbols, including the veil, from state-funded schools.[1] My central claim is that this measure was ill conceived. This is not because there are no plausible grounds for a ban, or because the veil is an 'easy case' (compare Spinner-Halev 2001a: 100). A practice should not be viewed as an innocuous personal choice simply because it appears not to cause physical harm. This assumption obscures the cultural significance of 'modest dress' symbols such as the hijab, as well as the questions that they raise concerning the conditions under which individuals adhere to their traditional practices. In response to these issues, I invoke the idea of reciprocity to argue that permitting the veil in schools would be likely to encourage a politically responsible discussion between diverse citizens concerning the complex matrix of social factors that shape their choices. To clarify, my claim is not that the veil is intrinsically good or bad, but that it raises highly significant issues in terms of the rights defended in this book.

Before proceeding, an explanation of veiling is in order. The garment takes a variety of forms: a scarf that covers the hair and the shoulders but reveals the face is known as a hijab; the niqab is a veil for the face that leaves the area around the eyes clear; the jilbab is a long garment that covers the entire body except for the hands, feet, face and head; and a garment worn by many Saudi women that covers the body, head and face is known as the burqa. The practice traditionally expresses norms of modesty that are mentioned in the Qur'an (Mookherjee 2008a)[2], and which have been speculated about by Western writers to the point where 'the veiled woman' has come to represent a synecdoche for Muslim culture as a whole (Pedwell 2007: 18). This is in spite of the fact that: (a) many Muslim women do not veil; (b) the practice is found in Hindu, Jewish and Christian cultures too; and (c) it was adopted in history by Greeks, Byzantines and Assyrians (Marmorstein 1954). Nonetheless, at the contemporary time the hijab is associated almost exclusively with Muslim communities, raising issues that vary according to different nations' experiences of colonisation and immigration. The symbol has been significant, for instance, in twentieth-century pro-Islamist movements in Egypt and Iran (Hirschmann 2003: 349).

Whilst acknowledging the wide-ranging issues raised by the hijab globally, one reason for limiting our focus to the French case in this chapter is that the country's tradition of republican citizenship, which aims to preserve homogeneity rather than acknowledge cultural differences (Schnapper 1991), brings into sharp relief my argument for permitting the veil in schools in terms of civic reciprocity. To be sure, there has been controversy about the veil in Britain too. For instance, a Manchester school briefly prohibited two girls from wearing the hijab in 1989 (Poulter 1997: 67); and, in 2006, the House of Lords upheld a school's refusal to permit a student to wear the jilbab.[3] However, a ban on the veil tends to appear extreme to Britons and Americans since the church–state separation in these countries is not generally thought to warrant prohibiting children from wearing religious headgear (Poulter 1994: Chapter 4). It is, moreover, apt to focus on France's less pluralistic political tradition, as the country has one of Europe's largest North African Muslim populations (Winter 2001).[4] The fact that the ban on religious symbols came into effect during the War on Terror, in the context of which Muslims have experienced increased discrimination (Wing 2003), suggests that the state's opposition to the veil is likely to have wide implications. The social problems experienced by Arab minorities contributed to unrest that was expressed in a fortnight of urban violence involving minority youths that spread throughout two hundred cities in France in 2005 (Amanpour 2005). In such a context, one concern is that banning the veil deepens the alienation of a community that already suffers its 'postcolonial' predicament acutely.

With these issues in mind, I proceed as follows. Section II explains the origins of the 'headscarves affair', focusing especially on the issues that it raises in terms of civic reciprocity. I define this idea through a reading of Tariq Modood's account of multicultural citizenship (Modood 2007; 2008). Section III further defines reciprocity in terms of non-alienation before returning to the presumption for educational accommodation, as outlined in Chapter 4. Since allowing the veil in schools would be likely to enable young Muslim women to integrate the different sources of their autonomy, prohibiting the veil in this context would not, I contend, support their core capacities and rights. Section IV further argues that women would be more likely to participate in the dialogues of the right to mediation if they have not been alienated from state education. Finally, Section V invokes a different conception of reciprocity in order to engage with the complicated issue of whether Muslim women endorse their decisions to wear the veil. In response to this problem, the political participation of diverse citizens in mediation could support a socially responsible debate concerning the subtle constraints arising from gender hierarchies cross-culturally.[5] The possibility of this debate sustains the hope of feminist engagement across cultural differences in a world of imperfectly reconcilable values and unequal relations of power.

II THE 'HEADSCARVES AFFAIR': FEMINIST CITIZENSHIP/MULTICULTURAL CITIZENSHIP

II (i) The Headscarves Affair and the French Ban

Contemporary re-veiling, represented by the increasing number of Muslim women wearing traditional dress in schools and workplaces around the world, has given rise in France to *l'affaire du foulard* or 'the headscarves affair'. This controversy is understood to have originated in 1989, when Ernest Chénière, the headmaster of a school near Paris, forbade three girls from wearing the veil in class. Already troubled by the manner in which Jewish children were absenting themselves on Saturdays, he believed that acceding to the Muslim girls' wishes would occasion a plethora of further claims from students of other faiths. The issue provoked a national controversy (Silverman 1992: 115), with the Education Minister, Lionel Jospin, eventually stating that, since *laïcité*, the republican principle of secular neutrality, entailed the protection of religious freedom, schools could prohibit religious symbols if they were used to pressurise persons reluctant to wear them (Johnson 1989). The commitment to *laïcité* was affirmed in France as a result of the country's historical struggle to free education from the dominant influence of the Catholic Church (Hazareesingh 1994). By distinguishing political and religious spheres, the republican state sought to guarantee religious freedom for all by establishing the Separation Law of 1905 (Laborde 2005: 305). In conformity with its historical commitments, the *Conseil d'Etat* thus responded to the controversy over the veil by declaring that religious freedom could be limited if it hindered the objectives of state education, which included inculcating in students respect for others and guaranteeing sex equality. The commitment to religious liberty could not entail allowing pupils to wear insignia which 'by the circumstances in which they are worn individually or collectively, or by their ostentatious and campaigning nature, constitute an act of pressure, provocation, proselytism or propaganda' (Poulter 1997: 58, citing L'Actualité Juridique: Droit Administratif AJDA 1999: 39).

The controversy continued for a number of years with anti-veiling sentiment increasing in the wake of reports of violence against unveiled Muslim girls by radical groups (Brun-Rovet 2000). Eventually, Jacques Chirac requested the formation of the Stasi Commission to investigate the issue of secularism.[6] Following its recommendations, in February 2004 an overwhelming majority in the National Assembly approved a ban on 'conspicuous' religious apparel in state education. The law is ostensibly neutral in that it prohibits not only the veil but also the Jewish skullcap, turbans and large crucifixes. However, concerns have been raised that it contravenes Article 9 of the European Convention for the Protection of Human Rights, which preserves individuals' freedom to manifest religious belief (Alibali 2004).[7] In addition, following Chirac's open criticism of the veil in 2003, a further worry is that the law is directed towards the hijab specifically (Richburg 2003). For this symbol is more conspicuous in French society than a crucifix, owing to the fact that it cannot be physically hidden and on account of its minority status (Galeotti 2002: 145). For these reasons, the distinction between discreet and prominent symbols in this context could well appear contrived (Barry 2001: 60).

Furthermore, even if we accept that a principle of neutrality is politically desirable, a key problem is how this term should be understood. On the one hand, a policy could be neutral in terms of its formal impact if it establishes a rule from which no one is allowed to deviate.[8] However, such a law may not be neutral in terms of its justification if it evinces a commitment to a comprehensive way of life (McKinnon 2006: 116). If the French ban is justified according to a secular conception of the good, and does not gain the support of those who adhere to a religious account, then its neutrality would be questionable. Moreover, the church–state separation is far from complete in practice, since the French government provides eighty per cent of the budget for Catholic schools, at which around two million children study (Cohen 2001). Finally, there is no benign way of eliminating ethnic differences from a common school. The interrelation between ethnic and religious issues in the hijab debate exposes the difficulty with the republican attempt to guarantee equality by eradicating visible differences in a way that even critics of identity politics such as Barry would find extreme. The precise meaning of neutrality is crucial, then, in light of the fact that religious diversity in France has increased significantly from the early twentieth century when the nation officially established its secular commitments (Brown, Garner and Bell 1993).

II (ii) Feminist and Multicultural Perspectives on the Hijab Controversy

Feminist responses to the veil are varied. Okin contests it on account of the ideology of female restraint on which it is based (1999b: 62). She is not alone. Many Western commentators have viewed Islam as a source of women's inequality, the ultimate symbol of which has been thought to be the veil (Stowasser 1994; Kandiyoti 1988–9). In the meantime, while some Muslim feminists support the veil or else view it as a minor issue compared to poverty, domestic violence and child custody (Ahmed 1992), Fatima Mernissi voices the concern that the symbol reveals the 'collective fantasy' of Muslim communities to relegate women to the domestic sphere and 'to highlight their illegal position on male territory by means of a mask' (Mernissi 1982: 189). Moreover, some Muslim women's organisations have campaigned against the veil in their home countries, with Arab intellectual Ghaiss Jasser responding angrily to multicultural defences of this symbol. 'If, then, you claim that the veil is a simply a manifestation of cultural particularity,' she argues, 'you lack solidarity with women opposing purdah . . . at the very cost of their lives' (Jasser 1999: 35).

For our current purposes, the most pertinent objection to the veil is found in the writings of republican feminists (see, for example, Zelensky and Vigerie 2003; Dauphin and Praud 2002), who contend that the recrudescence of religion in the late-modern era undermines women's interests by relegating them to second-class citizenship. Their specific concern is that women are often 'instrumentalized' by fundamentalist groups and, as Laborde (2006: 354) explains, the veiled Muslim woman has revived potent historical imagery of the Catholic nun as the antithesis of the republic, the 'anti-Marianne', whose irrational religiosity ostensibly symbolised rejection of the ideal of female autonomy by recalling the corporeal subservience that is anathema to feminists of the 1970s, who fought for control over their bodies. The alliance formed between laic intellectuals and immigrant women prior to the ban is significant in this context. In 2003, Muslim women participated in a nationwide march to denounce the blackmail to which they were too often subjected, according to which they were told: '[D]ress decently and wear the headscarf or else you are fair game for sexual harassment' (Guénif-Souilamas and Macé 2004: 8–10; see also Laborde 2006: 356). Moreover, the republican feminist critique of the veil is forcefully articulated by prominent public figure Elisabeth Badinter, who believes that the choice to wear this symbol signifies that Muslim women are 'closed up in their homes and confined to domestic tasks' (Badinter 1989, cited in Moruzzi 1994: 662). Even if Muslim girls choose this practice autonomously, this does not mean that they *are* autonomous; and the fact that they defend it simply makes no difference to the fact of their domination. Given the strong formative project to which republicans are committed, feminists of this tradition are concerned that permitting the hijab in schools gravely hinders Muslim girls' access to citizenship. For, on this account, the nation must be seen as a 'community of destiny', schools as a primary site in which allegiance to it is inculcated and all sexual and cultural discrimination therefore made to cease at the school door (Poulter 1997: 61). Indeed, feminist sentiment against the hijab was so strong prior to the ban that a group of French women signed a letter to *Elle* magazine in 2003, arguing that 'the veil sends us all, Muslim and non-Muslim, back to sex discrimination, which is intolerable' (cited in Delphy 2004).

To a degree, republican feminism is echoed in the comprehensive liberalism of J. S. Mill, who held that a person cannot submit to slavery or prefer a slothful life to one of Socratic questioning (Mill [1874] 1978). While Mill used the language of individuality rather than that of autonomy, his claim agrees with the republican idea that meaningful agency is possible only in a context of freedom to evaluate the merits of different ways of life, away from the tyranny of illiberal groups. Republican feminists endorse this claim by asserting a connection between personal autonomy and civic loyalty – a condition of freedom is the ability to identify with a just state, because this identification is the 'motivational anchorage essential to the . . . stability of a liberal society' (Laborde 2003: 170–1). Without this common anchorage, nobody's rights are secure. Accommodating young Muslim women's religious symbols would endanger their own and others' autonomy in a sense that recalls Macedo's concerns about the erosion of civic virtue in Chapter 4.

One problem with this critique, however, is that the republican feminist focus on the supposedly alienated condition of Muslim girls is not always accompanied by a thorough inquiry into gender domination in all areas. While they typically campaign for *parité*, or the equal political representation of the sexes, republican feminists have not focused uniformly on all sources of gender inequality in French society. Badinter, for instance, does not find fault with the pervasive pressures on women to conform to exacting standards of fashion (al-Hibri 1999) and, on the contrary, berates feminists who challenge the commodification of sex for reviving gender stereotypes (Badinter 2003). Moreover, the anxiety that republican feminists express about the repressive effects of religion fails to acknowledge the allegations of some sociologists who claim that the veil in Islam and anorexia nervosa in secular societies equally symbolise women's reactions to the contradictory messages that they receive concerning equality and sexual difference, to a point that both phenomena indicate their willing adherence to norms that undermine their interests (Nasser 1999: 411). In view of such charges, a broad appeal to autonomy would not support the banning of the veil specifically. As McKinnon contends, the argument is 'not very plausible in so far as it provides at least as strong a reason to prevent schoolchildren from mindlessly following fashion . . . as it does for banning the hijab' (McKinnon 2006: 116).

Whilst this is an important point, it does not, however, respond fully to feminist concerns about the veil. It does not lead to the conclusion that all allegations of sexual domination in this context are, in Galeotti's words, 'decidedly lame' (2002: 212). Although some critiques of veiling surely are driven by neo-orientalist agendas that have deepened owing to the War on Terror and the rise of Islamism (Amiri 2001: 19), consider Poulter's view:

> The most intriguing justification for a rule banning headscarves would be one which was . . . grounded in a concern for sexual equality amongst pupils and which adopted the position that the hijab reflects the subordinate position of women in Islam. Whether such an interpretation is right or wrong, it is clearly not so unreasonable that no sensible person could subscribe to it. (Poulter 1997: 69)

Raised some years before the French ban, Poulter's point recalls the *subversion of informal equality* objection to the presumption for educational accommodation. While we shall consider his point in that context shortly, I quote him here to emphasise that some republican feminist concerns are plausible. Freedom and force cannot be defined in the abstract; and there is evidence that some French Muslim women face pressures to wear the hijab which are arguably much more extreme than the pressures on women in the wider society to follow fashion. Organised groups of young men have reportedly congregated at school gates and used threats in working-class immigrant communities to impose norms of 'modest dress' on young women. According to one radio programme, '[t]he most horrific ritual is the *tournante*, the gang-rape of teenage girls who appear loose by wearing mini-skirts and going to the movies'.[9] The Stasi Commission corroborated these reports by affirming that there had been an 'alarming rise in sexist abuse' in schools, and that there was pressure, in the form of insults and violence, on Muslim girls to 'conform' by wearing the veil. Some pupils who had had their arms broken had lied to their parents to avoid denouncing their peers. The Commission also heard from Muslim fathers who had to transfer their daughters to Catholic schools where they were free from such pressures. According to Patrick Weil, one of the Stasi Commissioners, a 'clear majority' of Muslim girls who did not wear the veil asked the Commission to ban public displays of religious belief (Weil 2004). For these reasons, there is at least a plausible case in favour of the claim that the ban is a proportionate response to the problems that it seeks to address (Song 2007a: 175).

To reiterate, this is because judgements about the coerciveness of a practice only make sense in context. While a militant campaign against the hijab at a rural British university would be deeply disturbing, the proposal for a ban is not entirely incomprehensible in the French case. This is so, even though the fact that tens of thousands of Muslim women rallied in January 2004 to protest the ban should give us pause before accepting the Stasi Commission's conclusions too readily (McKinnon 2006: 113). While it is implausible to consider all women who wear the veil as tools for others' political mobilisation (Monnet 1990; Carens 2000: 159), simply appealing to the maxim *volenti non fit injuria* ('no harm is done a person when consent is given') would be irresponsible, since an interest theory of rights responsive to feminism and multiculturalism must be concerned with substantive capacities to resist coercion and not only with formal freedom. Moreover, the fact that pressure can be psychological rather than physical, as we saw in Chapter 3, suggests that even the traditional symbolism of the veil as a 'mobile form of purdah' (Werbner 2005) could be problematic, to the extent that it signifies women's seclusion from the wider world. While this symbolism may be no more harmful than that of Western garments such as the miniskirt, to make this point is, again, to fail to respond fully to feminist concerns. Thus, while the republican feminist worry that the veil represents a challenge to the state by a putatively inegalitarian group is not convincing (Carens 2000: 158; Lacoste-Dujardin 1990), the more nuanced concerns raised from this theoretical perspective cannot be dismissed by claiming that Muslim girls may not be alone in experiencing potentially coercive pressures.

We shall return to these issues in the course of the chapter. Before doing so, however, let us consider the contrasting *multicultural* perspective on this debate. Defenders of multicultural citizenship question the assumption that civic belonging is generally secured through privatising diversity. Tariq Modood, for instance, argues that policies of religious disestablishment in liberal states are liable to hamper the integration of groups in the context of deep inequalities of power (Modood 2005). The demand that citizens bracket their religious identities in public is often inequitable, given that the public culture of any society always expresses the norms of the majority society to some extent (ibid.: 11). Thus, while Modood does not take up the issue of the veil in detail, and while it is unlikely that he would contest the claim that the justifiability of restricting particular practices is a contextual question and that cultural freedom cannot be seen as a moral absolute, he and other defenders of multicultural citizenship generally argue in favour of exemptions from laws that penalise minority practices (see Kymlicka and Norman 2000: 11; Young 1997; Réaume 2000). The defence of the hijab that can be derived from their accounts does not appeal to a universal right to wear whatever one likes, depending on one's personal taste.[10] Equating the veil with a mere preference would fail to acknowledge the fact that, while the state might often have good reason to impose uniform laws, there are reasons to believe that ensuring equality can sometimes involve a right to express one's differences in public.

Modood claims that he is not wholly committed to the ethical-philosophical multiculturalisms of Parekh and Taylor that envisage dialogue between different groups as a means of increasing inter-cultural understanding (Modood 2007: 45). Yet his criticism of political philosophers' general tendency to privatise and, indeed, to ignore religious diversity belies a strong ethical and philosophical commitment to protecting the capacities of all citizens to affirm their political status without renouncing their moral sources. I thus draw from Modood's account the idea that the public affirmation of religious and cultural diversity is important in terms of bringing about reciprocity between diverse citizens. This is not reciprocity in the abstract liberal sense advocated by Gutmann and Thompson, which holds that citizens should be willing to offer others reasons that they could not reasonably reject (Gutmann and Thompson 1996: 64–5). Rather, it is a more concrete sense of reciprocity which holds that citizens should be in a mutual position to affirm their allegiance to the polity by drawing upon their distinctive values. Specifically, I extract from Modood's emphasis on religious diversity a commitment to the ideal of 'civic reciprocity in justification'.[11] This is the idea that, because citizens of a diverse polity do not all share moral sources, they can only affirm the polity and exercise citizenship if their diverse values are equally respected. As will be demonstrated, this argument serves to pre-empt the republican feminist criticism of the veil in terms of civic loyalty.

For consider again the conception of the loyal citizen presupposed by republicans, on the basis of which the French state historically demanded allegiance to the state above any affiliation to foreign religious authorities. Notably, Jewish elites responded successfully to this demand by toning down their doctrinal self-understanding as the 'chosen people' (Birnbaum 1992). However, much anxiety in France about the veil emanates from the assumption that it is difficult for Muslims to conform by pledging primary allegiance to a secular state, because Islam lacks a separation between spiritual and temporal spheres (Cohen 2001: 322; Laborde 2005: 320). Rather than sharing Christianity's other-worldliness, Islam evinces a belief in the possibility of building a just and prosperous social order in this world (Baumeister 2000: 65; Akhtar 1991). For these reasons, campaigns for the right to wear the veil are taken to indicate an anticipated inability by Muslims to integrate. We shall shortly see why Modood contests these general assumptions about Islam. However, for now, it is worth noting that this thick conception of the citizen is generally too extreme on his account. Not only does it lead states such as France to the dubious position of denying the existence of minorities and, thus, of requesting reservations on international minority rights (Lochak 1989: 114). Moreover, the republican denial that minority groups deserve any compensation or special treatment at all, on the grounds that no citizen is legally bound by the community of their birth, is, in Modood's view, sociologically naive (Modood 2007: 70). He therefore rightly queries the competitive state–religion relationship presupposed by the republican account, and emphasises that religions typically emphasise altruism, care of the sick and the homeless, mutuality and trust (ibid.: 76).

Modood asks, in essence, how the legitimacy and stability of the political order can be achieved if it is more costly for some citizens to integrate their private beliefs and public commitments. 'To become a citizen . . .' he insists, 'is to have a double right: to be recognised and to debate the terms of recognition' (Modood 2008). Here, a French republican could reply that a policy of strict secularism in the educational sphere ensures that all citizens accept liberal values for political purposes, whilst leaving their confessional loyalties sealed from state interference. However, this strategy has a problem because, while the state can teach young citizens the importance of tolerance, it cannot, without undermining its own neutrality, encourage them to adhere to any compelling justification for this value. Therefore, as Modood says, 'the state . . . may look to religious communities to inculcate virtues . . . without which a civic morality would have nothing to build on' (Modood 2005: 133). While a secularist might respond that heterogeneous groups in a pluralist state can never achieve mutual sympathy and, thus, that it is more realistic for all to commit to the polity in terms of a *modus vivendi*, republicans would not be appeased by this argument, given their desire for a political order that is held together by more than bargaining, compromise and an antagonistic system of rights.

Thus, whilst republicans typically insist on loyalty to the state as, in McKinnon's words, an 'antidote to liberal complacency about the fragility of just states which . . . is built in to the liberal account of a person's rights as being held against the state' (McKinnon 2006: 117), Modood replies that French strategies for ensuring this commitment are liable to demand too high a price of minority groups. His idea that religious values in particular can provide citizens with the motivational impetus to treat others with respect is borne out by the testimonies of other Muslim intellectuals such as Ghayasuddin Siddiqui, the leader of the 'Muslim Parliament' in Britain, and Merryl Wyn Davies, the writer and convert, who contends that Islam 'allows differences to flourish' and is 'inherently multicultural' (Wyn Davis, cited in Modood and Ahmad 2007: 189). While the claim that religious and political values are mutually reinforcing in a secular state is unstable for reasons that we shall shortly address, Modood correctly emphasises that the issue is not whether republicans should be concerned about civic loyalty, but how best this end can be achieved. His arguments are significant in light of the fact that the 'right to be different' has often been invoked in France by le Front National to justify the expulsion of Muslims (Hazareesingh 1994: 88); or has been considered unenforceable on the grounds that it is impossible to determine objectively what is involved in responding equitably to human differences (Laborde 2005: 314).

Lastly, Modood joins with other defenders of multicultural citizenship in challenging the republican emphasis on a stable world of public symbols, such as its national flag or language (Kymlicka and Norman 2000: 8). While republicans are not hostile in principle to expressions of difference in civil society in terms of language, dress and symbols, defenders of differentiated citizenship draw attention to the porous boundary between civil society and the public sphere. On their account, if the traditional dress of a minority is banned in public institutions, this act could be interpreted as 'an open declaration that some are not wanted as members of the state' (Levey 1997: 223). To Modood's mind, the (symbolic or actual) suppression of religious identity has the capacity to harm minority citizens if the restriction relates to images or practices that are perceived to define the group's self-conception, its source of collective pride or its 'mode of being' (Modood 2005: 99). Significantly, Modood invokes this term to explain the impassioned reaction of some Muslims against the portrayal of Mohammed in The Satanic Verses during the Rushdie Affair (ibid.: 112). The sense of humiliation and indignity arising from a ban on the hijab may be thought comparable, as it cannot but evoke movements of the colonial era, such as when Algerian women were unveiled by French women in a public event on 16 May 1958 (Bhabha 1986: viii). In light of these issues, Modood seems right to insist that 'citizenship is a number of coterminous processes: a framework of rights, practices of participation *and* ways of imagining . . . ourselves as a country' (Modood 2008). These claims present a convincing challenge to the republican criticisms of the veil in terms of civic loyalty – even if, as we shall see, the more subtle concerns raised from this perspective about the contextual nature of freedom remain to be addressed.

III RECIPROCITY, EDUCATIONAL ACCOMMODATION AND THE HIJAB

In order to see why the commitment to ensuring reciprocity yields a strong presumption in favour of accommodating the veil in the educational sphere, let us engage first with a potentially thorny problem with this commitment as we have conceived it so far. While reciprocity presupposes the possibility of uniting all persons in a common polity, regardless of the extent of value disagreements dividing them, Dagger usefully suggests that it need not demand thick consensus on a comprehensive conception of the good but only a sense of *fair play* (Dagger 1997: 46). This is to say that reciprocity demands only that anyone who takes part in a cooperative process must contribute to the production of its benefits. Following this account, the necessary condition for bringing about reciprocity between diverse citizens need only be that the laws of the state be minimally compatible with a citizen's deepest values, such that she is not alienated from state institutions and fails to have faith in their capacity to support her basic interests. This condition of non-alienation motivates a citizen to engage in public inter-actions without being stubborn, manipulative or dishonest. Put another way, non-alienation is the condition of civic reciprocity.

However, even if the commitment to reciprocity could be taken to be premised on the seemingly modest idea of non-alienation, a problem arises in relation to Modood's claim that religious and civic values are likely to be mutually supporting. What of the objection that the state cannot ensure the non-alienation of all citizens, because the notion of reciprocity is dependent on ideas of tolerance and equal dignity, to which not all belief systems subscribe? Republicans, as we have seen, are anxious about Islam's apparent rejection of a public–private distinction (Schapper 1991) and, thus, are wary of the possibility that this belief system opposes fundamental secular precepts. Modood replies, however, that moderate forms of Islam are compatible with a moderately secular state, and that the ideal of a relatively autonomous state historically shaped statecraft as much in the Muslim world as it did in European states (Modood 2005: 143–5). This claim is supported by the Turkish philosopher Ioanna Kuçuradi's characterisation of secularism not as a denial of religion but a 'temporal change' or an adjustment of religious faith to the 'experiences and exigencies of the age' (Kuçuradi 1999: 134). As this claim is well supported, Modood appears correct to insist that Muslims and republicans can both be secularists (Modood 2007: 77), and that adherents to Islam need not be alienated from a secular polity.

Yet a critic might insist that Islam's antipathy to, say, homosexuality conflicts with the egalitarianism of liberal states; and that this conflict undermines the possibility of evolving civic reciprocity between Muslims and secular citizens. The problem is equally reflected in the British Muslim Council's opposition to the repeal of 'Section 28' to allow schools to present same-sex marriages as valid alternatives (Modood and Ahmad 2007: 198). It is also evidenced in the belief of some Roman Catholics that the legal recognition of same-sex marriage would entail the state sanctioning the degradation of souls (see Wintemute 2002). These controversies emphasise that sexuality and the wider issue of sexual freedom are pivotal points of contention between liberals and many conservative religions; and, in the Muslim case, they highlight the opposition of this belief system to the liberal idea that all sexual orientations based on consent are worthy of respect. Modood concedes here that many Muslims would indeed find it hard to respect that which cannot be respected within Islam; and they would, therefore, not respect homosexuals as they do holders of different religious beliefs. However, he insists that Muslims can nonetheless tolerate homosexuals on the basis that each person has the right to his own sexual preferences. In contrast, liberals tend to respect sexual freedom but extend tolerance only to holders of different religious beliefs. Thus, Islam and liberalism 'distribute' tolerance and respect differently (Modood and Ahmad 2007: 199) but this difference does not alienate a Muslim from the values of a secular polity (see also Halstead 2005).

There are, however, a number of problems with this view. While I drew on it in Chapter 4 in order to challenge the prevalent liberal tendency to make somewhat stigmatising assumptions about minority faiths, a liberal state could be understood to demand equal respect between citizens and not mere tolerance. While you could 'merely' tolerate my beliefs, liberal principles require that you respect me as a citizen. Yet, if my sexual identity, or any other dimension of my identity, defines my personhood, it is not clear how my personal and civic values can be separated. To this extent, the distinction between toleration and respect is at least unstable in a liberal order. Furthermore, the state's acceptance of a Muslim's or Catholic's tolerance of homosexuality would appear to entail its acceptance of the claim that racists who do not persecute those whom they deem inferior are 'tolerant'. While the Muslim, the Catholic and the racist might *practise toleration* in the common-sense usage of the term, to the extent that they do not commit egregious harm that warrants legal intervention, the *virtue* of tolerance, strictly speaking, entails that a citizen's disapproval of that which they tolerate be justifiable in some sense (Horton 1996: 33). At the very least, the citizen must take responsibility for, by being ready to offer adequate grounds for, her disapproval of the conduct or identity that she opposes (see McKinnon 2006: 28–31). Here, what counts as a 'responsible belief' represents a thorny problem that cannot be ascertained in the abstract. Yet the crucial point for our purposes is that, apart from the difficulty of distinguishing tolerance from respect, simply restraining oneself from acting on one's prejudices does not obviously render one tolerant. These objections represent significant impediments to the claim that religious beliefs and secular values can generally be aligned in order to promote reciprocity between different groups. However, in a world in which states cannot determine a priori what counts as ethically responsible opposition to others' beliefs and identities, achieving reciprocity between diverse citizens might have to involve a provisional acceptance of a rough distinction between respect and tolerance, in Modood's common-sense usage of the term. This is so, even if part of what civic reciprocity should ideally involve is a willingness to *transform* one's beliefs through political engagement with others, and to participate in a discussion about what *should be* tolerated and respected (see Horton 1996: 37).

Thus, the commitment to reciprocity as non-alienation seems viable and important in the context of supporting the presumption for educational accommodation. While liberal states must recognise that tension can always arise between individual beliefs and political commitments (Spinner-Halev 2001a: 104), young citizens' core values should not be denigrated in or excluded from the educational sphere to a point that undermines their ability to engage with the state. If this is so, can we conclude with certainty that Muslim girls should be permitted to wear the hijab to school? Given that educational accommodation cannot be limitless, this issue should be ascertained by returning to the balancing test proposed in Chapter 4. The first question to consider is, to recall, that of *unjustified intolerance*. The rule to which a person objects would have to greatly burden her ability to commit to her private values. Now, on one view, it is difficult to accuse Muslim girls of unjustified intolerance, because the norms of piety and modesty traditionally justifying the hijab could indeed be matters of fundamental conscience even though there is, as Bennoune observes, an important difference between freedom of conscience (an internal affair) and freedom to manifest belief (an external matter) (Bennoune 2007). Poulter suggests that the issue be tested by means of English law's 'disproportionality' rule (Poulter 1997: 65), which holds that establishing whether a minority's claim is justifiable entails asking whether group-members are burdened by a rule in much greater proportion than members of the majority society. However, this means of testing 'justifiable intolerance' is not decisive if we consider that, while less than one per cent of the 500,000 female Muslim students in France wear the hijab (Silverman 1992: 145), one cannot therefore assume that the practice is of little consequence to those who do wear it. For one thing, it is likely that many young women do not wear it as a result of social pressures (Dwyer 1999). In sum, given the importance that secular states themselves attribute to the veil, it would be dubious to hold that Muslim girls who wish to wear the veil could easily compromise on this matter.

The hijab does not fall prey to the *subversion of formal rights* constraint either. It is not plausible to construe it as incitement to violence against other students in the way that wearing Nazi swastikas or black masks associated with American gang culture may be (Carens 2000: 139). It would also be implausible to object to it on the basis that its inclusion in a common school undermines the rights of other children to be treated with equal concern. While French Jews have also been historically required to de-emphasise their religious identity in the public sphere, it is unconvincing to claim that accommodating the hijab is anti-egalitarian, because the current ban on religious symbols does not prohibit small crucifixes or Stars of David, and, as I have said, because veils cannot be worn without being noticeable in French society (Galeotti 2002: 132). Finally, the claim that veiling jeopardises the rights of Muslims and others to a safe educational environment is uncompelling. In the Manchester controversy mentioned earlier, the school did contend that free-flowing veils endangered students in the science laboratory (Poulter 1997: 67). However, while such an objection could be plausible in relation to the burqa, in the case of the small hijab usually worn in France, the argument is, like the others under this heading, unpersuasive.

The most contentious question is, however, whether the veil falls prey to the *subversion of informal equality* objection, which I raised against *Mozert* in Chapter 4. Following the issues raised earlier in connection with the republican feminist critique, one could conceivably claim that *Mozert* and the hijab both involve students or parents who object to rules of which the rationale is to inculcate in young citizens a respect for sex equality. However, whilst the traditional symbolism of the veil cannot be disregarded, the assumption that it expresses sex inequality is contentious to a degree that the *Mozert* parents' proposal to shield their children from knowledge of progressive gender relations is not. Poulter is of course correct to say that a rule that seeks to prohibit the veil out of concerns for sexual equality would not be 'so unreasonable that no sensible person could subscribe to it' (Poulter (1997: 69); indeed, such a rule would be only too intelligible in Western societies, which typically associate the veil with oppression. However, 'modest dress' exemptions raise interpretive issues that should not be resolved by the state. What the veil signifies in terms of female identity is ambiguous to a point that, arguably, the state should not even assume that it is a religious symbol (al-Hibri 1982), or that, as a piece of cloth, it means anything at all. This is not to challenge the recent view of the European Court of Human Rights that national governments are generally better placed than supra-state bodies to determine whether a symbol poses threats to public order or to other citizens' rights (Bennoune 2007: 395). We can concede that states rightly have a 'margin of appreciation' on this issue (Hutchinson 1999) but still maintain that, in the context of ambiguity surrounding the extent of these threats, states should not interpret the meaning of minority symbols unilaterally. This is partly because, as I contended in Chapter 2, a liberal state must respond to the disadvantage that minorities experience in giving a 'voice' to values and meanings. In differentiating *Mozert* and the hijab on this basis, we need not disregard the fact that some evangelical women dispute their traditional identities in a way that is similar to the renegotiations of religious mandates undertaken by Muslim women (Bartkowski and Read 2003). However, the substance of *Mozert* falls prey to the 'subversion of informal equality' objection in a way that the hijab does not.

Moreover, consider the fact that Muslim women often reject the connotations of female inferiority that Westerners attribute to the veil, and that both sexes are enjoined in Islam to dress modestly (Franks 2000). Even if republicans are right to believe that special care should be taken to protect the equality of future citizens in the educational sphere, and that schools are a crucial environment in which they learn to think for themselves free from extraneous pressures, it is significant that the *Conseil d'État* refrains from interpreting religious doctrine and renounces the power to decide whether the hijab is gender discriminatory. The fact weakens the potential argument that, whatever emancipatory meaning Muslim women attribute to the veil, it is discriminatory in the eyes of the wider society. The point also draws attention to the possibility that, in prohibiting this symbol on the basis of its own interpretation of it, the state would deepen the discrimination that Muslim women encounter in the wider society. If these arguments are plausible, it then seems that banning the hijab in schools is ill considered. While these considerations do not allay all feminist concerns surrounding the conditions under which women adhere to their traditional practices, there is a strong case for the accommodation of this symbol in state education.

IV The Condition *and* Subject of Deliberation – the Hijab and the Right to Mediation

To appreciate the full significance of permitting the veil in schools, let us return to the group right to mediation. An additional reason for supporting the educational accommodation of the hijab is that it would most likely maintain young Muslim women in state education, and would therefore avail them of a greater opportunity to develop the understanding of ethical diversity necessary to participate in the dialogues of the right to mediation in the long term. One of the benefits of educational inclusion, then, would be that of enhancing Muslim women's capacities to participate in an interactive debate about their rights as adults to wear their religious symbols in their potential roles as public agents. This debate raises different issues from that concerning the right of students to wear religious symbols to school, as we shall see. While my defence of the right to mediation cannot, in itself, determine the precise way in which states should balance commitments to state neutrality and the religious freedoms of those who, as teachers, doctors and other civil servants, act in the name of the state, Muslim women's inclusion in a debate about this matter would, I contend, enhance the wider society's understanding of the issues at stake. The educational inclusion of the hijab is, then, likely to be a precondition for women's participation in mediation, even when the legitimacy of wearing hijab is the *subject* of the debate.

The point is important because in France all public agents are currently under a strict *'devoir de réserve'* (obligation of restraint) not to display signs of religious allegiance, in order that they show equal respect and impartiality to all users of state services. This principle was reasserted by the *Conseil d'État*'s statement in 2000 that *'laïcité* limits the right [of state agents] to express their religious convictions while engaged in public functions' (cited in *Stasi Report* 2). On this account, a Muslim tax inspector was recently banned from wearing the headscarf while on duty (Laborde 2005: 322). Such measures are not unique to France as, in Turkey, the veil has been prohibited in all public institutions since the 1920s (Secor 2005). It does not follow logically that, if the veil is deemed permissible in schools, there is no case for restricting public agents from wearing this garment, for it could be thought that public agents' duties are stronger than those of students who do not act in the name of the state. However, at the same time, *laïcité* holds that access to posts as public officials should be the same for all citizens, and that an application for a job as a school teacher or health professional cannot be rejected on the basis of the candidate's religion or culture (Auby 2001: 60). In this context, although the right to mediation cannot demand the equal representation of women in dialogue, if they do participate, the process would bring to light a balanced account of the interests of all parties when regulations concerning public sector neutrality are assessed. Indeed, it should be added here that Muslim women's articulation of the veil's meaning could have reoriented the Stasi Commission's recommendations, by undermining the contentious assumption that the women were too alienated to voice an independent perspective on this practice (Laborde 2006: 352). Their inclusion would have enabled the Commission to recognise that many believe that the veil affords women opportunities for going to university and that it can express self-protection against male pressure or rebellion against secular parents (Gaspard and Khosrokhavar 1995; Killian 2003). Listening to Muslim women's reasons for veiling would, in all likelihood, bring to light the porous borderline between liberal and non-liberal practices in a world of hyphenated or hybrid identities (Moruzzi 1994).

Whilst the practical difficulties involved in implementing group delibera-tion in a political culture that typically offers minorities only a limited voice must be acknowledged (Modood 2007: 75), let us proceed to consider the issues that could come to light in the event of an interactive political debate on this matter. At the preliminary stage of the dialogue where normative meanings are articulated, Muslim women could challenge republicans' account of the meaning of the veil, which relies on contentious interpreta-tions that are 'only based on a reconstruction of what . . . is thought to be known about Islam' (Laborde 2006: 361). Unsettling the received inter-pretation of veiling is important because that interpretation underwrites the case for religious restraint on the grounds that public agents should not demonstrate signs that connote inequality and unfreedom and, thus, which undermine their obligation to exhibit loyalty to republican values (Gau-demet 2000). Against this claim, Muslim women's testimonies could establish that, in view of the considerable pressure that exists in French society *not* to wear the veil, the choice to adopt it takes considerable courage, independence and personal autonomy (Laborde 2006: 361). Thus, this choice might express exactly the human capacities prized by the republican state. Dialogue could also highlight the extent to which Muslim women engage in feminist *ijtehad* (independent religious reasoning), which could yield a number of 'indigenous feminist' reasons for this practice, including the dignity that it offers and its tendency to ease the strain of multiple allegiances (ibid.: 363). To this degree, Muslim women's cultural reasons could form the basis of public reasons, which would help to liberate the debate from an exclusive focus on liberal conception of free choice (Chaudhary 2005: 362),[12] whilst also challenging the assumption that the symbol undermines republican values. One might of course object that, even without engaging in mediation, it is obvious that the veil has no single meaning for all women and that, while expressing its meanings in the public sphere is an interesting pursuit, this process cannot determine what public neutrality requires. However, it is important to see that attention to these alternative meanings, as empirically stated by women themselves, would alert all engaged in the debate to the precise reasons why they might be burdened by the state's insistence on a particular interpretation. These alternative meanings do not have abstract force or merit that stand free of the claims of real women. If neutrality is a principle of equality that ensures fairness, it is productive to acknowledge the possible (empirically stated) relationship of veiling to values such as equality and freedom from an insider's perspective. This is, in part, because states evidently do make assumptions about the meaning of this symbol; and, indeed, its 'over-determined' meaning is at the heart of the controversy about it (Galeotti 2002: 119).

Moving on to the second stage of the debate, Muslim women could also voice their views about the potential 'grave risks' to which wearing religious symbols as public agents might give rise. This is crucial because state institutions should treat agents and users alike with equal concern (Auby 2001: 66). It could therefore be thought contentious to allow teachers and other civil servants to wear the veil, if there is a serious risk of prejudice towards others. Yet the issue is complex because, just as it could be claimed that banning students from wearing the veil at schools is likely to perpetuate the inequality that it tries to combat by 'condemning Muslim girls to an almost certain educational death (*mort scolaire*)' (Laborde 2006: 360), restricting women from wearing the veil in their public roles in may lead to certain 'career death' for many and could undermine their equal opportunities for employment. In addition, while public schools under-standably seek to ensure that teachers do not show signs of prejudice, once again different considerations would need to be considered in dialogue with women themselves.[13] While the issue cannot be determined abstractly, one key question is why wearing any religious symbol should be believed to undermine the impartiality with which a schoolteacher carries out her role if, depending on the context, she may be the recipient of prejudice rather than the perpetrator of it. On the wider question of religious freedom in employment, Barry rightly contends that it would be unfair to take into consideration the wider society's negative perceptions of minority tradi-tions. However, in the case of public agents, it is more difficult to agree with his general point that the only question is whether a custom 'actually gets in the way of the efficient discharge of the task in hand' (Barry 2001: 60). It could be argued, for instance, that a student's perception of the meaning of a teacher's sectarian loyalty is relevant to determining the efficacy with which she carries out the function of her post.

However, recall that I argued in response to Shah Bano's case that, even if an injustice could be thought to arise through granting minority accommodation, the state should take steps to investigate whether the relevant problems could be addressed in ways that do not disproportionately burden those who adhere to minority values. In the debate about the veil, dialogue with Muslim women could reveal that providing equal rights to housing, employment and childcare might be more profitable than assuming that ensuring a just civil society must involve precluding public agents from demonstrating signs of religious allegiance. One reason for this is that the Islamophobia prevalent in European societies would hardly be addressed by sustaining the public view that to exhibit a sign of Muslim identity is ipso facto to oppose the state.[14] Moreover, recall that the final condition of the dialogue of mediation holds that, in the final analysis, any decision reached, such as a decision to allow Muslim schoolteachers to wear the hijab, should be revisited if it gives rise to serious threats to individual rights or public order at a later date. While the considerations raised here are speculative, the sketch they provide of potentially salient arguments demonstrates why the inclusion of Muslim women in the dialogues of the right to mediation is crucial. It emphasises, at least, that being female, a citizen *and* a Muslim is possible in a plural public sphere. In participating politically, they could challenge the official republican interpretation of neutrality, and assertions of their assumed sexual subordination (Cooke 2002: 158).

V ENDORSEMENT, FEMINIST CRITIQUE AND CITIZENS' RECIPROCAL INTERESTS

In conclusion, we can press harder on arguments from civic reciprocity to show that the advantages gained by Muslim women's inclusion in the dialogues of mediation speak to the deepest concerns raised by republican feminists. Their worries about the pressures on young women to adopt the veil in France today are compelling, even banning this symbol in school is not a persuasive response to them. To be specific, women's engagement in the dialogues of mediation promises to enable a cross-cultural dialogue about subtle issues arising from patriarchal social constraints to which all citizens should respond collectively, even if these constraints may not amount to extreme coercion requiring direct intervention in the form of prohibitive legislation, as discussed in Chapter 3. This final stage of my discussion therefore emphasises a further sense in which attention to cultural particularity provides a critical lens on universal issues of gender subordination as the subject of collective feminist concern.

As we saw in earlier chapters, if the category 'woman' is simply taken to designate a constituted group with uniform interests, then our assumption threatens to erase the complexities of how people suffer discrimination and exercise agency across cultures, by 'finding oppression a priori' (Young 1994: 715; see also Mohanty 1991). However, as I also explained at the outset, Young does not reject the possibility that the structures of gender subordination are real and, in a certain sense, universal. In fact, she leaves room for the possibility of recognising a creative interplay between the particularity and universality of women's interests. Accepting her insights in the context of the debate considered here indicates that the right to mediation could enhance women's collective awareness of subtle issues concerning patriarchal social control across cultures. In particular, it could involve women's common understanding of how their *reciprocal interests* in avoiding domination and in endorsing their decisions might be protected. To support this view, recall Young's criticism of Spelman's conception of 'multiple genders' (Spelman 1988: 170-8), or the assumption that gender-relations are structured entirely within a class, race or any other social group. This approach, Young contends, wrongly assumes the stability of communities in a world in which all groups are relationally constituted and internally differentiated (Young 1995). Moreover, the assumption of 'multiple genders' obscures the fact that gender discrimination often cuts across different groups. It is not true, for instance, that a Muslim woman's gendered experience is properly identified only by comparing her situation to Muslim men, since much of her experience is also likely to be conditioned by her relation to men and women in the wider world. Therefore, while women cannot be said to be a self-conscious group, they are likely to have what Sartre calls 'unity in flight', or a passive unity discernible through the bearing that their actions have on material and practico-inert histories that partially transcend their local context. To understand women as a *latent* group, then, keeps in view the possibility of evolving mutual concern between citizens through dialogue.

While the conditions for a politically responsible dialogue between diverse women are hard to actualise for reasons that I shall shortly explain, the possibility of locating common concerns on subtle issues of gender domination is vital. Doing so would respond to republican feminist anxieties concerning the matrix of factors that might, in some cases, inhibit women from truly endorsing their decisions to wear the veil. To be sure, it is implausible to claim that the hijab limits women's freedom in the direct sense that being forced into marriage is likely to do. However, given the complexity of the pressures to which Muslim women are often subject in this respect, it is necessary to acknowledge the social constraints that might shape their choices. As Bennoune argues, 'headscarves . . . cannot be seen as mere innocent symbols of personal religious beliefs nor simply flags for gender discrimination' (Bennoune 2007: 391). This is because the contexts in which choices are made are always relevant to determining questions of freedom and force. While it is true that constraints on choice are ubiquitous, republican concerns about social domination indicate that we need to go beyond the extreme view that conceives veiling as oppressive per se, as well as the defensive response that holds that any criticism of the conditions under which it is adopted is imperialistic (Green 2006: 37). While legal prohibitions are usually not a credible response to subtle pressures that all individuals might experience in an imperfect world, focusing on these factors supports a broader project of responding to all citizens' *reciprocal interests* in endorsing their decisions.

This point can be supported further by considering Reidy's contention that it does not suffice to conceive the legitimacy of a liberal order solely in terms of the notion of *reciprocity of justification* (Reidy 2007). Legitimacy does not only rest on citizens' capacities to justify the polity, but also on the capacity of state institutions to protect important human interests. Following Rawls, Reidy argues that all citizens have 'reciprocal' interests in freedom of expression and social primary goods. Drawing from Habermas, Forst argues similarly in favour of 'reciprocal' or universal rights (Forst 2001). It is worth pressing harder on this idea, however, since Reidy and Forst arguably do not acknowledge fully the interplay between the particularity and universality of human interests. Reciprocal interests should be viewed not in terms of a set of thick liberal goods or procedural freedoms but as the interests of all citizens to endorse their decisions, whatever they may be. An interest theory of rights that responds to feminism and multiculturalism must be critical of situations in which individuals take decisions out of fear and anxiety and act in ways that they do not endorse, as we saw in Chapter 3.

My point in emphasising the social pressures on some French Muslim women to take up the veil is not to undercut my previous argument in favour of accommodating this symbol in schools. Moreover, the violence that has been committed against unveiled Muslim girls should be separated from the question of veil's legitimacy per se.[15] However, the struggle against patriarchy is a legitimate ground for all women, and all citizens. Laborde rightly warns that celebrating 'a postmodern sociology of subjectivity that reduces agency to the individual "negotiation" . . . of different normative orders . . . potentially legitimizes the perpetuation of domination' (Laborde 2006: 367). If the psychological use of force can be just as potent as physical pressure, the complex matrix of social conditions under which religious and cultural conventions are taken up raise inescapable feminist questions. In this context, the inclusion of Muslim women in the dialogues of the right to mediation could lead to productive discussion about the subtle structural constraints that they experience and, in the long term, could enhance the strategies for resisting and overcoming them. The potential domination of these fora by male community elites could be mitigated by ensuring women-only focus groups in certain situations on the issue of social pressures on individuals and the measures, in addition to education, that could counter-act them. Much care would have to be exercised to ensure that the dialogue does not merely confirm intellectualised reactions against practices such as the veil, nor entrench stereotypes, such as the 'false equation of Terrorist = Fundamentalist = Muslim = Veiled Woman' (Bennoune 2007: 394). However, the need for a serious discussion of the relevant issues is high-lighted by considering Hirschmann's analysis of Abu-Lughod's study of the veiling practices of Bedouin women (Hirschmann 1988). Abu-Lughod claims that, for the Bedouin, veiling is seen as an expression of indepen-dence; and women view their segregation as honourable, since it signifies that they do not need the company of men (Abu-Lughod 1986: 84). While Hirschmann concedes that this study gives pause to Western anxieties that the veil undermines women's autonomy, she also expresses the concern that women who interpret veiling in an emancipatory light, just as those who believe that they freely choose to wear cosmetics or miniskirts, do not necessarily acknowledge the structures that mandate these choices. While conceding that Western women's criticisms of the veil often undermine the attempts of Muslim women to affect change in their communities (see Ahmed 1992), she maintains that it would be contentious not to engage in a deeper inquiry because:

> how much leeway most women really have [about whether to veil] is hazy because [these decisions are made] within normative parameters which women may support through their actions, but have not created . . . Abu-Lughod rightly asserts that 'veiling is voluntary' . . . but the fact of cultural sanction . . . means this choice is to some significant degree coerced. (Hirschmann, 2003: 357)

I do not cite Hirschmann here in order to make the implausible suggestion that the situation of Bedouin and that of immigrant women in France can be perfectly aligned. Rather, my point is to emphasise her key insight that women of all cultural locations might do well to question the assumption that, because they re-appropriate the meaning of their practices in creative or non-traditional ways, their decisions therefore raise no issues of justice. Whatever meaning individual Muslim women independently locate in veiling, patriarchy may be pervasive enough to ensure that it 'remains invested with meanings of purity, suggesting a fragile heterosexual desirability' (Dwyer 1999: 18). Given that the veil is heavily laden with connotations ranging from eroticism to political fanaticism, it is likely to be almost impossible for an individual to control the meaning that she wishes to communicate, not least because symbolic meanings often exceed individual capacities (ibid.). This point does not lead us to the extreme and counter-intuitive conclusion that the decision to wear this symbol can never be classified as free (Abu-Odeh 1993). However, a full recognition of the complexity of this issue involves retaining a Foucauldian understanding of the fact that social control can work through the 'colonization of desire', and the redefinition of coercion as freedom (Hirschmann 2003: 357; see Foucault 1983). It entails keeping in mind the subtle influences of power which liberal theories of autonomy generally fail to acknowledge (Hirschmann 2003: 38; Chambers 2008). While these subtle influences are pervasive, there is reason to think that they sometimes require a collective feminist response. Thus, if an interest theory of rights is to react appropriately to the deepest issues of structural disadvantage presented by women's choices to comply with community norms, it would be productive to use the civic fora made available by the right to mediation as a means to discuss the relevant issues.

This point can emphasised further in the case of the hijab by considering the decisions of the Cairene women, discussed by MacLeod, who veil in order to earn a living without unwanted attention from men (MacLeod 1991). 'Rather than placing the blame . . . on to men [for harassing unveiled women],' Hirschmann observes, 'women accommodate by altering their dress to fit the prevailing norm' (Hirschmann 2003: 359). Clearly, if autonomy is culturally constituted, as I argued in Chapter 3, there is no neat theoretical solution to this problem. At the minimum, it is important to protect the opportunities of all citizens who participate in dialogue to ask whether their negotiations of their traditions reproduce power relations rather than effect real change in terms of equality (MacLeod 1991: 15). Instituting dialogue about these issues is clearly a difficult endeavour in practice, since it involves ensuring, first and foremost, that women do not feel alienated from their communities or challenged on key questions of faith. Moreover, in the case we are considering, since it is precisely racism or religious prejudice that often makes it hard for Muslim women to discard a defensive attitude, feminists may seem naive to assume that increased understanding can be evolved through cross-cultural dialogue. As Hirschmann suggests, 'given that Muslim women's networks have specifically engaged in cross-cultural exchange amongst Muslim countries to challenge gender-oppressive laws as non-Islamic, perhaps Western feminists should simply stay out of the matter' (Hirschmann 2003: 197). Yet recall Said's point in Chapter 4 that 'indigenous' feminist movements that seal themselves entirely from a broader engagement with movements for social justice *may* end up as discriminatory as the apparently elite discourses that they contest. Therefore, on the assumption that cross-cultural dialogue does indeed have value, it should be stressed that approaching the issue of the hijab must involve, at the minimum, a concession on the part of Western women that the veil does not hinder equality and autonomy in principle any more than their own garments, and that liberal societies continue to support patriarchy. As a condition of reciprocal debate, all citizens would have a responsibility to recognise that 'the veiled woman' is no more dominated in principle than they themselves may be. Under these conditions, women might, as Elspeth Probyn puts it, 'speak with attitude' – that is, speak not merely about themselves or the other but 'speak *within the space* between [themselves] and other selves' (Probyn 1993: 140, my emphasis).

While I therefore concede its demanding political conditions in the real world, cross-cultural dialogue between women should be seen as a dynamic possibility promised by the framework of rights defended in this book. As Bennoune insists, a broad concern for gender equality should remain at the heart of the debate about the veil, precisely because one of the consequences of Islamophobia can be the 'silencing of self-criticism and the slide into defending the indefensible' (Bennoune 2007: 382). Here, dialogue would increase a polity's understanding of the systemic nature of gender subordination, and would enable women to transcend their serialised position on certain issues. The point would not be to dismiss Muslim women who counter Western stereotypes by claiming that the veil is a fashion accessory rather than a capitulation to a conservative ideology. Instead, it is to recognise together that the Western fashion/beauty complex poses barriers to women's access to citizenship and justice too (Chambers 2008). The purpose is to acknowledge different cultural configurations of power and to identify, through the exchange of experiences, issues that warrant a collective response. From the spectacle of sati to the subtlety of the hijab, the various debates that we have entered into in this book indicate that, while women's reactions to their gendered identities cannot be generalised, their actions are likely to be united in a web of histories that are related to material structures such as the division of labour and normative heterosexuality (Young 1994:

738; Stone 2004). Thus, Hirschmann rightly characterises cross-cultural communication as 'global feminism's most radical card' (Hirschmann 2003: 196); and postcolonial writers such as Bulbeck (1998), Spivak (1990) and Gunning (1992) similarly recommend a dialogue which both recognises the similarity of the other, as well as her separation from oneself as a result of power-relations. As Spivak insists, 'there has to be a simultaneous other focus: not merely who am I? but who is the other woman? How am I naming her? How does she name me?' (Spivak, cited in Hardacre and Manderson 1990: 17). There has to be an awareness, in other words, of Foucault's 1983 point that emancipation begins in the recognition that the more one resists one's context, the more one inscribes oneself in the terms of its power.

Admittedly, hard questions persist concerning how common problems could be addressed. While addressing all policy questions lies outside the purview of this book, my aim in this concluding section has been to reinforce the central claim that a rights-protecting state requires a politically responsible dialogue, as a state cannot guarantee high-priority entitlements if it fails to engage with the normative perspectives of those to whom they apply. Whilst the elasticity of rights discourse suggests its radical potential, rights are, in themselves, too abstract to determine when state intervention promotes or denies justice. Rights are not trumps in any straightforward sense, as I argued in Chapter 1, but are continually mediated by those whose lives they regulate. Women's participation in the dialogues of mediation is therefore crucial because experiences of the post-war era give the lie to the idea that patriarchy or racism entirely wither away through increased state regulation or the provision of economic rights. While I do not disregard the importance of such rights and, on the contrary, have emphasised their role in responding to gender injustice in different contexts, I emphasise that securing gender and cultural justice simultaneously involves recognising that human beings require differentiated, as well as a universal, baskets of goods.

We have seen that, although a commitment to fostering political deliberation per se does not guarantee individuals' freedom from coercion, to defend deliberation as a condition for discovering the meaning of rights is apt. One reason for this it is that more state intervention would not bring about a condition of Promethean freedom or unfettered individual choice. This is not only because there is no non-sinister sense in which we can be 'forced to be free', as Berlin warned, but also because choice is practically always mediated by cultural expectations, social norms or religious beliefs. Therefore, protecting women's reciprocal civic interests requires an inclusive dialogue that recognises the cultural particularity of interests and vulnerabilities as well as their relation to universal structures of gender hierarchy. The purpose of dialogue in relation to the veil would not be to determine whether this symbol is as oppressive as Western fashion or to assert simply, with some neo-Foucauldians, that, since all individuals are subject to social control, the very notion of choice is impossible. While unfettered choice is indeed highly unlikely in all but the rarest cases, the framework of rights that we have defended confronts the problem of choice in a non-ideal world directly, takes human beings as it finds them, and engages with them in their particularity. It begins with the 'ontological starting point of multiplicity' (Pedwell 2007), in an attempt to theorise the claims of all citizens and, through such reciprocal concern, to struggle for justice and, eventually, common ground.

VI CONCLUSION

In this final chapter, I have affirmed the importance of configuring women's rights as multicultural claims in political philosophy, undertaking this task by appealing to ideas of civic reciprocity. In doing so, I have sought to avoid the disciplining of minority communities that often accompanies republican accounts of citizenship, without capitulating to 'the indifference of an overly legalistic liberalism' (Benhabib 2004: 297) that is often accused of prioritising individuals' rights to satisfy their preferences in a superficial sense. My arguments against banning the veil in the educational sphere were grounded in the long-term benefits accruing from Muslim women's engagement in mediation. Such engagement would enhance all citizens' awareness of the need to protect reciprocal civic interests in endorsing their decisions. By thinking critically but sympathetically about the diverse experiences of women who 'bargain with patriarchy' (Kandiyoti 1988), and by examining the different patterns of disadvantage arising in relation to the material structures of gender subordination, opportunities for solidarity and change could evolve. While the dialogue recommended here admittedly requires conditions of mutuality and reciprocity between citizens that are often elusive in the real world, retaining faith in the endeavour is important, precisely in view of our common residence in an imperfect world.

NOTES

1. Law No. 2004-22 of 15 March 2004. Journal Officiel de la République Francaise (JO) [Official Gazette of France] 17 March 2004, p. 5190.
2. 'And tell the believing women to lower their gaze and be modest and to display their adornment only that which is apparent, and to draw their veils over their bosoms' (Qur'an, sura 24, ajat 3).
3. R v. Governors of Denbigh High School [2006] UKHL 15.

4. The Muslim population of France has been estimated at 5 million, though it is impossible to ascertain this figure because the French government does not officially categorise citizens in terms of ethnicity.

5. To be clear, I am not proposing that mediation would only involve women. See Section V, below.

6. The Stasi Commission was composed of twenty experts, mostly lawyers and academics, who interviewed educational and religious representatives over three months (see the 'Stasi Report' at http://lesrapports.ladocumentation-francaise.fr/BRP/034000725/0000/pdf).

7. The cases that have been taken to the European Court of Human Rights (for example, *Leyla Sahin* v. *Turkey* European Court of Human Rights Grand Chamber, Application no. 44774/98, 10 November 2005) have involved adult women who have alleged violations of Articles 8 (right to private life), 9 (right to religious expression), 10 (freedom of expression) and Article 2 of Protocol 1 (right to education).

8. Republicans historically attempted to appease Catholic hostility towards the Separation Law by allowing them the free use of state-owned churches (Kaltenbach and Tribalat, 2002: 118).

9. See Bennoune 2007: 414, citing 'French Muslims Fail to Enter Mainstream and Suffer from Poverty, Discrimination and Sexism' (National Public Radio Broadcast, 26 February 2003).

10. Thanks to John Horton for this point.

11. It is worth emphasising that this exact phrase is my own, and is not found in Modood's writings.

12. On one view, authorities try 'to make out that the hijab is a religious symbol but it is much more that. It is compulsory for practising Muslim women' (Mitchell, 2004).

13. In the UK, Aishah Azmi, a teaching assistant was refused the right to wear niqab at work and was dismissed from her position, even though she was awarded £1,100 in compensation for indirect discrimination (see 'Schools Sack Woman After Veil Row', BBC News 24 November 2006). In *Dahlab* v. *Switzerland* [Application No. 42393/98 15th February 2001], a Muslim Swiss schoolteacher took her case concerning dismissal to the European Court of Human Rights. The Court found that the ban pursued legitimate aims, namely the freedom of others and public order. The court also asked whether the restriction is relevant, sufficient and proportionate to the law's aim, and concluded that 'it cannot be denied that the wearing of a headscarf might have some kind of proselytising effect'.

14. To be sure, the Stasi Commission recognised that banning the veil would not remedy all the problems encountered by minority communities. It listed at least twenty further reforms aimed at improving the social position of minority groups.

15. The organisation 'Neither Whores nor Submissives' was formed in the wake of the immolation of a Muslim girl in a garbage receptacle in a Paris suburb in 1993. One of the reasons given for her murder was allegedly her refusal to submit to the pressures to wear the veil.

Epilogue

Women's rights are, then, best conceived as multicultural claims. The idea behind this proposition is not simply the evident point that human beings are diverse, but that there is a crucial interplay to be revealed between the interests of women in their lived social contexts and universal ideals of gender justice. In recognising this interplay, attention to the particular in an interest theory of rights should be taken as a means to reconfigure taken-for-granted assumptions of universal justice at any given historical time. Moreover, attending to a back-and-forth interplay between the universal an the particular (Benhabib 2002) helps to defuse the assumption of a fundamental conflict between rights to sex equality and cultural autonomy in liberal theory, and its concomitant assumption that the goods pursued by members of non-liberal cultures are, in some sense, exceptionally sexist, irrational, unreasonable or exceptionally discriminatory. While it is un-doubtedly true that few liberals would deny that rights must be interpreted in the light of actual human beings' experiences, emphasising the complex-ities involved in doing so enables us to respond to charges within feminism concerning substitutionalism, as well as to the now pervasive question of whether multiculturalism is bad for women. By exploring issues arising in liberal states around the world, each of which appears to exemplify the 'dilemma' that liberal philosophers perceive at the intersection of commit-ments to gender equality and cultural diversity, I presented women's rights as inherently multicultural by building upon Young's account of the 'serialised' condition of women's existence. From that conceptual starting point, I defended an interest theory of rights that integrates feminist and multicultural discourses in a world of imperfectly reconcilable values and uneven relations of power.

While the issues surrounding the recognition of minority divorce in India in Chapter 2 demonstrated that a deliberative approach could usefully reveal the cultural particularity of women's interests, such an approach does not necessarily suffice where structural inequalities run so deep that women lack the ability to speak out in political debate. The imperative for intercultural deliberation must therefore be supplemented by the universal protection of rights to self-direction and the substantive capacities of all individuals to challenge underlying disadvantages and power disparities that sometimes manifest themselves in acutely harmful practices such as forced marriage, as we saw in Chapter 3. While my exploration of education and the issues raised by the hijab led to the conclusion that women's serialised condition should not rule out the possibility of evolving common feminist responses to subtle constraints arising from patriarchy cross-culturally, this dimension of the interplay between universality and particularity in feminist justice accepts that there may be political factors – not least the delight with which the international media reports dramatic instances of violence against minority women – that undermine efforts to redress structural inequalities collectively. Thus, the full complexity of the issues raised by the idea of 'women's rights as multicultural claims' is clarified in the various debates that we have considered – sati, divorce, forced marriage, civic education and the veil.

The theoretical insights of this study are twofold. First, in a world characterised by unequal power and imperfectly reconcilable values, attention to the particularity of women's interests and vulnerabilities provides a critical corrective to the tendency of liberal feminists to respond to the issues confronting women of different cultural contexts simply by redoubling efforts to apply uniform or similar laws. The basket of goods protected under their ideal account of gender identity typically contains a capacity to make non-conformist choices and to achieve material success in a market economy. Liberal feminists tend to take these goods to constitute the essence of gender justice, from which minority practices are taken to deviate especially. This assumption underlies Okin's forceful assertion that the problems of 'other women' are like 'ours', only *more so*. Yet the universal purchase of liberal feminist ideals is continually unsettled by women who sometimes reject the secular egalitarianism of liberalism and, rationally and plausibly, de-emphasise the pursuit of liberal autonomy and economic prosperity in favour of other goods. Women's priorities and goals differ across (contested and permeable) cultural, religious and ethnic boundaries, as do the forms of discrimination that they experience. It cannot always be assumed that women of the majority society suffer less discrimination than those in minority groups, since oppression is often not a matter of physical severity or quantity, but of modality. Thus, the simple effort to protect women through uniform rights does not always respond adequately to women's interests and vulnerabilities.

The second crucial insight arising from this book's central proposition is that the cultural particularity of women's experiences relate in meaningful ways to structures of gender subordination that exist across cultures. This underlying awareness of the systemic nature of gender inequality, and, therefore, of the implausibility of blaming culture for bad behaviour, encourages feminists to conceptualise women as connected, not necessarily in terms of everyday objectives but in terms of webs or 'chains' of an ongoing history (Stone 2004). One basic rationale behind stressing this interconnectedness is the fact that the gendered experience of a native American, Muslim or Mormon woman cannot be fully understood by examining gender relations within her community, as she may be subject to discrimination at work or sexual harassment in the wider society too. One might argue, then, that women's experiences of disadvantage cross-culturally are united through the bearing that their actions commonly have upon material structures such as the sexual division of labour and their rule-bound bodies. To argue that women's rights are multicultural claims is therefore not to reject the universality of ideals of gender justice or to deny that these ideals should be pursued institutionally through a schedule of high-priority rights. However, it urges consciousness of the situated-ness and historicity of any conception of justice, which must, in the final analysis, give rise to the question: 'What is the *genealogy* of the essentializing discourse that established a normative feminist subject, woman, that excluded, devalued, or found deviant the lives of many women?' (Young 1994: 717, my emphasis).

As claims concerning 'multiple genders' fail to grasp the complexity of the relation between women's differences and similarities internationally, a more nuanced approach is needed in feminist theory, involving a strong commitment to universality that is continually mediated by the claims of cultural particularity. In a multicultural world, feminists need to attempt to 'see connections', in the Wittgensteinian sense, between local experiences of gender disadvantage and a broader, cosmopolitan view of the issues at stake. Feminism is a fighting creed that must be continually, and universally, critical of oppression and injustice. However, it gains its strength and credibility through its capacity to engage with the concerns, beliefs and priorities that structure the lives of diverse human beings. Where certainty about the ideal form of justice is unavailable, we may at least presume the universal *relevance* of aiming at the ideal. By bracketing the question of ultimate, justificatory truth, but by keeping faith in the pursuit of the ideal, multicultural states can defend a schedule of rights for all in imperfect conditions, mindful of their ultimate historicity.

Bibliography

Abraham, M. (2000), *Speaking the Unspeakable: Marital Violence among South Asian Immigrants in the United States*, Piscataway: Rutgers University Press.

Abu-Lughod, Lila (1986), *Veiled Sentiments*, Berkeley: University of California Press.

Abu Odeh, Lama (1993), 'Postcolonial Feminism and the Veil', *Feminist Review*, 43, pp. 26–37.

Ackerman, Bruce (1980), *Social Justice in the Liberal State*, New Haven: Yale University Press.

Agarwal, Bina (1988), *Structures of Patriarchy: State, Community and Household in Modernising Asia*, London: Zed Books.

Ahmad, Fauzia, Tariq Modood and Stephen Lissenburgh (2003), *South Asian Women and Employment in Britain*, London: Policy Studies Institute.

Ahmad, Imtiaz (2003), *Divorce and Remarriage among Muslims in India*, Delhi: Manohar.

Ahmed, Leila (1982), 'Feminism and Feminist Movements in the Middle East', in Azizah al-Hibri (ed.), *Women and Islam*, New York: Pergamon Press.

Ahmed, Leila (1992), *Women and Gender in Islam*, New Haven: Yale University Press.

Akhtar, S. (1991), *The Final Imperative*, London: Bellew Publishing.

Aks, Judith (2004), *Women's Rights in Native North America*, New York: LFB Scholarly Publishing.

al-Hibri, Azizah (1982), 'A Study of Islamic Herstory: Or How Did We Ever Get into this Mess?', in Azizah al-Hibri (ed.), *Women and Islam*, New York: Pergamon Press.

al-Hibri, Azizah (1999), 'Is Western, Patriarchal Feminism Good for Third-World/ Minority Women?', in S. M. Okin (with respondents), pp. 41–7.

Ali, S. S. (2000), *Gender and Human Rights in Islam and International Law*, The Hague: Kluwer.

Alibali, A. (2004), 'French ban on faith symbols would contravene international rights law', 13 February 2004 (available at www.alb-net.com/pipermail.albsa-info/2004-Februrary/003483.html).

Alibhai-Brown, Yasmin (2000a), *After Multiculturalism*, London: Foreign Policy Centre.

Alibhai-Brown, Yasmin (2000b), 'The Truth about Forced Marriage', *The Guardian*, 3 July 2000, p. 3.

Amanpour, Christiane (2005), 'French Riot Police "Beat Youths"', 10 November 2005 (available at www.cnn.com/2005/WORLD/europe/11/10/france.riots.index.html).

Amato, P. R. (1994), 'The Impact of Divorce on Men and Women in India and the United States', *Journal of Comparative Family Studies*, 24:2, 207–21.

Amiri, Rina (2001), 'Muslim Women as Symbols and Pawns', *New York Times*, 27 November 2001, p. 1.

An-Na'im, Abdullahi (1999a), 'The Cultural Mediation of Human Rights', in Joanne Bauer and David A. Bell (eds), pp. 147–68.

An-Na'im, Abdullahi (1999b), 'Promises We Should All Keep in Common Cause', in S. M. Okin (with respondents), pp. 59–65.

Anthias, Floya, (2002), 'Beyond Feminism and Multiculturalism', *Women's Studies International Forum*, 25:3, pp. 275–86.

Arneil, Barbara, Monique Deveaux, Rita Dhamoon and Avigail Eisenberg (eds) (2006), *Sexual Justice/Cultural Justice*, London: Routledge.

Arneson, R. 1989, 'Equality and Equal Opportunity for Welfare, *Philosophical Studies*, 56, pp. 77–93.

Arneson, R. and I. Shapiro (1996), 'Democratic Autonomy and Religious Freedom', in I. Shapiro and R. Hardin (eds), *NOMOS 38: Political Order*, New York: New York University Press, pp. 356–411.

Attwood, Bain (1992), 'Introduction', in Attwood Bain and John Arnold (eds), *Power, Knowledge and Aborigines*, Melbourne: La Trobe.

Auby, Jean-Bernard (2001), 'Administrative Law in France', in R. Seerden and F. Stroink (eds), *Administrative Law of the European Union*, Antwerp: Intersentia, pp. 59–89.

Audi, Robert and Nicholas Wolterstorff (eds) (1997), *Religion in the Public Square*, London: Rowman and Littlefield.

Babb, Lawrence A. (1975), *The Divine Hierarchy*, New York: Columbia University Press.

Babbitt, Susan (1993), 'Feminism and Objective Interests', in Linda Alcoff and Elizabeth Potter (eds), *Feminist Epistemologies*, New York: Routledge, pp. 245–64.

Bader, Veit (2005), 'Associative Democracy and Minorities within Minorities', in A. Eisenberg and J. Spinner-Halev (eds), pp. 319–39.

Badinter, Elisabeth (1989), Interview with L. Joffin, *Le Nouvel Observateur*, pp. 9–15 November 1989, pp. 7–11.

Badinter, Elisabeth (2003), *Fausse route*, Paris: Odile Jacob.

Bainham, Andrew (1995), 'Family Law in a Pluralistic Society', *Journal of Law and Society*, 22:2, pp. 234–47.

Baker, Nancy, Peter Gregware and Margery Cassidy (1999), 'Family Killing Fields: Honor Rationales in the Murder of Women', *Violence against Women*, 5:2, pp. 164–84.

Balibar, Etienne (2004), 'Dissonance dans la laïcité', *Mouvements*, 33:34, pp. 148–61.

Ballard, Roger (ed.) (1994), *Desh Pardesh: The South Asian Presence in Britain*, London: Hurst & Co.

Bannerji, H. (2000), *The Dark Side of the Nation: Essays on Multiculturalism, Nationalism and Gender*, Toronto: Canadian Scholars' Press.

Barlow, Tani (2000), 'International Feminism of the Future', *Signs*, 25:4, pp. 1094–105.

Barry, Brian (1995), 'John Rawls and the Search for Stability', *Ethics*, 105:4, pp. 874–915.

Barry, Brian (1996), 'Spherical Justice and Global Injustice', in David Miller and Michael Walzer (eds), *Pluralism, Justice and Equality*, Oxford: Oxford University Press, pp. 67–78.

Barry, Brian (2001), *Culture and Equality*, Cambridge: Polity Press.

Bartkowski, J. P. (1999), 'One Step Forward, One Step Back: "Progressive Traditionalism" and the Negotiation of Domestic Labor within Evangelical Families', *Gender Issues*, 17:4, pp. 40–64.

Bartowski, John P. and Jen'nan Ghazal Read (2003), 'Veiled Submission: Gender, Power and Identity among Evangelical and Muslim Women in the United States', *Qualitative Sociology*, 26:1, pp. 71–92.

Bates, Stephen (1993), *Battleground: One Mother's Crusade, the Religious Right and the Struggle for Control of our Classrooms*, New York: Simon and Schuster.

Bauer, Joanne and Daniel Bell (eds) (1999), *The East Asian Challenge for Human Rights*, Cambridge: Cambridge University Press.

Baum, Bruce (2004), 'Feminist Politics of Recognition', *Signs*, 29:4, pp. 1073–102.

Baumeister, Andrea (1998), 'Cultural Diversity and Education: The Dilemma of Political Stability', *Political Studies*, 46:5, pp. 919–36.

Baumeister, Andrea (2000), *Liberalism and the 'Politics of Difference'*, Edinburgh: Edinburgh University Press.

Baumeister, Andrea (2003a), 'The Limits of Universalism', in Bruce Haddock and Peter Sutch (eds), *Multiculturalism, Identity and Rights*, London: Routledge.

Baumeister, Andrea, (2003b), 'Habermas: Discourse and Cultural Diversity', *Political Studies*, 51:4, pp. 740–58.

Baumeister, Andrea (2003c), 'Ways of Belonging: Ethnonational Minorities and Models of Differentiated Citizenship', *Ethnicities*, 3:3, pp. 369–92.

Baumeister, Andrea (2006), 'Gender Equality and Cultural Justice: The Limits of Transformative Accommodation', *Critical Review of International Social and Political Philosophy*, 9:3, pp. 399–417.

Bell, Daniel (1993), *Communitarianism and its Critics*, Oxford: Clarendon.

Bellah, R. N., R. Madsen, W. M. Sulllivan, A. Swidler and S. M. Tipton, (1985), *Habits of the Heart*, Berkeley: University of California Press.

Bendroth, M. L. (1993), *Fundamentalism and Gender, 1875 to the Present*, New Haven: Yale University Press.

Benhabib, Seyla (2002), *The Claims of Culture*, Princeton: Princeton University Press.

Benhabib, Seyla (2004), *The Rights of Others*, Cambridge: Cambridge University Press.

Benn, Stanley (1988), *A Theory of Freedom*, New York: SUNY Press.

Bennoune, Karima (2007), 'Secularism and Human Rights: A Contextual Analysis of Headscarves, Religious Expression and Women's Equality under International Law', *Columbia Journal of Transnational Law*, 45:2, pp. 376–99.

Benson, Paul (1990), 'Feminist Second Thoughts about Free Agency', *Hypatia*, 5:3, pp. 47–64.

Benson, Paul (1991), 'Autonomy and Oppressive Socialization', *Social Theory and Practice*, 17:3, pp. 385–408.

Benson, Paul (2005), 'Taking Ownership', in John Christman and Joel Anderson (eds), *Autonomy and the Challenges to Liberalism*, Cambridge: Cambridge University Press, pp. 101–26.

Berlin, Isaiah (1969), 'Two Concepts of Liberty', in Isaiah Berlin, *Four Essays on Liberty*, Oxford: Oxford University Press, pp. 167–72.

Bhabha, Homi (1986), 'Remembering Fanon', in Franz Fanon, *Black Skin, White Masks*, London: Pluto Press, pp. vii–xxvi.

Bhabha, Homi (1999), 'Liberalism's Sacred Cow', in S. M. Okin (with respondents), pp. 79–84.

Bhabha, Homi (2000), 'On Minorities: Cultural Rights', *Radical Philosophy*, 100, pp. 3–6.

Bhardwaj, A. (2001), 'Growing Up Young, Asian and Female in Britain: A Report on Self-Harm and Suicide', *Feminist Review*, 68:1, pp. 52–67.

Bhopal, Kalwant (1989), 'South Asian Women and Arranged Marriages in East London', in R. Barot, H. Bradley and S. Fenton (eds), *Ethnicity, Gender and Social Change*, Basingstoke: Macmillan.

Birnbaum, Pierre (1992), *Les fous de la République*, Paris: Fayard.

Blackstock, C. (2002), 'Blunkett in clash over marriages', *The Guardian*, 8 February 2002.

Bloch, Ruth (1993), 'A Culturalist Critique of Trends in Feminist Theory', *Contention*, 2:3, pp. 79–106.

Bloom, Allan (1987), *The Closing of the American Mind*, New York: Simon and Schuster.

Bou-Habib, Paul (2006), 'A Theory of Religious Accommodation', *Journal of Applied Philosophy*, 23:1, pp. 109–26.

Brah, Avtar (1996), *Cartographies of Diaspora*, London: Routledge.

Brasher, B. (1988), *Godly Women*, New Brunswick: Rutgers University Press.

Brems, Eva (1997), 'Enemies or Allies? Feminism and Cultural Relativism as Dissident Voices in Human Rights Discourse', *Human Rights Quarterly*, 19:1, pp. 136–64.

Breyer, Hugh (1991), 'Cinderella, The Horse God and the Wizard of Oz', *Journal of Law and Education*, 20:1, pp. 63–93.

Brown, L., J. Garner and J. Bell (1993), *French Administrative Law*, Oxford: Oxford University Press.

Brun-Rovet, M. (2000), 'A Perspective on the Multiculturalism Debate: L'Affaire Foulard and Laïcité in France 1989–1999', Seminar paper, Harvard University, Department of Government.

Bulbeck, Chilla (1998), *Re-orienting Western Feminisms*, Cambridge: Cambridge University Press.

Bunting, Annie (1993), 'Theorizing Women's Cultural Diversity in Feminist International Human Rights Strategies', *Journal of Law and Society*, 20:1, pp. 6–22.

Burke, Jason (2000), 'Love, honour and obey – or die', *The Observer*, Sunday, 8 October 2000.

Burtt, Shelley (1994), 'Religious Parents, Secular Schools', *The Review of Politics*, 56:1, pp. 51–70.

Burtt, Shelley (1996), 'In Defense of Yoder', in R. Hardin and I. Shapiro (eds), *NOMOS 38: Public Order*, New York: New York University Press, pp. 412–37.

Calhoun, Cheshire (2008), 'Losing Oneself', paper presented to the Colloquium of the AHRC Centre for Law, Gender and Sexuality, Keele University, 28 February 2008.

Callan, Eamonn (1995), 'Rejoinder: Pluralism and Polarization', *Canadian Journal of Education*, 20, pp. 325–9.

Callan, Eamonn (1996), 'Political Liberalism and Political Education', *Review of Politics*, 58:1, pp. 5–33.

Callan, Eamonn (1997), *Creating Citizens*, New York: Clarendon.

Carens, Joseph (2000), *Culture, Citizenship and Community*, Oxford: Oxford University Press.

Carter, Stephen (1993), *The Culture of Disbelief*, New York: Anchor Books

Cassatella, Andrea (2006), 'Multicultural Justice: Will Kymlicka and Cultural Recognition', *Ratio Juris*, 19:1, pp. 80–100.

Chambers, Clare (2008), *Sex, Culture and Justice*, Pennsylvania: Penn State University Press.

Chandler, David (2001), 'Universal Ethics and Elite Politics', *International Journal of Human Rights*, 5:4, pp. 72–91.

Charlesworth, Hilary (1995), 'Human Rights as Men's Rights', in Julie Peters and Andrea Wolper (eds), *Women's Rights as Human Rights*, London: Routledge, pp. 103–13.

Charlesworth, Hilary (2000), 'Martha Nussbaum's Feminist Internationalism', *Ethics*, 111:1, pp. 64–78.

Chatterjee, Partha (1995), 'Religious Minorities and the Secular State', *Public Culture*, 8:1, pp. 11–39.

Chaudhary, Ajay Singh (2005), '"The Simulacra of Morality": Islamic Veiling, Religious Politics and the Limits of Liberalism', *Dialectical Anthropology*, 29, pp. 349–72.

Chirac, Jacques (2003), 'Address to the Nation', 17 December 2003, http://network.bbc.co.uk/mpapers/pasetools/print/news.bbccouk/1/hi/europe/3330659.stm

Christman, John (2004), 'Relational Autonomy, Liberal Individualism and the Social Constitution of Selves', *Philosophical Studies*, 117, pp. 143–64.

Code, Lorraine (2000), 'The Perversion of Autonomy and the Subjection of Women', in C. Mackenzie and N. Stoljar (eds), pp. 189–209.

Cohen, G. A. (1999), 'Expensive Tastes and Multiculturalism', in R. Bharghava, A. Baghchi and R. Sudarshan (eds), *Multiculturalism, Liberalism and Democracy*, Oxford: Oxford University Press, pp. 80–115.

Cohen, Martine (2001), 'L'intégration de l'islam et les musulmans en France: modèles du passé et pratiques actuelles', in La laïcité, une valeur d'aujourd'hui ? Contestations et renégociations du modèle français, sous la direction de Jean Baudouin et Philippe Portier, Presses Universitaires de Rennes, 2001, p. 322.

Cossman, Brenda and Ratna Kapur (1999), *Secularism's Last Sigh?*, Delhi: Oxford University Press.

Cooke, M. (2002), 'Multiple Critique', in L. E. Donaldson and K. Pui-Lan (eds), *Postcolonialism, Feminism and Religious Discourse*, London: Routledge, pp. 142–61.

Crocker, David (1995), 'Functioning and Capability', in Martha Nussbaum and Jonathan Glover (eds), pp. 153–98.

Crosette, B. (1991), 'Disgruntled India', *New York Times*, 17 June 1991, p. 1.

Dagger, Richard (1997), *Civic Virtues*, Oxford: Oxford University Press.

D'Agostino, Fred (1991), 'Some Modes of Public Justification', *Australasian Journal of Philosophy*, 4, pp. 390–414.

Daly, Mary (1978), *Gyn/Ecology*, Boston: Beacon Press.

Damon, William (2001), 'To Not Fade Away: Restoring Civic Identity Among the Young', in D. Ravitch and J. P. Viteritti (eds), *Making Good Citizens*, New Haven: Yale University Press, pp. 122–41.

Das, Veena (1992), *Critical Events*, Delhi: Oxford University Press.

Datta, V. N. (1998), *Sati*, Delhi: Manohar.

Dauphin, S. and J. Praud (2002), 'Debating and Implementing Gender Parity in French Politics', *Modern and Contemporary France*, 10:1, pp. 5–11.

Deakin, A. (1986), *God's Choice: The Total World of a Fundamentalist Christian School*, New York: Schuster.

Delaney, C. F. (1979) (ed.), *Rationality and Religious Belief*, Indiana: University of Notre Dame Press.

Delphy, C. (2004), 'La suppression d'une liberté comme la défense d'une autre liberté?', *Revue Politique Mensuelle*, (January–February).

Deneulin, Séverine (2002), 'Perfectionism, Paternalism and Liberalism in Sen and Nussbaum's Capability Approach', *Review of Political Economy*, 14:4, pp. 497–518.

Denny, Frederick (1994), 'Islamic Theology in the New World', *Journal of the American Academy of Religion*, 62:4, pp. 1069–84.

de Sousa Santos, Boaventura (2002), 'Toward a Multicultural Conception of Human Rights', in Berta Hernandez-Truyol (ed.), *Moral Imperialism*, New York: New York University Press.

Deveaux, Monique (2005), 'A Deliberative Approach to Conflicts of Culture', in A. Eisenberg and J. Spinner-Halev (eds), pp. 340–62.

Deveaux, Monique (2006), *Gender and Justice in Multicultural Liberal States*, Oxford: Oxford University Press.

Dewey, John (1956), *The Child and the Curriculum*, Chicago: University of Chicago Press.

Dhamoon, Rita (2006), 'The Politics of Cultural Contestation', in Barbara Arneil et al. (eds), pp. 30–49.

Dickie, E. (1988), '(Mis)representing Roop: Natality, Femininity and Subjectivity in the Debate about Sati', *Scottish Journal of Religious Studies*, 19:1, pp. 5–18.

Dirlik, A. (1990), 'Culturalism as Hegemonic Ideology and Liberating Practice', in J. Mohammed and D. Lloyd (eds), *The Nature and Context of Minority Discourse*, New York: Oxford University Press, pp. 50–61.

Dodson, Mark (1996), 'Power and Cultural Differences in Native Title Mediation', *Aboriginal Law Bulletin*, 61:3, p. 84.

Donnelly, Jack (1989), *Universal Human Rights in Theory and Practice*, Ithaca: Cornell University Press.

Donnelly, Rachel (1999), 'Arranged Marriages not Cultural Heritages but Man-Made Law', *The Irish Times*, 3 June 1999, p. 13.

Dumont, L. (1980), *Homo Hierarchicus*, Chicago: University of Chicago Press.

Düttmann, Alexander Garcia (2000), *Between Cultures: Tensions in the Struggle for Recognition*, London: Verso.

Dworkin, Gerald (1989), 'The Concept of Autonomy', in John Christman (ed.), *The Inner Citadel*, Oxford: Oxford University Press.

Dworkin, Ronald (1979), *Taking Rights Seriously*, London: Duckworth.

Dworkin, Ronald (1981), 'What is Equality? Part II, Equality of Welfare', *Philosophy and Public Affairs*, 10: 4, pp. 283–345.

Dworkin, Ronald (1984), 'Rights as Trumps', in J. Waldron (ed.), *Theories of Rights*, Oxford: Oxford University Press, pp. 153–67.

Dworkin, Ronald (2000), *Sovereign Virtue*, Cambridge, MA: Harvard University Press.

Dwyer, Claire (1999), 'Veiled Meanings: Young British Muslim Women and the Negotiation of Difference', *Gender, Place and Culture*, 6:1, pp. 5–26.

Dwyer, J. (1996), 'The Children We Abandon', *North Carolina Law Review*, 74, pp. 4321–42.

Eckert, Penelope (1993), 'Cooperative Competition in Adolescent Girl Talk' in Deborah Tannen (ed.), *Gender and Conversational Interaction*, Oxford: Oxford University Press, pp. 32–61.

Eisenberg, Avigail (2003), 'Diversity and Equality: Three Approaches to Cultural and Sexual Difference', *Journal of Political Philosophy*, 11:1, pp. 41–64.

Eisenberg, Avigail (2005), 'Identity and Liberal Politics: The Problem of Minorities within Minorities', in A. Eisenberg and J. Spinner-Halev (eds), pp. 249–70.

Eisenberg, Avigail (2006), 'Identity, Multiculturalism and Religious Arbitration', in B. Arneil et al. (eds), pp. 211–31.

Eisenberg, Avigail and Jeff Spinner-Halev (eds) (2005), *Minorities within Minorities*, Cambridge: Cambridge University Press.

Ellison, Ralph (1952), *Invisible Man*, New York: Random House.

Engineer, A. A. (1985), *The Shah Bano Controversy*, Hyderabad: Orient Longman.

Enslin, Penny (2003), 'Liberal Feminism, Diversity, and Education', *Theory and Research in Education*, 1, pp. 73–85.

Enslin, Penny and Mary Tjiattas (2004), 'Liberal Feminism, Cultural Diversity and Comparative Education', *Comparative Education*, 40:4, pp. 503–16.

Estlund, David (1996), 'The Survival of Egalitarian Justice', *Journal of Political Philosophy*, 69, pp. 390–414.

Ewing, Katherine (1991), 'Can Psychoanalytic Theories Explain the Pakistani Woman?', *Ethos*, 19, pp. 131–60.

Farley, M. A. (1993), 'Feminism and Universal Morality', in G. Outka and J. P. Reeder (eds), *Prospects for a Common Morality*, Princeton: Princeton University Press, pp. 174–91.

Fish, Stanley (1997), 'Boutique Multiculturalism, or Why Liberals Are Incapable of Thinking about Hate Speech', *Critical Inquiry*, 23:2, pp. 378–95.

Fish, Stanley (1999), 'Mutual Respect as a Device for Exclusion', in Stephen Macedo (ed.), *Deliberative Politics*, New York: Oxford University Press, pp. 8–102.

Fiske, Edward (1987), 'The Push for Smarter Schoolbooks', *New York Times Education, Life Section*, 12 August 1987, pp. 20–3.

Foner, Nancy (1997), 'The Immigrant Family: Cultural Legacies and Cultural Changes', *International Migration Review*, 31:4, pp. 961–74.

Forst, Rainer (2001), 'Towards a Critical Theory of Transnational Justice', *Metaphilosophy*, 32:1, pp. 160–171.

Foucault, Michel (1983), 'Afterward: The Subject of Power', in *Michel Foucault: Beyond Structuralism and Hermeneutics*, Hubert Dreyfus and Paul Rabinow (eds), Chicago: University of Chicago Press.

Frankfurt, Harry (1988), *The Importance of What We Care About*, Cambridge: Cambridge University Press.

Franks, M. (2000), 'Crossing the Borders of Whiteness', *Ethnic and Racial Studies*, 23:5, pp. 917–29.

Fraser, Nancy (1997), *Justice Interruptus*, London: Routledge.

Fraser, Nancy (2003), 'Contributions to *idem* and Axel Honneth', *Redistribution or Recognition*, London: Verso.

Frazer, Elizabeth (1999), 'Introduction: The Idea of a Political Education', *Oxford Review of Education*, 25:2, pp. 5–22.

Freedman, Jane (2006), 'The Headscarf Debate: Muslim Women in Europe and the War on Terror', in Krista Hunt and Kim Rygiel (eds), *(En)Gendering the War on Terror*, Aldershot: Ashgate.

Freeman, Samuel (2000), 'Deliberative Democracy: A Sympathetic Comment', *Philosophy and Public Affairs*, 29:4, pp. 317–418.

Friedman, Marilyn (2003), *Autonomy, Gender and Politics*, Princeton: Princeton University Press.

Frye, Marilyn (1983), 'In and Out of Harm's Way', in Marilyn Frye (ed.), *The Politics of Reality*, New York: Crossing Press, pp. 14–32.

Gabriel, G. (1993), *Being a Woman of God*, Nashville: Thomas Nelson.

Galeotti, A. E. (2002), *Toleration as Recognition*, Cambridge: Cambridge University Press.

Gallie, W. B. (1968), 'Essentially Contested Concepts', in his *Philosophy and Historical Understanding*, New York: Schocken Books, pp. 157–91.

Galston, William (1991), *Liberal Purposes*, Cambridge: Cambridge University Press.

Galston, William (1995), 'Two Concepts of Liberalism', *Ethics*, 105:3, pp. 516–34.

Gaspard, F. and F. Khosrokhavar (1995), *Le Foulard et la République*, Paris: Découverte.

Gatens, Moira (1996), *Imaginary Bodies*, London: Routledge.

Gaudemet, Yves (2000), *Traité de droit administratif*, Paris: LGH.

Gedalof, Irene (1999), 'Agency, the Self and the Collective in Indian Feminisms', in Irene Gedalof, *Against Purity*, London: Routledge.

Gehring, Verna and William Arthur Galston (eds) (2002), *Philosophical Dimensions of Public Policy*, London: Transaction Publishers.

Gilligan, Carol (1982), *In a Different Voice*, Cambridge, MA: Harvard University Press.

Gillis, Stacy, Gillian Howie and Rebecca Munford (eds) (2004), *Third Wave Feminism*, Palgrave: Macmillan.

Glazer, Nathan (1997), *We Are All Multiculturalists Now*, Cambridge, MA: Harvard University Press.

Glendon, M. (1991), *Rights Talk: The Impoverishment of Political Discourse*, New York: Free Press.

Goodwin, Robin and Duncan Cramer (2000), 'Marriage and Social Support in a British Asian Community', *Journal of Community and Applied Social Psychology*, 10:1, pp. 49–62.

Govier, Trudy (1993), 'Self-Trust, Autonomy and Self-Esteem', *Hypatia* (Winter), 8, pp. 99–120.

Gray, John (1995), *Isaiah Berlin*, London: Fontana.

Gray, Leslie and Michael Kevane (1999), 'Diminished Access, Diverted Exclusion', *African Studies Review*, 42:2, pp. 15–39.

Greatbatch, D. and R. Dingwall (1999), 'The Marginalization of Domestic Violence in Divorce Mediation', *International Journal of Law, Policy and the Family*, 13:2, pp. 174–90.

Green, Leslie (1995), 'Internal Minorities and their Rights', in Will Kymlicka (ed.), pp. 256–75.

Green, Sarah (2006), 'Unveiling Liberty', *Hinckley Journal of Politics*, 7, pp. 37–42.

Guénif-Souilamas, N. and Macé, E. (2004), *Les féministes et le garçon arabe*, Paris: Editions de l'Aube.

Gunew, Sneja (1997), 'Postcolonialism and Multiculturalism', *The Yearbook of English Studies*, 27, pp. 22–39.

Gunning, Isabelle (1992), 'Arrogant Perception, World-Travelling and Multicultural Feminism', *Columbia Human Rights Law Review*, 23:2, pp. 189–248.

Gutmann, Amy (1980), 'Children, Paternalism and Education', *Philosophy and Public Affairs*, 9, pp. 338–58.

Gutmann, Amy (1989), 'Undemocratic Education', in Nancy Rosenblum (ed.), *Liberalism and the Moral Life*, Cambridge, MA: Harvard University Press.

Gutmann, Amy (1995a), 'Communitarian Critics of Liberalism', *Philosophy and Public Affairs*, 14:3, pp. 308–22.

Gutmann, Amy (1995b), 'Civic Education and Social Diversity', *Ethics*, 105:3, pp. 557–79.

Gutmann, Amy (1999), *Democratic Education*, Princeton: Princeton University Press.

Gutmann, Amy and Dennis Thompson (1996), *Democracy and Disagreement*, Cambridge, MA: Harvard University Press.

Habermas, Jurgen (1990), *Moral Consciousness and Communicative Action*, Cambridge, MA: MIT Press.

Habermas, Jurgen (1995), 'Reconciliation Through the Public Use of Reason', *The Journal of Philosophy*, 92:3, pp. 109–31.

Halstead, J. M. (1995), 'Voluntary Apartheid? Problems of Schooling for Religious and Other Minorities in Democratic Societies', *Journal of the Philosophy of Education*, 29:2, pp. 257–72.

Halstead, J. M. (2005), 'Islam, Homophobia, and Education', *Journal of Moral Education*, 34:1, pp. 37–42.

Hardacre, Helen and Lenore Manderson (1990), 'The Hall of Mirrors', paper prepared for the International Workshop on the Construction of Gender and Sexuality in Southeast Asia, University of California, Los Angeles, 9–11 December 1990.

Hardgrove, Anne (1999), 'Sati Worship and Marwari Public Identity in India', *Journal of Asian Studies*, 58:3, pp. 723–52.

Hare, R. M. (1975), 'Autonomy as an Educational Ideal – Chairman's Remarks', in S. C. Brown (ed.), *Philosophers Discuss Education*, London: Macmillan.

Harris, Angela (1990), 'Race and Essentialism in Feminist Legal Theory', *Stanford Law Review*, 42, pp. 581–616.

Hauptman, Judith (1998), *Re-reading the Rabbis*, Boulder, Boulder: Westview.

Hawley, John Stratton (ed.) (1994), *Sati: the Blessing and the Curse*, Oxford: Oxford University Press.

Hazareesingh, Sudhir (1994), *Political Traditions in Modern France*, Oxford: Oxford University Press.

Heilman, S. (1992), *Defenders of the Faith*, New York: Schocken Books.

Hellsten, Sirkku Kristina (1999), 'Pluralism in Multicultural Liberal Democracy and the Justification of Female Circumcision', *Journal of Applied Philosophy*, 16:1, pp. 69–83.

Hellum, Anne (1999), 'Women's Human Rights and African Customary Laws', in Christian Lund (ed.), *Development and Rights*, London: Routledge, pp. 88–104.

Heyd, David (ed.) (1996), *Toleration: An Elusive Virtue*, Princeton: Princeton University Press.

Hickley, M. (2006), 'Plans to Outlaw Forced Marriages Shelved', *Daily Mail*, 7 June 2006, p. 2.

Hirschmann, Nancy (1988), 'Western Feminism, Eastern Veiling and the Question of Free Agency', *Constellations*, 5:3, pp. 345–68.

Hirschmann, Nancy (2003), *The Subject of Liberty*, Princeton University Press.

Hoffman, John P. and Alan S. Millar (1997), 'Social and Political Attitudes Among Religious Groups', *Journal for the Scientific Study of Religion*, 36:1, pp. 52–70.

Holmes, Stephen (1995), *Passions and Constraints*, Chicago: University of Chicago Press.

Home Office (UK Government) (2000), *A Choice By Right: The Report of the Working Group on Forced Marriage*, Home Office Communications Directorate (available at http://www.fco.gov.uk).

Home Office (UK Government) (2005), *Forced Marriage: A Wrong not a Right*, Home Office Communications Directorate (available at http://www.homeoffice. gov.uk/comrace/race/forcedmarriage/htm).

Honneth, Axel (1995), *The Struggle for Recognition*, London: Polity Press.

Horton, John (1996), 'Toleration as a Virtue', in David Heyd (ed.), pp. 28–43.

Horton, John (2009, forthcoming), 'Reasonable Disagreement', in M. Dimova-Cookson and P. Stirk (eds), *Multiculturalism and Moral Conflict*, London: Routledge.

Hundal, Sunny (2007), 'Forced Marriage Farce', *The Guardian*, 2 August 2007.

Hutchings, Kimberly (2005), 'Speaking and Hearing: Habermasian Discourse Ethics, Feminism and International Relations', *Review of International Studies*, 31:1, pp. 155–65.

Hutchinson, M. (1999), 'The Margin of Appreciation Doctrine in the European Court of Human Rights', *The International and Comparative Law Quarterly*, 48:3, pp. 638–50.

Huntingdon, Patricia (1995), 'Toward a Dialectical Concept of Autonomy', *Philosophy and Social Criticism*, 21, pp. 37–55.

Huntington, G. (1993), 'Health Care', in D. B. Kraybill (ed.), *The Amish and the State*, Baltimore: The Johns Hopkins University Press.

Hutchings, Kimberly (2000), 'Towards a Feminist International Ethics', *Review of International Studies*, 26:5, pp. 111–30.

Hyman, Paula (1995), *Gender and Assimilation in Modern Jewish History*, Washington: University of Washington Press.

Ignatieff, Michael (2001), *Human Rights as Politics and Idolatry*, Princeton: Princeton University Press.

Ignatieff, Michael (2003), 'Human Rights, Sovereignty and Intervention', in N. Owen (ed.), *Human Rights and Human Wrongs*, Oxford: Oxford University Press.

Ingram, Attracta (1996), 'Rawlsians, Pluralists and Cosmopolitans', in David Archard (ed.), *Philosophy and Pluralism*, Cambridge: Cambridge University Press, pp. 147–61.

Ishay, Micheline (2004), *The History of Human Rights*, California: University of California Press.

Ivison, Duncan (1997), 'The Secret History of Public Reason', *History of Political Thought*, 18:1, pp. 126–47.

Ivison, Duncan (2002), *Postcolonial Liberalism*, Cambridge: Cambridge University Press.

Jaggar, Alison (2006), 'Reasoning about Well-being', *Journal of Political Philosophy*, 14: 3, pp. 301–22.

Jarman, Francis (2002), 'Sati: From Exotic Custom to Relativist Controversy', *Culture Scan*, 2:5, pp. 1–18.

Jasser, Ghaiss (1999), 'The Twin Evils of the Veil', *Social Identities*, 5:31, pp. 35–7.

Johnson, R. W. (1989), 'Wars of Religion', *New Statesman*, 15 December, 1989, pp. 13–14.

Jones, Peter (1990), 'Respecting Beliefs and Rebuking Rushdie', *British Journal of Political Science*, 20:4, pp. 415–37.

Jones, Peter (1994), 'Bearing the Consequences of Belief', *Journal of Political Philosophy*, 2: 1, pp. 24–43.

Jones, Peter (1996), 'International Human Rights: Philosophical or Political?', in Simon Caney, David George and Peter Jones (eds), *National Rights, International Obligations*, Boulder: Westview, pp. 183–204.

Jones, Peter (1999a), 'Human Rights, Group Rights and People's Rights', *Human Rights Quarterly*, 21:1, pp. 80–107.

Jones, Peter (1999b), 'Group Rights and Group Oppression', *Journal of Political Philosophy*, 7: 4, pp. 353–77.

Jones, Peter (2001), 'Human Rights and Diverse Cultures: Continuity or Discontinuity?', in Simon Caney and Peter Jones (eds), *Human Rights and Global Diversity*, London: Routledge, pp. 27–50.

Kach, N. and I. DeFaveri (1987), 'What Every Teacher Should Know About Multiculturalism', in L. L. Stewin and S. J. H. McCann (eds), *Contemporary Educational Issues*, Toronto: Copp Clark Pitman.

Kakar, Sudhir (1978), *The Inner World*, Oxford: Oxford University Press.

Kaltenbach, Jeanne-Hélène and Michèle Tribalat (2002), *La République et l'islam*, Paris: Gallimard.

Kandiyoti, Deniz (1988), 'Bargaining with Patriarchy', *Gender and Society*, 2:3, pp. 274–90.

Kandiyoti, Deniz (1988–9), 'Women and Islam: What are the Missing Terms?', *Dossier*, 5:6: pp. 5–9.

Kaplan, Esther (2005), *With God on their Side: George W. Bush and the Christian Right*, New York: New York University Press.

Kastoryano, Riva (2006), 'French Secularism and Islam', in Tariq Modood, Anna Triandafyllidou and Ricard Zapata-Barrero (eds), *Multiculturalism, Muslims and Citizenship*, London: Routledge

Kasturirangan, Aarati, Sandhya Krishnan and Stephanie Riger (2004), 'The Impact of Culture and Minority Status on Women's Experience of Domestic Violence', *Trauma, Violence and Abuse*, 5:4, pp. 318–32.

Keller, Evelyn Fox (1985), *Reflections on Gender and Science*, New Haven: Yale University Press.

Kelly, Paul (ed.) (2002), *Multiculturalism Reconsidered*, Oxford: Polity Press.

Khory, K. R. (1993), 'The Shah Bano Case', in Ronald Baird (ed.), *Religion and Law in Independent India*, Delhi: Manohar, pp. 43–64.

Killian, Caitlin (2003), 'The Other Side of the Veil', *Gender and Society*, 17:4, pp. 567–590.

Kingdom, Elizabeth (1996), 'Transforming Rights: Feminist Political Heuristics', *Res Publica*, 2:1, pp. 63–75.

Kishwar, Madhu (1986), 'Pro-Women or Anti-Muslim?', *Manushi*, 32, pp. 4–13.

Kishwar, Madhu, and R. Vanita (1987), 'The Burning of Roop Kanwar', *Manushi* 42–3, pp. 15–29.

Kristinsson, S. (2000), 'The Limits of Neutrality', *Canadian Journal of Philosophy*, 30:2, pp. 257–86.

Krosenbrink-Gelissen, L. E. (1991), *Sexual Equality as an Aboriginal Right*, Saarbrucken, Germany: Verlag Breitenbach.

Kuçuradi, Ioanna (1999), 'Secularism and Human Rights', in Bhuvan Chandel and Ioanna Kuçuradi (eds), *Cultural Traditions and the Idea of Secularization* (Paris: Govier).

Kukathas, Chandran (1995), 'Are There Any Cultural Rights?', in Will Kymlicka (ed.), pp. 133–53.

Kukathas, Chandran (1997), 'Multiculturalism as Fairness', *Journal of Political Philosophy*, 5:4, pp. 406–27.

Kukathas, Chandran (2001), 'Is Feminism Bad for Multiculturalism?', *Public Affairs Quarterly*, 15:2, pp. 83–98.

Kukathas, Chandran (2003), *The Liberal Archipelago*, Oxford: Oxford University Press.

Kymlicka, Will (1989), *Liberalism, Community and Culture*, Oxford: Clarendon.

Kymlicka, Will (1995a), *Multicultural Citizenship*, Oxford: Oxford University Press.

Kymlicka, Will (ed.) (1995b), *The Rights of Minority Cultures*, Oxford: Oxford University Press.

Kymlicka, Will (1996), 'The Good, the Bad and the Intolerable', *Dissent*, pp. 22–30.

Kymlicka, Will (1999a), 'Liberal Complacencies', in S. M. Okin (with respondents), pp. 31–4.

Kymlicka, Will (1999b), 'Comments on Shachar and Spinner-Halev: An Update on the Multiculturalism Wars', in C. Joppke and S. Lukes (eds), *Multicultural Questions*, Oxford: Oxford University Press, pp. 112–29.

Kymlicka, Will and Wayne Norman (2000), 'Citizenship in Culturally Diverse Societies', in W. Kymlicka and W. Norman (eds), pp. 1–43.

Kymlicka, Will and Wayne Norman (eds), (2000), *Citizenship in Diverse Societies*, Oxford: Oxford University Press.

Kymlicka, Will (2002), 'Multiculturalism and Minority Rights: West and East', *Journal of Ethnopolitics and Minority Issues in Europe*, 4, pp. 1–25.

Laborde, Cécile (2003), 'Toleration and laïcité', in Catriona McKinnon and Dario Castiglione (eds), *The Culture of Toleration in Diverse Societies*, Manchester: Manchester University Press.

Laborde, Cécile (2005), 'Secular Philosophy and Muslim Headscarves in Schools', *Journal of Political Philosophy*, 13: 3: pp. 305–29.

Laborde, Cécile (2006), 'Female Autonomy, Education and the *Hijab*', *Critical Review of International Social and Political Philosophy*, 9:3, pp. 351–77.

Laborde, Cécile (2008), *Critical Republicanism*, Oxford: Oxford University Press.

Lacey, Nicola (1998), *Unspeakable Subjects*, Oxford: Hart.

Laclau, Ernesto and Chantal Mouffe (2001), *Hegemony and Socialist Strategy*, London: Verso.

Lacoste-Dujardin, Camille (1990), 'Les Fichus Islamistes', *Hérodote*, 56, pp. 14–44.

Laden, Antony (2001), *Reasonably Radical*, Ithaca: Cornell University Press.

Laden, T. (1991), 'Freedom, Preference and Objectivity', Harvard University, mimeo.

Langlois, Anthony (2001), *The Politics of Justice and Human Rights*, Cambridge: Cambridge University Press.

Larmore, Charles (1986), *Patterns of Moral Complexity*, Princeton: Princeton University Press.

Larson, Gerald. (2001), *Religion and Personal Law in Secular India*, Indiana: Indiana University Press.

Lebreton, G. (1993), 'Port de signes religieux et laïcité de l'enseignement Public', 62, *Petites Affiches*, 4, pp. 4–10.

Levey, Geoffrey B. (1997), 'Equality, Autonomy and Cultural Rights', *Political Theory*, 25: 2, pp. 215–48.

Levinson, Meira (1997), 'Liberalism versus Democracy: Schooling Private Citizens in the Public Square', *British Journal of Political Science*, 27:3, pp. 333–60.

Levy, Jacob (1997), 'Classifying Cultural Rights', in Will Kymlicka and I. Shapiro (eds), *Ethnicity and Group Rights*, New York: New York University Press.

Lieberman, M (1993), *Public Education: An Autopsy*, Cambridge, MA: Harvard University Press.

Lindley, Richard (1986), *Autonomy*, London: Macmillan.

Lochak, Danièle (1989), 'Les Minorités et le Droit Public Français', in Alain Fenet and Gérard Soulier (eds), *Les minorités et leurs droits depuis 1789*, Paris: Harmattan, pp. 111–84.

Locke, John [1689] (1985), *A Letter Concerning Toleration*, Indianapolis: Hackett.

Loomba, A. (1993), 'Dead Women Tell No Tales', *History Workshop Journal*, 36:1, pp. 230–66.

Lorde, Audre (1984), *Sister Outsider*, California: Crossing Press.

Lubienski, Chris (2000), 'Wither the Common Good? A Critique of Homeschooling', *Peabody Journal of Education*, 75:1–2, pp. 207–32.

Macedo, Stephen (1990), *Liberal Virtues*, Oxford: Clarendon.

Macedo, Stephen (1995a), 'Liberal Civic Education and Religious Fundamentalism: the Case of God v. John Rawls', *Ethics*, 105, pp. 468–96.

Macedo, Stephen (1995b), 'Liberal Civic Education and its Limits', *Canadian Journal of Education*, 20:3, pp. 304–14.

Macedo, Stephen (2000), *Diversity and Distrust*, Cambridge, MA: Harvard University Press.

MacIntyre, Alasdair (1981), *After Virtue*, London: Duckworth.

Mackenzie, Catriona (2000), 'Imagining Oneself Otherwise', in Catriona Mackenzie and Natalie Stoljar (eds), pp. 1–2.

Mackenzie, Catriona and Natalie Stoljar (2000), 'Introduction: Autonomy Reconfigured', in Catriona Mackenzie and Natalie Stoljar (eds) (2000), pp. 3–31.

Mackenzie, Catriona and Natalie Stoljar (eds) (2000), *Relational Autonomy: Feminist Perspectives on Autonomy, Agency and the Social Self*, New York: Oxford University Press.

Mackenzie, Catriona (2006), 'Relational Autonomy, Sexual Justice and Cultural Pluralism', in Barbara Arneil et al. (eds), pp. 103–21.

Mackie, Gerry (2000), 'Ending Footbinding and Infibulation: A Convention Account', *American Sociological Review*, 61, pp. 999–1017.

MacKinnon, Catharine (1987), *Feminism Unmodified*, Cambridge, MA: Harvard University Press.

MacKinnon, Catharine (2007), *Are Women Human?*, Cambridge, MA: Harvard University Press.

MacLeod, Arlene (1991), *Accommodating Protest: Working Women, the New Veiling and Change in Cairo*, New York: Columbia University Press.

MacLeod, Colin (1997), 'Conceptions of Parental Autonomy', *Politics and Society*, 25:1, pp. 117–40.

Mahajan, Gurpreet (1988), *Identities and Rights*, New Delhi: Oxford University Press.

Mahajan, Gurpreet (2005), 'Can Intra-Group Equality Co-exist with Cultural Diversity?', in A. Eisenberg and J. Spinner-Halev (eds), pp. 90–112.

Mahoney, Martha (1994), 'Victimization or Oppression?', in M. Fineman and R. Mykitiuk (eds), *The Public Nature of Private Violence*, New York: Routledge, pp. 62–77.

Major, Andrea (2006,) 'A Question of Rites?', *History Compass*, 4:5, pp. 780–99.

Mani, Lata (1989), 'Contentious Traditions', in K. Sangari and S. Vaid (eds), pp. 88–126.

Manning, Christel (1999), *God Gave Us the Right*, Piscataway: Rutgers University Press.

Margalit, Avishai (1996), 'The Ring: On Religious Pluralism', in David Heyd (ed.), pp. 147–57.

Margalit, Avishai and Moshe Halbertal (1994), 'Liberalism and the Right to Culture', *Social Research*, 61:3, pp. 491–510.

Margalit, Avishai and Joseph Raz (1990), 'National Self-Determination', *European Journal of Philosophy*, 87: 9, pp. 439–61.

Marmorstein, E. (1954), 'The Veil in Judaism and Islam', *Journal of Jewish Studies*, 5:1, pp. 1–11.

Marshall, Jill (2006), 'Freedom of Religious Expression and Gender Equality: *Sahin v. Turkey*', *Modern Law Review*, 69, pp. 452–61.

Marx, K. (1844), 'On the Jewish Question', first published in Paris under the German title *Zur Judenfrage*, reprinted in Jeremy Waldron (ed.), (1987) *Nonsense Upon Stilts: Bentham, Burke and Marx on the Rights of Man*, London: Methuen, pp. 137–50.

Mashhour, Amira (2005), 'Islamic Law and Gender Equality', *Human Rights Quarterly*, 27:2, pp. 562–96.

Mawdsley, Ralph and Alice Mawdsley (1988), 'Diminished Status of Religious Liberty in Public Education', *West's Education Law Reporter*, 46:3, pp. 897–912.

Mayer, Ann Elizabeth (2000), 'A "Benign" Apartheid', *UCLA Journal of International Law and Foreign Affairs*, 5, pp. 237–338.

McCarthy, Thomas (1994), 'Kantian Constructivism and Reconstructivism', *Ethics*, 105, pp. 44–63.

McIntyre, J. (1981), 'Multi-cultural and Multi-faith Societies: Some Examinable Assumptions', in E. Hulmes (ed.), *Occasional Papers 3*, Oxford: Farrington Institute for Christian Studies.

McKinnon, Catriona (2000), 'Civil Citizens', in C. McKinnon and I. Hampsher-Monk (eds), pp. 144–64.

McKinnon, Catriona (2006), *Toleration: A Critical Introduction*, London: Routledge.

McKinnon, Catriona and Iain Hampsher-Monk (eds) (2000), *The Demands of Citizenship*, London: Continuum.

Mejia, Melanie (2007), 'Gender Jihad: Muslim Women, Islamic Jurisprudence and Women's Rights', *Kritike*, 1:1, pp. 1–24.

Mendus, Susan (1986), 'Liberty and Autonomy', *Proceedings of the Aristotelian Society*, 87, pp. 107–20.

Mendus, Susan (2000a), 'Out of the Doll's House: Reflections on Autonomy in Political Philosophy', in Susan Mendus, *Feminism and Emotion*, Basingstoke: Macmillan, pp. 127–40.

Mendus, Susan (2000b), 'To Have and to Hold: Liberalism and the Marriage Contract', in Susan Mendus, *Feminism and Emotion*, Basingstoke: Macmillan, pp. 83–97.

Mendus, Susan (2002), 'Choice, Chance and Multiculturalism', in Paul Kelly (ed.), pp. 31–44.

Menon, Usha (2000), 'Does feminism have Universal Relevance? The Challenges Posed by Oriya Hindu Family Practices', *Daedalus*, 129:4, pp. 77–99.

Mernissi, Fatima (1982), 'Virginity and Patriarchy', in A. al-Hibri (ed.), *Women in Islam*, New York: Pergamon Press.

Merry, Sally Engle (2006), *Human Rights and Gender Violence*, Cambridge: Cambridge University Press.

Merry, Sally Engle and Rachel Stern (2005), 'The Female Inheritance Movement in Hong Kong', *Current Anthropology*, 46:3, pp. 387–409.

Meyers, Diana Teitjens (1989), *Self, Society and Personal Choice*, New York: Columbia University Press.

Meyers, Diana Teitjens (1993), 'Cultural Diversity: Rights, Goals and Competing Values', in David Goldbert and Michael Krauz (eds), *Jewish Identity*, Philadelphia: Temple University Press.

Meyers, Diana Teitjens (2000), 'Feminism and Women's Autonomy: The Challenge of Female Genital Cutting', *Metaphilosophy*, 31: 5, pp. 469–91.

Milde, Michael (1998), 'Critical Notice of James Tully: *Strange Multiplicity*', *Canadian Journal of Philosophy*, 28:1, pp. 119–43.

Mill, John Stuart [1864] (1978), *On Liberty*, Cambridge, MA: Hackett.

Miller, David (2001), 'Distributing Responsibilities', *Journal of Political Philosophy*, 9:4, pp. 453–71.

Miller-McLemore, Bonnie (1997), 'Faith, Family and Feminism', *Pastoral Psychology*, 46:2, pp. 107–18.

Mitchell, Susan (2004), 'Inside Story: Veiled Threat', *Sunday Business Post*, 18 January 2004, p. 3.

Mitnick, Eric (2003), 'Individual Vulnerability and Cultural Transformation', *Michigan Law Review*, 101:6, pp. 1636–60.

Modood, Tariq (2000), 'Anti-Essentialism, Multiculturalism, and the "Recognition" of Religious Groups', in W. Kymlicka and W. Norman (eds), pp. 175–98.

Modood, Tariq (2005), *Multicultural Politics*, Edinburgh: Edinburgh University Press.

Modood, Tariq (2007), *Multiculturalism: A Civic Idea*, Cambridge: Polity Press.

Modood, Tariq (2008), 'Multicultural Citizenship and the Anti-Sharia Storm', *Open Democracy* (available at www.opendemocracy.net/article/faith_ideas/ europe/islam/anti_sharia_storm).

Modood, Tariq and Fauzia Ahmad (2007), 'British Muslim Perspectives on Multiculturalism', *Theory, Culture and Society*, 24:2, pp. 187–213.

Modood, Tariq, R. Berthoud, J. Lakey, J. Nazroo, P. Smith, S. Virdee and S. Beishon (eds), (1997), *Ethnic Minorities in Britain: Diversity and Disadvantage*, Basingstoke: Macmillan.

Mohanty, Chandra Talpade (1991), 'Under Western Eyes', in C. T. Mohanty, A. Russo and L. Torres (eds), *Third World Women and the Politics of Feminism*, Bloomington: Indiana University Press.

Molyneux, Maxine and Shahra Razavi (eds) (2002), *Gender Justice, Development and Rights*, Oxford: Oxford University Press.

Monnet, Jean-François (1990), 'A Creil, l'origine de "l'affaire des foulards"', *Hérodote*, 56, pp. 45–54.

Moody-Adams, Michele (1994), 'Culture, Responsibility and Affected Ignorance', *Ethics*, 104, pp. 291–309.

Mookherjee, Monica (2005), 'Affective Citizenship', *Critical Review of International Social and Political Philosophy*, 8:1, pp. 31–50.

Mookherjee, Monica (2008a), 'Multiculturalism', in Catriona McKinnon (ed.), *Issues in Political Theory*, Oxford: Oxford University Press, pp. 218–40.

Mookherjee, Monica (2008b, forthcoming), 'Autonomy, Force and Cultural Plurality', *Res Publica*, 8:2.

Moore, Dahlia (2000), 'Gender Identity, Nationalism, and Social Action among Jewish and Arab Women in Israel', *Gender Issues*, 18:2, pp. 3–28.

Moore, Henrietta (2000), 'Difference and Recognition', *Signs*, 25:4, pp. 1129–32.

Moruzzi, Norma (1994), 'A Problem with Headscarves', *Political Theory*, 22, pp. 653–72.

Mukhopadhyay, A. (1969), 'Sati as a Social Institution in Bengal', in Calcutta Historical Society's *Bengal Past and Present*, Calcutta: Firma KLM, pp. 34–52.

Mullally, Siobhan (2004), 'Feminism and Multicultural Dilemmas in India', *Oxford Journal of Legal Studies*, 24:4, pp. 671–92.

Mullally, Siobhan (2006), *Gender, Culture and Human Rights*, Oxford: Oxford University Press.

Mumtaz Ali, Syed (1994), 'The Review of the Ontario Civil Justice System The Reconstruction of the Canadian Constitution and The Case for Muslim Personal/Family Law A Submission to The Ontario Civil Justice Review Task Force', Canadian Society of Muslims (available at http://muslim-canada.org/submission.pdf).

Murphy, R. F. (1964), 'Social Distance and the Veil', *American Anthropologist*, 66:6, pp. 1257–74.

Nagel, Thomas (1987), 'Moral Conflict and Political Legitimacy', *Philosophy and Public Affairs*, 16:3, pp. 215–40.

Nandy, Ashish (1994), 'Sati as Profit Versus Sati as Spectacle', in John Stratton Hawley (ed.), pp. 56–75.

Narayan, Uma (1997), *Dislocating Cultures*, London: Routledge.

Narayan, Uma (2000), 'Essence of Culture and a Sense of History', in U. Narayan and S. Harding (eds), pp. 80–100.

Narayan, Uma (2002), 'Minds of Their Own: Choices, Autonomy, Cultural Practices, and Other Women', in Louise Antony and Charlotte Witt (ed.), *A Mind of One's Own: Feminist Essays in Reason and Objectivity*, Boulder: Westview, pp. 418–32.

Narayan, Uma and Sandra Harding (eds) (2000), *Decentering the Center*, Bloomington: Indiana University Press.

Nasser, Mervat (1999), 'The New Veiling Phenomenon – is it an Anorexic Equivalent?', *Journal of Community and Applied Social Psychology*, 9, pp. 407–21.

Newnham Asian Women's Project (2007), 'Forced Marriage Civil Protection Bill: Response to the Consultation on Amendments to the Family Law Act', March 2007 (available at http://www.endviolenceagainstwomen.org.uk/documents/NAWP%20forced%marriage%20%Civil%20%Bill%20.pdf).

Nicholson, Linda (1996), 'To Be or Not to Be: Charles Taylor and the Politics of Recognition', *Constellations*, 3:1, pp. 1–16.

Nussbaum, Martha (1995), 'Human Capabilities, Female Human Beings', in Martha Nussbaum and Jonathan Glover (eds), pp. 61–104.

Nussbaum, Martha (1999a), *Sex and Social Justice*, Oxford: Oxford University Press.

Nussbaum, Martha (1999b), 'A Plea for Difficulty', in S. M. Okin (with respondents), pp. 105–14.

Nussbaum, Martha (2000), *Women and Human Development*, Cambridge: Cambridge University Press.

Nussbaum, Martha (2002), 'Women's Capabilities and Social Justice', in Maxine Molyneux and Shahra Razavi (eds), (2002), pp. 44–75.

Nussbaum, Martha (2003), 'Capabilities as Fundamental Entitlements', in B. Agarwal, J. Humphries and Ingrid Robeyns (eds), *Amartya Sen's Work and Ideas: A Gender Perspective*, London: Taylor and Francis, pp. 35–61.

Nussbaum, Martha (2004), 'On Hearing Women's Voices', *Philosophy and Public Affairs*, 32:2, pp. 193–205.

Nussbaum, Martha and Jonathan Glover (eds) (1995), *Women, Culture and Development*, Oxford: Clarendon.

Nussbaum, Martha and Amartya Sen (eds) (1993), *The Quality of Life*, Oxford: Clarendon.

Obando, Ana Elena (2004), 'How Effective Is a Human Rights Framework in Addressing Gender-Based Violence?', *Women's Human Rights Net* (available at www.whrnet.org.docs/issue-genderviolence.html).

O'Connor, Karen and Gregg Ivers (1988), 'Creationism, Evolution and the Courts', *PS: Political Science and Politics*, 21:1, pp. 10–17.

Okin, Susan Moller (1989), *Justice, Gender and the Family*, London: Basic Books.

Okin, Susan Moller (1994), 'Gender Inequality and Cultural Differences', *Political Theory*, 22:1, pp. 5–24.

Okin, Susan Moller (1995), 'Inequalities Between the Sexes in Different Cultural Contexts', in M. Nussbaum and J. Glover (eds), pp. 274–97.

Okin, Susan Moller (1998a), 'Feminism, Women's Human Rights and Cultural Differences', *Hypatia*, 13:2, pp. 32–52.

Okin, Susan Moller (1998b), 'Feminism and Multiculturalism: Some Tensions', *Ethics*, 108, pp. 661–84.

Okin, Susan Moller (with respondents) (1999a), *Is Multiculturalism Bad for Women?*, Princeton: Princeton University Press.

Okin, Susan Moller (1999b), 'Is Multiculturalism Bad for Women?', in S. M. Okin (with respondents).

Okin, Susan Moller (1999c), 'Reply', in S. M. Okin (with respondents), pp. 117–31.

Okin, Susan Moller (2002), ' "Mistresses of their own Destiny": Group Rights, Gender and Realistic Rights of Exit', *Ethics*, 112: pp. 205–30.

Okin, Susan Moller (2003), 'Poverty, Wellbeing and Gender: What Counts? Who's Heard?', *Philosophy and Public Affairs*, 3:3, pp. 205–30.

Okin, Susan Moller (2005), 'Multiculturalism and Feminism: No Simple Question, No Simple Answers', in Avigail Eisenberg and Jeff Spinner-Halev (eds), pp. 67–89.

Oldenburg, Veena (1994), 'The Continuing Invention of the Sati Tradition', in J. Stratton Hawley (ed.), pp. 40–57.

Olsaretti, Serena (2005), 'Endorsement and Freedom in Amartya Sen's Capability Approach', *Economics and Philosophy*, 21, pp. 89–108.

O'Neill, Onora (1993), 'Justice, Gender and International Boundaries', in Martha Nussbaum and Amartya Sen (eds), *The Quality of Life*, Oxford: Clarendon, pp. 324–35.

Oshana, Marina (1988), 'Personal Autonomy and Society', *Journal of Social Philosophy*, 29:1, pp. 81–102.

Ozorak, Elizabeth Weiss (1996), 'The Power, but not the Glory', *Journal for the Scientific Study of Religion*, 35:1, pp. 17–29.

Owen, David (1999), 'Political Philosophy in a Post-Imperial Voice', *Economy and Society*, 28:4, pp. 520–49.

Parekh, Bhikhu (1993), 'The Cultural Particularity of Liberal Democracy', in David Held (ed.), *Prospects for Democracy*, Cambridge: Polity Press, pp. 156–175.

Parekh, Bhikhu (1995), 'Education for a Multicultural Society', *Papers for the Philosophy of Education Society of Great Britain*, 31 March–2 April 1995, pp. 1–10.

Parekh, Bhikhu (1999), 'A Varied Moral World', in S. M. Okin (and respondents), pp. 69–75.

Parekh, Bhikhu (2000a), *Rethinking Multiculturalism*, Basingstoke: Macmillan.

Parekh, Bhikhu (2002b), 'Review of A. Shachar's *Multicultural Jurisdictions*', *American Political Science Review*, 96:4, pp. 811–12.

Parekh, Bhikhu (2002c), 'Barry and the Dangers of Liberalism', in P. Kelly (ed.), pp. 133–50.

Patel, Pragna (2000) 'Southall Black Sisters: domestic violence campaigns and alliances across the divisions of race, gender and class', in Jalna Hanmer and Catherine Itzin (eds), with S. Quaid and D. Wigglesworth, *Home Truths about Domestic Violence*, London: Routledge, pp. 167–83.

Pathak, Zakia and Rajeswari Rajan (2001), '"Shahbano"', in Elizabeth Castelli (ed.), *Women, Gender and Religion: A Reader*, New York: Palgrave, pp. 195–215.

Pedwell, Carolyn (2007), 'Tracing "The Anorexic" and "The Veiled Woman"', *LSE Gender Institute Working Paper Series*, 20, pp. 1–45.

Perez, Nahshon (2002), 'Should Multiculturalists Oppress the Oppressed?', *Critical Review of International Social and Political Philosophy*, 5:3, pp. 51–79.

Peshkin, Alan (1986), *God's Choice: The Total World of the Fundamentalist Christian School*, Chicago: University of Chicago Press.

Pham, J. Peter (2006), 'Beyond Power Politics', *Human Rights and Human Welfare* (available at http://hrhw/volumes/2006/pham-2006a/pdf).

Phillips, Anne (2001), 'Feminism and Liberalism Revisited: Has Martha Nussbaum Got It Right?' *Constellations*, 8:2, pp. 249–66.

Phillips, Anne (2002), 'Multiculturalism, Universalism and the Claims of Culture', in Maxine Molyneux and Shahra Razavi (eds), pp. 115–38.

Phillips, Anne (2003), 'When Culture Means Gender', *Modern Law Review*, 66:4, pp. 510–31.

Phillips, Anne (2005), 'Dilemmas of Gender and Culture', in A. Eisenberg and J. Spinner-Halev (eds), pp. 113–34.

Phillips, Anne (2006) 'What is Culture?' in B. Arneil et al. (eds), pp. 15–29.

Phillips, Anne (2007), *Multiculturalism without Culture*, Princeton: Princeton University Press.

Phillips, Anne (2008, forthcoming), 'Free to Decide for Oneself', in D. O'Neill, I. M. Young and M. Shanley (eds), *The Illusion of Consent*, Pennsylvania: University of Pennsylvania Press.

Phillips, Anne and Moira Dustin (2004), 'UK Initiatives on Forced Marriage: Regulation, Dialogue and Exit', *Political Studies*, 52:3, pp. 531–51.

Pichler, Pia (2007), 'Talking Traditions of Marriage', *Women's Studies International Forum*, 30:3, pp. 201–16.

Platiel, Rudy (1992), 'Gender Issue Sparks Native Disunity', *Globe and Mail*, 20 July 1992.

Post, Robert (1999), 'Between Norms and Choices', in S. M. Okin (with respondents), pp. 64–8.

Poulter, Sebastian (1994), 'Minority Rights', in C. McCrudden and G. Chambers (eds), *Individual Rights and the Law in Britain*, Oxford: Oxford University Press.

Poulter, Sebastian (1997), 'Muslim Headscarves in School: Contrasting Legal Approaches in England and France', *Oxford Journal of Legal Studies*, 17:1, pp. 43–74.

Probyn, Elspeth (1993), *Sexing the Self*, London: Routledge.

Putnam, Ruth Anna (1993), 'Michael Walzer: Objectivity and Social Meaning', in M. Nussbaum and A. Sen (eds), pp. 64–8.

Putnam, Ruth Anna (1995), 'Why Not a Feminist Theory of Justice?', in M. Nussbaum and J. Glover (eds), pp. 298–331.

Quong, Jonathan (2002), 'Are Identity Claims Bad for Deliberative Democracy?' *Contemporary Political Theory*, 1:3, pp. 307–28.

Quong, Jonathan (2007), 'Political Liberalism without Scepticism', *Ratio*, 20:3, pp. 320–40.

Radoszkowicz, A. (2004), 'A Woman Chained', *The Jerusalem Post*, 3 December 2004: p. 27.

Rahman, Aminur (1999), 'Microcredit Initiatives of Equitable and Sustainable Development: Who Pays?', *World Development*, 1:2, 125–54.

Rajan, Rajeswari S. (1993), *Real and Imagined Women*, London: Routledge.

Rajan, Rajeswari S. (2003), *The Scandal of the State*, Durham, NC: Duke.

Ramazanoglu, Caroline (1989), *Feminism and the Contradictions of Oppression*, London: Routledge.

Rao, Arati (1999), 'Speaking/Seeking a Common Language', in C. Gustafson and P. Juviler (eds), *Religion and Human Rights*, Armonk: M. E. Sharpe, pp. 117–39.

Rao, Shakuntala (1999), 'Woman-as-Symbol', *Women's Studies International Forum*, 22:3, 317–28.

Rawls, John (1971), *A Theory of Justice*, Oxford: Oxford University Press.

Rawls, John (1993), *Political Liberalism*, New York: Columbia University Press.

Rawls, John (1995), 'Reply to Habermas', *Journal of Philosophy*, 92:3, pp. 109–26.

Rawls, John (1996), 'Introduction to the Paperback Edition', *Political Liberalism*, New York: Columbia University Press.

Rawls, John (1997), 'The Idea of Public Reason Revisited', *University of Chicago Law Review*, 64:3, pp. 765–807.

Rawls, John (1999), *The Law of Peoples*, New York: Columbia University Press.

Rawls, John (2001), *Justice as Fairness: A Restatement*, Cambridge, MA: Harvard University Press.

Raz, Joseph (1984), 'On the Nature of Rights', *Mind*, 93, pp. 194–214.

Raz, Joseph (1986), *The Morality of Freedom*, Oxford: Clarendon.

Raz, Joseph (1994), *Ethics in the Public Domain*, Oxford: Clarendon.

Raz, Joseph (1999), 'How Perfect Should One Be? And Whose Culture Is?', in S. M. Okin (with respondents), pp. 95–9.

Razack, Sherene (1984), 'What is to be Gained by Looking White People in the Eye?', *Signs*, 1:19, pp. 894–923.

Razack, Sherene (2004), 'Imperilled Muslim Women, Dangerous Muslim Men and Civilised Europeans', *Feminist Legal Studies*, 12:2, pp. 129–74.

Réaume, D. (2000), 'Official-Language Rights', in W. Kymlicka and W. Norman (eds), pp. 245–73.

Reich, Rob (2002), *Bridging Liberalism and Multiculturalism in American Education*, Chicago: University of Chicago Press.

Reich, Rob (2005), 'Minors within Minorities', in A. Eisenberg and J. Spinner-Halev (eds), pp. 209–26.

Reidy, David A. (2000), 'Rawls' Wide View of Public Reason: Not Wide Enough', *Res Publica*, 6:1, pp. 49–72.

Reidy, David A. (2007), 'Reciprocity and Reasonable Disagreement', *Philosophical Studies*, 132:2, pp. 243–91.

Reitman, Oonagh (2000), 'Feminism and Multiculturalism', *International Feminist Journal of Politics*, 2:2, pp. 297–316.

Reitman, Oonagh (2005a), 'On Exit', in Avigail Eisenberg and Jeff Spinner-Halev (eds), pp. 189–208.

Reitman, Oonagh (2005b), 'Multiculturalism and Feminism: Incompatibility, Compatibility or Synonymity', *Ethnicities*, 5:2, pp. 216–48.

Rich, Adrienne (1984), *On Lies, Secrets and Silence*, London: Virago.

Richburg, Keith B. (2003), 'French President Urges Ban on Head Scarves in Schools', *Washington Post*, 18 December 2003.

Robison, Richard (1996), 'The Politics of Asian Values', *Pacific Review*, 9:3, pp. 309–27.

Rodgers, M. E. (2004), *Understanding Family Law*, London: Routledge.

Roland, A. (1996), *Cultural Pluralism and Psychoanalysis*, London: Routledge.

Rosenblum, Nancy (1998), *Membership and Morals*, Princeton: Princeton University Press.

Rosenblum, Nancy (2000), *Obligations of Citizenship and Demands of Faith*, Princeton University Press.

Rotella, Sebastian (2003), 'Chirac Proposes Ban on Head Scarves', *Los Angeles Times*, 18 December 2003.

Rowell, Glennon (1987), 'Implications of the Tennessee Textbook Controversy for Public Education', *Educational Leadership*, 44:8, pp. 14–5.

Roy, Arundhati (1996), *The God of Small Things*, New Delhi: Flamingo.

Sager, Lawrence (2000), 'The Free Exercise of Culture: Some Doubts and Distinctions', *Daedalus*, 129:4, pp. 193–208.

Saharso, Sawitri (2000), 'Female Autonomy and Cultural Imperative', in W. Kymlicka and W. Norman (eds), pp. 224–44.

Saharso, Sawitri (2003a), 'Feminist Ethics, Autonomy and the Politics of Multiculturalism', *Feminist Theory*, 4:2, pp. 199–214.

Saharso, Sawitri (2003b), 'Culture, Tolerance and Gender', *European Journal of Women's Studies*, 10:1, pp. 7–27.

Saharso, Sawitri (2006), 'Is Freedom of the Will But a Western Illusion?', in B. Arneil et al. (eds), pp. 122–38.

Sahgal, Gita (1992), 'Secular Spaces: The Experience of Asian Women Organizing', in G. Sahgal and N. Yuval-Davis (eds), *Refusing Holy Orders*, London: Virago, pp. 163–97.

Sahgal, Nayantara (1985), *Rich Like Us*, New Delhi: W. W. Norton & Co.

Sangari, Kumkum and Sudesh Vaid (1989), *Recasting Women*, Delhi: Kali for Women.

Sangari, Kumkum and Sudesh Vaid (1991), 'Institutions, Beliefs, Ideologies', *Economic and Political Weekly*, 26, WS2–18.

Sartre, Jean-Paul (1976), *Critique of Dialectical Reason – I, Theory of Practical Ensembles*, trans. A. Sheridan-Smith, London: New Left Books.

Schimmel, David (1988), 'Religious Freedom and the Public School Curriculum', *West's Education Law Reporter*, 42:4, pp. 1047–57.

Schnapper, D. (1991), *La France de l'intégration*, Paris: Huppert.

Schrag, Francis (1988), 'Diversity, Schooling and the Liberal State', *Studies in Philosophy and Education*, 17:1, pp. 29–46.

Schrag, Francis (1998), 'Diversity, Schooling and the Liberal State', *Studies in the Philosophy of Education*, 17:1, pp. 29–46.

Schwartzman, Lisa (1999), 'Liberal Rights Theory and Social Inequality: A Feminist Critique', *Hypatia*, 14:2, pp. 26–47.

Schwartzman, Lisa (2006), *Challenging Liberalism*, Pennsylvania: Penn State University Press.

Scott, David (2003), 'Culture in Political Theory', *Political Theory*, 31:1, pp. 92–115.

Secor, Anna (2005), 'Islamism, Democracy and the Political Production of the Headscarf Issue in Turkey', in Ghazi-Walid Falah and Caroline Ross Nagel (eds), *Geographies of Muslim Women*, London: Guilford Press, pp. 203–25.

Sen, Amartya (1982), *Choice, Welfare and Measurement*, Oxford: Blackwell.

Sen, Amartya (1985a), 'Wellbeing, Agency and Freedom', *Journal of Philosophy*, 82:4, pp. 169–221.

Sen, Amartya (1985b), 'The Moral Standing of Markets', *Social Philosophy and Policy*, 2:2, pp. 200–28.

Sen, Amartya (1995a), *Inequality Reexamined*, Oxford: Oxford University Press.

Sen, Amartya (1995b), 'Gender Inequality and Theories of Justice', in Martha Nussbaum and Jonathan Glover (eds), pp. 259–73.

Sen, Amartya (1999), *Development as Freedom*, Oxford: Oxford University Press.

Sen, Mala (2002), *Death by Fire*, Piscataway: Rutgers University Press.

Shachar, Ayelet (1999), 'The Paradox of Multicultural Vulnerability', in C. Joppke and S. Lukes (eds), *Multicultural Questions*, Oxford: Oxford University Press, pp. 87–111.

Shachar, Ayelet (2000), 'Should Church and State be Joined at the Altar?', in W. Kymlicka and W. Norman (eds), pp. 199–242.

Shachar, Ayelet (2001), *Multicultural Jurisdictions*, Cambridge: Cambridge University Press.

Shah Bano (1985), 'Shah Bano's Open Letter to Muslims', published in *Inquilab* 13 November 1985, translated into English by A. Karim Shaikh.

Shahid, W. A. and P. van Koningsveld (1995), *Religious Freedom and the Position of Islam in Western Europe*, Berlin: Kampen.

Shain, Farzana (2003), *The Schooling and Identity of Asian Girls*, Stoke-on-Trent: Trentham Books.

Silverman, M. (1992), *Deconstructing the Nation*, London: Routledge.

Smock, P., W. Manning and S. Gupta (1999), 'The Effect of Marriage and Divorce on Women's Economic Wellbeing', *American Sociological Review*, 64, pp. 794–812.

Smolin, D. (1995), 'Will International Human Rights Be Used as a tool of Cultural Genocide?', *Journal of Law and Religion*, 12:1, pp. 143–71.

Song, Sarah (2005), 'Majority Norms, Multiculturalism and Gender Equality', *American Political Science Review*, 99:4, pp. 473–89.

Song, Sarah (2006), 'Religious Freedom vs. Sex Equality', *Theory and Research in Education*, 4:1, pp. 23–40.

Song, Sarah (2007a), *Justice, Gender and Politics of Multiculturalism*, Cambridge: Cambridge University Press.

Song, Sarah (2007b),'The Subject of Multiculturalism', paper presented at the Stanford Political Theory Workshop, November 2007.

Spelman, Elizabeth (1988), *Inessential Woman*, Princeton: Princeton University Press.

Spinner-Halev, Jeff (2000), 'Extending Diversity', in Will Kymlicka and Wayne Norman (eds), pp. 68–99.

Spinner-Halev, Jeff (2001a), *Surviving Diversity*, Princeton: Princeton University Press.

Spinner-Halev, Jeff (2001b), 'Feminism, Multiculturalism, Oppression and the State', *Ethics*, 112, pp. 84–113.

Spinner-Halev, Jeff (2005), 'Autonomy, Association and Pluralism', in A. Eisenberg and J. Spinner-Halev (eds), pp. 157–71.

Spivak, Gayatri (1988), 'Can the Subaltern Speak?' in B. Ashcroft et al. (eds), *The Postcolonial Studies Reader*, London: Routledge.

Squires, Judith (2000), 'The State in (and of) Feminist Visions of Political Citizenship', in C. McKinnon and I. Hampsher-Monk (eds), pp. 35–50.

Squires, Judith (2002), 'Culture, Equality and Diversity', in Paul Kelly (ed.), pp. 114–32.

Srivastava, Kavita (2004), 'Justice Immolated', *The New Nation*, 30 June 2004, Editorial Page.

Stankiewicz, Greg (1991), 'The Controversial Curriculum', Case Study, Woodrow Wilson School, Princeton University

Steans, Jill (2007), 'Debating Women's Human Rights as a Universal Feminist Project', *Review of International Studies*, 33, pp. 11–27.

Steiner, Hillel (1994), *An Essay on Rights*, Oxford: Blackwell.

Stephen, Andrew (2008), 'How would Jesus vote?', *New Statesman*, 4 February 2008.

Stolzenberg, Nomi Maya (1993), '"He Drew a Circle that Shut Me Out": Assimilation, Indoctrination and the Paradox of a Liberal Education', *Harvard Law Review*, 106, pp. 581–667.

Stone, Alison (2004), 'Essentialism and Anti-Essentialism in Feminist Philosophy', *Journal of Moral Philosophy*, 1:2, pp. 135–53.

Stowasser, Barbara Freyer (1994), *Women in the Qur'an, Traditions, and Interpretation*, New York: Oxford University Press.

Strauss, Leo (1989), 'Relativism', in Leo Strauss, *The Rebirth of Classical Political Rationalism*, Chicago: University of Chicago Press.

Subrahmanian, Ramya (2002), 'Engendering Education: Prospects for a Rights-Based Approach to Female Education Deprivation in India', in M. Molyneux and S. Razavi (eds), pp. 204–33.

Sunstein, Cass (1995), 'Gender, Caste and Law', in M. Nussbaum and J. Glover (eds), pp. 332–59.

Sunstein, Cass (1999), 'Should Sex Equality Law Apply to Religious Institutions?', in S. M. Okin (with respondents), pp. 85–94.

Sunstein, Cass (2001), *Designing Democracy: What Constitutions Do*, Oxford: Oxford University Press.

Swaine, Lucas (2001), 'How Ought Liberal Democracies to Treat Theocratic Communities?' *Ethics*, 111:1, pp. 302–43.

Symodides, Janusz (1998), 'Cultural Rights: A Neglected Category of Human Rights', *International Social Science Journal*, 50:158, pp. 559–72.

Tamir, Yael (1990), 'Whose Education Is It Anyway?' *Journal of the Philosophy of Education*, 24:2, pp. 161–70.

Tamir, Yael (1993), *Liberal Nationalism*, Princeton: Princeton University Press.

Tamir, Yael (1995), 'Two Concepts of Multiculturalism', *Journal of the Philosophy of Education*, 29:2, pp. 161–72.

Taylor, Charles (1979), 'What's Wrong with Negative Liberty?', in A. Ryan (ed.), *The Idea of Freedom*, New York: Oxford University Press.

Taylor, Charles (1991), *The Ethics of Authenticity*, Cambridge, MA: Harvard University Press.

Taylor, Charles (1992a), 'The Politics of Recognition', in C. Taylor (with respondents), pp. 25–74.

Taylor, Charles (with respondents) (1992b), *Multiculturalism and the Politics of Recognition*, A. Gutmann (ed.), Princeton: Princeton University Press.

Taylor, Charles (1993), *Reconciling the Solitudes*, Montreal: McGill-Queen's University Press.

Taylor, Charles (1999), 'Conditions of an Unforced Consensus on Human Rights', in J. Bauer and D. Bell (eds), pp. 124–44.

Thompson, Simon (2006), *The Political Theory of Recognition*, London: Polity Press.

Thurman, Robert (1996), 'Human Rights and Human Responsibilities', in Irene

Bloom, J. Paul Martin, Wayne Proudfoot (eds), *Religious Diversity and Human Rights*, New York: Columbia University Press, pp. 87–114.

Tomasi, J. (2001), *Liberalism Beyond Justice*, Princeton: Princeton University Press.

Torbisco Casals, Neus (2006), *Group Rights as Human Rights*, Dordrecht: Springer.

Toubia, Nahid (1995), *Female Genital Mutilation: A Call for Global Action*, New York: RAINBO.

Tully, James (1995), *Strange Multiplicity*, Cambridge: Cambridge University Press.

Tully, James (1999), 'The Agonic Freedom of Citizens', *Economy and Society*, 28:2, pp. 161–82.

Tully, James (2000), 'The Challenge of Reimagining Citizenship and Belonging in Multicultural and Multinational Societies', in C. McKinnon and I. Hampsher-Monk (eds), pp. 212–34.

Tully, James (2004), 'Recognition and Dialogue', *Critical Review of International Social and Political Philosophy*, 7:3, pp. 84–106.

Turpel-Lafond, Mary Ellen (1997), 'Patriarchy and Paternalism', in C. Andrew and S. Rogers (eds), *Women and the Canadian State*, Montreal: McGill-Queen's University Press, pp. 64–78.

Underhill, D. (1987), 'Voltaire Arraigned in Alabama', *Christian Century*, 104:15, pp. 438–44.

Valadez, Jorge (2001), *Deliberative Democracy, Political Legitimacy and Self-Determination in Multicultural Societies*, Boulder: Westview.

Van Dyke, Vernon (1982), 'Collective Entities and Moral Rights', *Journal of Politics*, 44:1, pp. 21–40.

Vojak, Colleen (2003), '*Mozert v. Hawkins*: A Look at Self-Knowledge and the Best Interests of the Child', *Educational Theory*, 53:4, pp. 401–49.

Volpp, Leti (2000), 'Blaming Culture for Bad Behavior', *Yale Journal of Law and the Humanities*, 12, pp. 89–116.

Wadhwa, Soma (2002) 'Waifs of the Gutter', in *Outlook* (available at www.outlookindia.com/full.asp?fodname=20020708&fname=Alwar+%28).

Waldron, Jeremy (1989), 'Rights in Conflict', *Ethics*, 99:3, pp. 503–19.

Waldron, Jeremy (1993), 'Liberal Rights: Two Sides of the Coin', in *Liberal Rights; Collected Papers 1981–1991*, Cambridge: Cambridge University Press, pp. 40–62.

Walker, Alice [1982] 1998, *The Color Purple*, Florida: Harcourt Books.

Walzer, Michael (1987), *Spheres of Justice*, Oxford: Blackwell.

Walzer, Michael (1993), 'Objectivity and Social Meaning', in Martha Nussbaum and Amartya Sen (eds), pp. 165–77.

Walzer, Michael (1994), *Thick and Thin*, Indianapolis: Notre Dame University Press.

Walzer, Michael (1997), *On Toleration*, New Haven: Yale University Press.

Wedeen, Lisa (2002), 'Conceptualising Culture', *American Political Science Review*, 96:4, pp. 713–28.

Weil, Patrick (2004), 'A Nation in Diversity', *OpenDemocracy*, 25 March 2004 (available at www.opendemocracy.net/faith_europe_islam/article_1811.jsp).

Weinstock, Daniel (2006), 'Is "Identity" A Danger to Democracy?' in Igor Primoratz and Aleksandar Pavkovic (eds), *Identity, Self-Determination and Secession*, Aldershot: Ashgate, pp. 15–26.

Weller, P. (1993), *Religions in the UK*, Derby: University of Derby.

Wellman, Carl (1999), *The Proliferation of Rights*, Boulder: Westview.

Werbner, Pnina (2000), 'What Colour 'Success'?', in Hans Vermeulen and Joel Perlmann (eds), *Immigrants, Schooling and Social Mobility*, London: Palgrave.

Werbner, Pnina (2005), 'Honour, Shame and the Politics of Sexual Embodiment Amongst South Asian Muslims in Britain and Beyond', *International Social Science Review*, 6:1, pp. 25–47 (available at p.werbner.googlepages.com/Honor.Beersheva.pdf).

Wikan, Unni (2002), *Generous Betrayal: The Politics of Culture in the New Europe*, Chicago: Chicago University Press.

Wilson, Amrit (2007), 'The Forced Marriage Debate and the British State', *Race and Class*, 49:1, pp. 25–38.

Wing, Adrien Katherine (2003), 'Civil Rights in the Post-9/11 World', *Louisiana Law Review*, 63, pp. 717–57.

Wintemute, Robert (2002), 'Religion v. Sexual Orientation: A Clash of Human Rights?', *Journal of Law and Inequality*, 1:2, 125–54.

Winter, Bronwyn (2001), 'Fundamental Misunderstandings: Issues in Feminist Approaches to Islamism', *Journal of Women's History*, 13:1, pp. 9–41.

Wittgenstein, Ludwig (1968), *Philosophical Investigations*, trans. G. E. M. Anscombe, Oxford: Blackwell.

Wolf, Susan (1992), 'Comment', in C. Taylor (with respondents), pp. 75–87.

Wolf, Susan (1995), 'Commentary: Martha C. Nussbaum: Human Capabilities, Female Human Beings', in Martha Nussbaum and Jonathan Glover (ed.), pp. 105–115.

Woodberry, R. D. and C. S. Smith (1998), 'Fundamentalism et al: Conservative Protestants in America', *Annual Review of Sociology*, 24:1, pp. 25–56.

Wuff, E. (1972), *Psychiatrie und Klassengesellschaft*, Frankfurt A M: Anthenaum Fischer Taschenbuch Verlag.

Yasuaki, Onuma (1999), 'Towards an Inter-civilizational Approach to Human Rights', in Joanne Bauer and Daniel Bell (eds), pp. 103–123.

Young, Iris Marion (1994), 'Gender as Seriality: Thinking about Women as a Social Collective', *Signs*, 19:3, pp. 713–38.

Young, Iris Marion (1995), *Justice and the Politics of Difference*, Princeton: Princeton University Press.

Young, Iris Marion (1996), 'Communication and the Other', in Seyla Benhabib (ed.), *Democracy and Difference*, Princeton: Princeton University Press.

Young, Iris Marion (1997), 'Polity and Group Difference', in R. Goodin and P. Pettit (eds), *Contemporary Political Philosophy: An Anthology*, Oxford: Blackwell, pp. 248–64.

Young, Robert (1980), 'Autonomy and Socialization', *Mind*, 89:536, pp. 565–76

Young, Robert (1986), *Personal Autonomy: Beyond Positive and Negative Liberty*, New York: Croom Helm.

Yuval-Davis, Nira (1980), 'The Bearers of the Collective', *Feminist Review*, 4, pp. 15–27.

Zelensky, A. and A. Vigerie (2003), 'Laïcardes, puisque féministes', *Pro-Choix*, 25, pp. 11–13.

Index